This volume is published in co-operation with

 Centre International des Sciences de l'Homme
International Centre for Human Sciences
المـــركــز الــدولي لعلوم الانســان

as part of the research project "Culture and Democracy"

Studien zu Ethnizität, Religion und Demokratie

herausgegeben von
Theodor Hanf
Jakob Rösel

Band 4

Theodor Hanf and Nawaf Salam (eds.)

Lebanon in Limbo

Postwar Society and State in an Uncertain Regional Environment

Nomos Verlagsgesellschaft
Baden-Baden

Bibliografische Information Der Deutschen Bibliothek

Die Deutsche Bibliothek verzeichnet diese Publikation in
der Deutschen Nationalbibliografie; detaillierte bibliografische
Daten sind im Internet über http://dnb.ddb.de abrufbar.

Bibliographic information published by Die Deutsche Bibliothek

Die Deutsche Bibliothek lists this publication in the Deutsche
Nationalbibliografie; detailed bibliographic data is available
in the Internet at http://dnb.ddb.de.

ISBN 3-8329-0310-0

1. Auflage 2003
© Nomos Verlagsgesellschaft, Baden-Baden 2003. Printed in Germany. Alle Rechte,
auch die des Nachdrucks von Auszügen, der photomechanischen Wiedergabe und der
Übersetzung, vorbehalten. Gedruckt auf alterungsbeständigem Papier.

This work is subject to copyright. All rights are reserved, whether the whole or part of the material is concerned, specifically those of translation, reprinting, re-use of illustrations, broadcasting, reproduction by photocopying machine or similar means, and storage in data banks. Under § 54 of the German Copyright Law where copies are made for other than private use a fee is payable to »Verwertungsgesellschaft Wort«, Munich.

Contents

Acknowledgements	6
Toward a New Perspective on Secularism in Multicultural Societies ILIYA HARIK	7
Taif Revisited NAWAF SALAM	39
The Postwar Political Process: Authoritarianism by Diffusion FARID EL KHAZEN	53
A Note on Confessionalism AHMAD BEYDOUN	75
A Polity in an Uncertain Regional Environment SAMIR KASSIR	87
On Roots and Routes: The Reassertion of Primordial Loyalties SAMIR KHALAF	107
The New Social Map SALIM NASR	143
The Deepening Cleavage in the Educational System MUNIR BASHSHUR	159
The Postwar Economy: A Miracle That Didn't Happen BOUTROS LABAKI	181
The Sceptical Nation. Opinions and Attitudes Twelve Years after the End of the War THEODOR HANF	197

Acknowledgements

The editors express their gratitude to the co-authors for their contributions, which were first presented at a panel of the World Congress for Middle Eastern Studies in Mainz in September 2002. The panel was sponsored by UNESCO and the German Academic Exchange Service (DAAD). The empirical study was funded by the International Centre for Human Sciences, Byblos, Lebanon.

Thanks go to the sponsors, to John Richardson for translations and revisions and to Angela Herrmann for editorial organisation, layout and generally midwifing this book.

Toward a New Perspective on Secularism in Multicultural Societies

ILIYA HARIK

Introduction: The Agony of Multiculturalism

The agony of ambiguous identity has always afflicted a Lebanese population torn by attachments of local, national and ideological nature. To the extent that such attachments cut across communal, state, and national boundaries they make the question of identity problematic, especially in a turbulent region prone to external intervention and a high sensitivity toward the need for social coherence and national unity. In the diverse spectrum of Lebanese society, religious communalism is the primary identity, which has for long inspired a counter demand for secularism, understood in a conventional way as a distancing of any religious feature from the political arena.

But how important is identity, anyway? Has it at any time been the central concept in explaining political behaviour? Under what conditions do national, class, sectarian, or ethnic identities assume great importance? Is it fair to claim that a person's communal identity would sum him or her up politically? Can there be something more in identity terms beyond the observable attitude, which people don in a contextual setting? It is at times suggested that *there is*; a claim made strong especially in the political literature of nationalists. No doubt, something strong is associated with that verbal act of soul-searching. By referring to identity, one is not just indicating how one looks, or how one thinks. Something I wish I know what it is. And that "is" has been so badly belaboured by academics and intellectuals over the years that it has become the gambit in which philosophical discourse lost its trail.

Let this essay then be a note of caution *not* to lose our trail of thought in dissipating existential lures when dealing with the ever-recurring issue of identity.

I shall therefore be tentative here and think out loud[1] when I suggest at the outset that the significance of the phenomenon is entirely sociological, and therefore subject to considerable variations. Rather than being an existential inquiry, evoking the concept of

---

[1] Let me make it clear that this is an essay and not a study. I am openly trying to develop positions, which I had previously expressed in various contexts on the subject of political integration in multi-cultural societies. References will be made to the place and time at which these views were expressed.

identity seems like tinkering with matters of images[2] and role-playing. Was it not true that as chancellor, Beckett was the loyal royalist of Henry II, and as Archbishop of Canterbury he became the protector of the Church against Henry? Does the formal role change the identity so easily? If so, which is the more important to study: the social structure within which we find ourselves, the attachments we make to others, the constituencies we represent, or the illusive concept of identity presented to us as essential, autonomous and continuous in successive time spans?

Is it not true that a citizen of Lebanon can be a Muslim with a universal outlook and a Lebanese patriot at one and the same time? Was Gibran Kahlil Gibran a Maronite, a Lebanese, a naturalized American, a humanist or what? Is a Catalan, a Catholic, an ethnic, a Spaniard, or a European?

Whether the answer is none, some, or all of these things, we will still be faced by a theoretical and practical problem: the sorting out of people according to their social attributes, and the difficulties associated with efforts to integrate diverse groups into one commonwealth. The fact that shares of power and of public goods are to a significant extent a function of such a social map stimulates group awareness.

Secularization and the Signature Identity

The Overlap of Multiple Identities

Like a traveller landing in a foreign city, we are hurled into an environment with a clearly delineated social map, in which the signposts are collectivities. For the most part, the individual owes the image of him/herself to the spatial divisions on the social map. The social map injects in us certain simple but imponderable facts which we are not at liberty to alter. It tells us where we belong, and identifies the accessible and forbidden spaces. Respect, status, and favour are allocated by spatial designation. Imagine the "Negro" in America, his/her geographical and psychological spaces as shaped by the "other." Think of the ghetto and the servile attitude of its dwellers amounting to submissive self-images imprinted on them by the larger society. Is the prostitute's demeaning and low self-image part of his/her character, or a reflection of the public's perception of the profession? In all these cases, the "other" defines our social image, an act in which we are partners as accomplices. How else would one explain the fact that an atheist in Lebanon is socially identified as a member of the religious community to which he/she was born? Individualism here is the weaker driver; no one has an unfettered choice to fully define him/herself.

Now let us think along those lines in spatial terms and find the place on the social map of women, of blue collar workers, of the landed gentry, barons of business, Anglo-Saxon wasps, Kurds in Beirut or Ankara, Shiites or Maronites in Lebanon and so on.

---

2 Not the same thing as imagining in the Benedict Anderson sense.

Not that the individual is never recognized as an autonomous social being, but rather that social formations have a predetermined bearing on the outcome of interaction.

When citizens are seen and defined as members of a group over above what they are as individuals, they feel compelled to respond in the same way to the challenges of the public arena. No surprise that many Lebanese who are not religious find it extremely difficult to dissociate from their signature identity group. When power, privilege, advantage, and role acceptance are all affected by group membership, it is not to the individual to buck the system. The individual can indeed make in-roads, but not a social revolution.

Add to this complicated social picture the fact that blocks on the map constitute overlapping sets. It may be possible for one and the same person in a certain location to claim spots in another block or blocks. In such a case, the reference is made to multiple identities.

The Signature Identity

While all identities borne by one and the same person are relevant, and each of which is evoked contextually, it is usually the case that a person bears on his sleeves a *signature identity* as a primary label, to wit, ethnicity in Turkey, the religious sect in Lebanon[3], race in the United States, etc. A signature identity is the distinctive label that stands out among all other defining social attributes, which locate the primary position of a person on the social map. Let us remember at this point that for analytical necessity, consideration will be limited to (a) natural features such as colour or race, and (b) to features of heritage such as regionalism, language, culture, or religion. It is true that all the heritage features can be acquired individually and often are, but they mostly are passed on from parent to child, and only exceptionally modified by the individual.

A signature identity may be transitive in character when it takes on the form of a magnet around which other social attributes of a community cluster. For instance, being Kurdish in Iraq or in Turkey is associated with other attributes such as territoriality, religious sect, way of life, social class, and educational status. When one utters the word "Kurd", the listener conjures up those other categories and designates the person's place on the social map without the aid of his/her official identity card (Harik 1972 (2)).

Transitive and Competitive Identities

Transitivity is the characterization we give to the tendency for social traits to cluster around a signature identity, such as the quality of being a Kurd carries with it other attributes. The greater the extent to which a signature identity is transitive, the more intense and wide is the social cleavage. Inversely, the greater the transitive character, the

---

[3] Sometimes ethnicity is the signature identity in Lebanon such as the case is with Armenians and Kurds.

lesser the possibilities of secularization. To bear the signature identity as a Kurd in Iraq is to carry with it several other attributes such as a territorially separate location, an Indo-European language, rural and/or pastoral way of life, and Sunni Islam. Thus the gap between an Iraqi Kurd in Kirkuk and an Iraqi Shiite in Basra is very wide.

The competitive character of identity is the obverse of transitivity. The more competitive the various identities are with the signature identity, the greater is the overlapping of the sets on the social map and the stronger the possibilities are for secularization. Being Arab, for example, provides a Christian in Lebanon or in Egypt with a social attribute that competes with his identity as a Christian. The Arabic language and culture create for a Christian Arab a space that overlaps with that of Arab Muslims. In short, a Maronite in certain contexts finds him/herself in the same identity set as Muslims, a fact which dilutes the purity of his signature identity as a Christian. Similarly in Iraq, Shiites share Arab language and identity with other Iraqi Arabs of other sects. Thus, there are more overlapping spaces in which Shiites in Iraq share a common ground with non-Shiite Arabs. As we shall see later, competing identities play an important role in attenuating the intensity of signature identities in multicultural communities.

In Lebanon, one can observe a weakness in the transitive power of communalism as a signature identity. The Arabic language, culture, and urbanization have competed with religious communalism. Consider here the residential patterns that were developing in Beirut[4] and the istiyaf towns[5]. Muslims were finding it agreeable to move into Christian Ashrafiyeh, Christians were increasingly choosing quarters in West Beirut such as Ras Beirut and Mazra'ah for residence or work. Just as highland Christians and Druze were making homes in the Sunni Muslim towns, so were the latter spending joyful summer times in highland towns. Not only has the movement to urban centres, mainly Beirut, been attractive to Christians and Druze, but included Shiites as well (Khuri 1975).

Among other forces that weaken the transitive quality of identity, social engineering stands out with special significance. The Lebanese electoral system is such an instance which contributed considerably to the establishment of cross-cutting ties among the various communities (Harik 1980, 1972 (2), 1972 (1)). It has been a common and more advantageous practice for candidates from different communities to run on the same election ticket. Supporters were thus drawn from multiple communities and worked earnestly in tandem to make the composite ticket win.

How far did that communal cross-cutting experience extend? It depends. We know that it did extend to business cooperation and to the market place in general. Some businesses and some markets were more mixed than others. A social geographer can draw us a more extensive and developed inter-communal map of Beirut, or Lebanon in general, and how it was transformed after the war. Lacking such studies, we have no choice but to make an educated guess regarding the nature of the post civil war social map. Static analysis has produced fairly impressive ethnographic maps of Lebanon, but less

---

[4] For the national role of Beirut, see below
[5] Summer resort towns.

of how competing identities had transformed the social map, what multiple identities look like now, and how elastic are boundary lines. What is certain is that competing identities from 1943 to 1975 created divisions within communities and built bridges across communal lines (Harik 1972 (1)).

The social geographer can observe the development of overarching spaces that are socially inclusive and bring under their umbrella members of diverse spatial blocks. One of the most significant special blocks, which formed broad umbrellas is that of *wataniyah*, or state community identification.

As political scientists, or students of nation-building, our sights are set on the overlapping zones of social and political spaces. Some prefer to call this phenomenon of overlapping social spaces integration, but I prefer to describe it as a *secularization* process. The "integration" concept refers most typically to a top-down design, which has the quality of imprinting a dominant culture on smaller and "deviant" ones. That is not the case with the overlapping spaces of identity in Lebanon. In the last resort, integration amounts to a process of assimilating the weaker status group to the dominant culture. Under secularism, cultures retain their identities regardless of status rank

The fact that in relatively advanced societies, individuals and groups entertain multiple identities makes it possible to achieve horizontal and vertical mobility (Harik 1972 (2)). In other words, a citizen can (a) move across cultural lines of separation, and/or (b) upwards within his own group. Vertical integration is the tendency of some groups, especially minorities, who seek to establish links directly with the central governmental structures and less with citizens from other group.

The interesting question, however, is whether all the various identities borne by a person are active at one and the same time, or is it the case that one identity is activated while others remain dormant? How do various identities interact and how are boundaries shared or penetrated. In other words, to be dynamic, the subject of inquiry has to focus on patterns of co-existence, why and how.

The Two Rival Models of Co-Existence

Ideologues, and social engineers as well, have reacted in a variety of ways to the challenges of multiculturalism and changing social spaces. Two of those reactions make a serious difference to Lebanon and its neighbours. In trying to understand the process of bridging social distances among diverse groups belonging to the same commonwealth, we encounter two models, which compel our attention: (1) the overriding model, and (2) the contextual identity model (Harik 1972 (2)).

The Overriding Model

In the case of the overriding model, leaders subsume other groups under the fold of their own signature identity by means of indoctrination, force, or persuasion. The most common forms of the overriding model in modern times have been nationalism and individualism. Individualism as a contrived ideological imposition tears apart the natural ties that bind, while nationalism tends to submerge hereditary social ties under a thick layer of ice. It may be reasonable in this context to consider nationalism as the more dominant force, because individualism or socialism, seem to be associated to a lesser or greater degree with the nation state.

The obsession with one overriding persuasion suffers from being less democratic, if democratic at all. It almost always downgrades other identities and seeks to supersede, or exclude them all together. When faced with multicultural identities inside one commonwealth, advocates of the overriding model seek to transform the social clay in the image of the dominant solidarity. Transformation is, however, a mythological journey, whose true purpose of domination is thinly concealed under a foggy blanket of reform. It is mythical because it almost always remains a pretence, and almost never succeeds.

Whether the signature identity under the overriding model is nationalism, religious fundamentalism, Leninism-Stalinism, or fascism, the violation of values of most citizens is a common practice. A strongly coherent and undifferentiated solidarity makes a group in a multicultural setting unsuited for a secular and democratic way of life.

The Contextual Model

The contextual model, in contrast, assumes a pluralist form and is more likely to be democratic, though not necessarily always so. Basically, it may be viewed as a public park with open spaces. In this model, social differences (colour, kinship, language, national origin, religion, class, political persuasion, etc.) are acknowledged as equally legitimate parts of one commonwealth. Legitimacy though is not enough, for in some advanced societies, say the United States before the Civil Rights Act of 1964, recognition was limited to designated spaces, a tendency, which is not democratic, nor agreeable to minorities.

Under the contextual model, recognition of multicultural differences extends into the public sphere. Accessibility is not circumscribed to designated areas, to the individual's home, or to his local community picnics, but includes interplay among members of communal solidarities in the public arena. The separate but equal rule, which was once advocated in the US, is greatly circumscribed. No segregated units in the military services, or any other official agency would be tolerated.

Fluctuation in the Value of Identity

Various societies, which adhere to the contextual model, allow individuals and groups to assign different values to identities to which they subscribe. Some individuals or groups may put religion above loyalty to the state (*wataniya*); others reverse the order of significance. Implied in the model is the recognition of fluctuation in the value of an attachment, depending on the context. It is indeed of the essence of the contextual model that no attachment has the same value, or the same function, under different conditions. The decision rests with the individual who determines the fluctuating values of his/her priorities in the multicultural world in which one lives.

Fluctuation in the values of identities in pluralist societies implies meeting of the minds among some individuals across the isle. Two citizens from different sects may disagree on the importance they attach to religious communalism, but agree on the extent to which they value human rights, or kinship ties. Lebanese from diverse religious communities share a sense of strong identification with democratic norms, but differ in the extent to which they ascribe legitimacy to primordial ties. In another instance of overlap in political positions, many Lebanese Maronites who had fought *à l'outrance* against Lebanese Muslims over Palestinian political and armed presence in the country during the seventies and eighties, have recently joined with the same Muslim citizens in supporting the armed Palestinian *intifada* in the Occupied Territories.

The history of independent Lebanon provides very few instances of unpolluted solidarity among signature identity groups. It contributes rather strong evidence of mutability in social adherence across spatial boundaries. There is a great deal of coalescence and proliferation, separation and realignment. The borders separating identity groups in Lebanon are porous; the lines fade then thicken, and the traffic across separation lines on the political map is at times quite heavy.

The difference between the overriding and the contextual patterns is very clear: In the first model, multiplicity of identities is the social evil, while the public good is associated with unity under a preferred signature identity. In the contextual model, the issue of multiple identities is neither an evil nor a public good. The focus is rather on the problematic, and the problematic in the pluralist approach is the attitude assumed toward political and social diversity in addition to the uses that are made of it. If deep cleavages characterize social diversity and the component parts lack common denominators, then the polity is obviously fragile and unstable. In addition, if the system management of diversity is inadequate and/or unfair, pluralism would not be practical and is bound to lose legitimacy.

A case in point of inadequate management is adherence to a rigid quota system, as has become the case in Lebanon. Rigidity results in losses of other values such as merit, efficiency, and progress. Such a situation is adverse to the common interest of state and society. What matters is not multiple or diverse adherence to identities but how diversity is dealt with and managed in the process of establishing public peace and upholding the common good.

Secularism

The blurring of communal borderlines is an indication of increasing secularization, whereby an individual enjoys the right and ability to take positions, which are not exclusively associated with one's signature identity. Such behaviour does not necessarily mean divesting oneself from one's community, or replacing one identity for another. It is rather an expansion of the multiple identity spectrum, often to a more inclusive sphere. Thus secularism is *an additional, not a replacement identity*.

An ambiguity in the meaning of secularism prevails in Western literature. In one sense, secularism refers to an attitude of hostility toward religion, while in another sense it refers to a position of distancing the political from religious involvement and vice versa (Marty 1969; Bradbury and Gilbert 1989; Van Ness 1996). In both cases, whether hostility or jurisdictional separation, secularism constitutes an alternative ideology and a replacement of another identity.

When thus used in conventional terms, secularism stands for a substantive doctrine comparable in that respect to religious ideologies, such as that of the Muslim Brotherhood, the Turkish Rafah Party, and of the Christian Right in the US. It is not what its adherents make it out to be, a sanitized tendency of a neutral nature. In the French and American political lexicon, it is a common practice to present secularism as a cleaning of the slate from other unfavourable and obtrusive tendencies in politics. Conventionally understood, secularism is an exclusionary political movement, and hence reflects a strongly non-democratic trait. If democracy means hearing all voices expressed in the public place, how come religious or ethnic voices are the ones to be shut out of the public arena. The identification of secularism with an ideological position makes of it a partisan persuasion, a rival not a neutral voice.

The nationalist regimes of Iraq, Syria, and Tunisia,[6] which are known in the Arab world as secularist, are also autocratic systems of government. They are the regimes that provide citizens with hardly any access to the public arena. In Turkey, a developing democracy, secularism is an official ideology of an exclusionary nature. Though showing more democratic traits than its Arab neighbours, Turkey has nevertheless continuously oppressed its religious and ethnic communities in the name of secularism and nationalism.

Keeping religion at a distance or subordinating it to other ideologies is not necessarily an aspect of democracy. Twentieth century history has shown that the most oppressive and exclusionary regimes fall under what is conventionally referred to as "secularists", namely nationalist and communist regimes.

Under the contextual model, and in contrast to the Franco-American usage, secularism is viewed as a mode of behaviour, not a fixed substantive position. It stands for the ability of a citizen to be mobile in the public space by defining one's position and course of action according to context, uninhibited by one's signature identity or by coercive means.

The secularist is a bearer of a cross-cultural embassy, enjoying free traffic across political and cultural lines. Secularism is the ability of culturally diverse individuals and/or groups to freely coalesce or dissociate in the public arena, depending on the issues and contexts. An actor who finds that he/she shares the same political position prevalent among members of a different group is able to join sides with them on that issue. Under

---

6 Algeria may fit in here too but is a more complex case.

secularism, individuals from different signature identity groups may find it possible socially and psychologically to be party to social deliberation and agreement regarding a public issue.

Secularism, as it is defined here, is a procedural matter not a substantive doctrine; it means the freeing of the access to the public sphere and accepting the results of the democratic process.

The more diverse the views expressed and the positions taken by members of a signature identity group the greater is the potential for secularization. Recent surveys have confirmed a retrogressive tendency toward secularization during and after the civil war period (El-Amine and Faour, 1997). Results have shown that the breakdown in attitudes along signature identity lines is strikingly higher than in the pre-war era (Theodor Hanf 1986; El-Amine 1997; Hudson 1968; Harik 1980). This tendency of group distinctiveness according to community adherence is confirmed by an informal observation of the post-war period, especially as manifested in demographic retreat from mixed residential areas.

Al-Amine and Faour study uncovers another tendency of more intriguing nature. Christian respondents in a sample of university students reflect political diversity of views, with a breakdown usually to two, three, or four attitudinal patterns. In contrast, Muslim student respondents have shown a very highly homogeneous attitude across the board. If this tendency is confirmed in future studies, it would show that Christians entertain more mobile identity perspectives, and therefore are more readily amenable to the secularization process than their Muslim counterparts.

However, considering that the surveys were conducted in the nineties, right after hostilities ended, it is not surprising to see persisting distances separating the communities. More encouraging is the common commitment to democracy reflected in the surveys on both sides of the aisle (El-Amine 1997; Qa'i 2000).

There has been, of course, a tradition of proliferation of political attitudes among Christians and less communal cohesiveness than has usually been the case with Lebanese Muslims. However, internal divisions and competing identities have been and still are in evidence within Muslim as well as Christian sects. Thus, the tendency of the electoral laws, adopted since independence in 1945, to create internal rivalry and competition at the same time as building bridges across communal lines persists. However, the importance of this tendency has become defused and its future threatened by the post-Taif manipulation of the electoral laws. The most critical factor has been the enlargement of constituencies rendering voters' choices almost meaningless, except as a support gesture to the most prominent communal leaders.

Secularism in the Neutral Sense

Secularism in the classical and broader sense of neutrality[7] vis-à-vis color, sect, class, national origin, sex etc. is untenable, and where tried, tends to be oppressive. The neutralism idea has been more theoretical than actual, a fact less recognized sometimes in the literature (Rawls 1971) than in experience. The *actual* tendency under so-called neutral positions has been to favour one signature identity (usually of the nation state) over other less "worthy", or less "potent" identities. The violations of other peoples' values which result from the so-called neutrality position is usually covered up by cultural complicity (Harik 1997). The association of the so-called neutralism with nationalism tends to be oppressive. We see it clearly today in Turkey, Iran, Iraq, and Syria *vis-à-vis* the Kurds and other minorities, and in Algeria toward the Berbers. This has, of course, been the typical experience of most minority groups elsewhere including Britain, France, and Italy, to mention only a few cases, where the signature identity group gave its name and character to the nation-state. The minorities were forced to assimilate.

In turn, socialist and nationally oriented groups have reason to be critical of communalism in multicultural societies (and in largely homogeneous ones too) for an assortment of unfavourable features. First, communalist regimes are more prone to place clientelism over merit, motivate leaders to arouse primordial sentiment and hostility toward others, and weaken national resolve by their divisiveness. Such a criticism is legitimate and fair, but it may also be pointed out that those same flaws are known to occur in multiparty systems in all societies, but more in politically less advanced countries.

The record of so-called progressive or modernist political parties in Lebanon, it can be argued, is worse than anything we have seen from the traditional and locally oriented politicians. Clientelism, ideological bigotry, hostility, and corruption are common features of political party politics in general. As for national divisions, conflicts and even civil wars, political parties have had their share of disrepute, especially in pre-World War II Europe. The locus of reform may be misplaced when the blame is put on the political party system or on communalism as such. The nature of political power coupled with an un-civic political culture presses those involved in politics toward committing objectionable and corrupt practices.

Advocating secularism as a neutral ideology does not resolve problems arising from multiculturalism. Neutralism in such cases comes down to being no more than an act of dissimulation.

---

7 What is usually referred to as color blind form of justice. The blindness concept is adequate as a legal term, but should be used with qualification politically.

Liberalism and the Politics of Identity

Up to this point, identity and secularism have been viewed from the position of the right and left; now we turn to the liberal perspective.

The shift in favour of the politics of identity more recently in the literature has provoked some liberal thinkers (Dworkin 2000; Barry 2001; Rawls and Kelly 2001). Not that they do not allow for a plurality of views among citizens; on the contrary, pluralism is the badge they wear. The problem for conventional liberals is that the politics of identity runs contrary to the classical liberal creed of equality and individualism.

At present though it has almost become politically and ideologically correct to speak of the politics of identity, i.e. of recognizing communalism and group solidarity as distinctive and co-existent within an over-arching community – the nation-state.[8] It was not always the case, though. In the tradition of liberally rooted democratic thought, recognition of difference, which implies an extra-individual identity whether ethnic, sectarian, class or regional, was considered an anathema. The correct civic culture of the liberals recognized only citizenship as a legitimate framework for political participation.

The liberal tradition has for long strongly affected Lebanese intellectuals and academics by virtue of their dependence on Western thought. As a result, one observes the presence of a hiatus separating the pragmatic founders of the Lebanese polity from the post-independence *café trottoir* intellectuals. The fear of political divisions and the antipathy shown toward communal recognition is matched only by the suppression and dehumanization inflicted on political life by integrationist regimes.

The nationally advocated philosophy of integration meant in the Middle East, as in the United States, transforming minorities socially and culturally in the image of the dominant group. To see this in Middle Eastern terms, imagine, integration of the Kurds in Turkey (Cizre 2001) or Iraq to the national culture. The hapless Kurds would only be allowed to be Turks, or Arabs respectively, not free citizens with cultural identities of their own. This type of cultural integration is what the politics of recognition rejects.

There is a common thread, which links integrationist regimes in developing and industrially advanced societies. The most obvious example of that tradition is manifest in the century old struggle for integration in the USA. The rock bottom line of the liberal credence was that a black citizen has equal rights and obligations as a white one. There was never any doubt that that was the proper civic attitude in a democracy, and on the face of it there should not be. However, when it became clear that not all blacks looked at that position as the sufficient solution to their problem, a kind of shock overtook liberals. They fought selflessly to free the blacks from being treated differently, then it turned out that the blacks cherished the difference, after all.

---

8 When I wrote in that vein in 1972, the subject was not yet a part of orthodoxy in the political science parlors of the US, whereas in Lebanon and the Arab world the politics of recognition was considered offensive and reactionary.

While the principle of individual equality before the law is impregnable in a juridical sense, politically it may become the source of negating group identity, and the cause of denial of its fair role in society. In terms of jurisprudence, justice requires equality, but politically justice requires recognition of difference also. There is no fairness in equality rights granted to an Afro-American citizen in an electoral constituency where he/she will remain an ineffective and unfulfilled political minority for as long as one could see. Equality as a solution advanced in favour of individuals in a deprived community is meaningless unless it is linked to group rights.

In short, some blacks viewed equality as a way of short-changing them in a competitive society, which is based on individual merit and class structure, both of which are stacked against them. The legal framework aside, the scales were bent against them in the market place and in the political arena for centuries. Treating them on the basis of "one man one vote," was in principle right, but it was not going to redress the lop-sided political and economic structure, or generate meaningful equality. Culturally, Afro-Americans viewed integration as it was really meant to be – assimilation. Assimilation is a form of cultural nationalism, an intrusion into one's way of life and self-image, deprivation of identity, if you wish. They did not necessarily want to become a replica of white people, nor be submerged into white history.

The Alliance of Liberalism with Nationalism

The universalism and uniformity in such liberal concepts as liberty, equality and fraternity abruptly fade when they reach the outer boundaries of the nation-state. The symbiosis of liberalism and nationalism, though is becoming weaker, has persisted since the dawn of the democratic era. In recent years, the troublesome but perennial alliance between liberalism and nationalism has been subjected to criticism, not only from outside but from within the liberal tradition itself. Inability of the liberal-national symbiosis to accommodate the doctrine of individual equality to fairness toward group identities makes it a very difficult model to implement, especially in multicultural societies, such as Lebanon and other Third World countries.

Though himself coming from a classically liberal tradition, Charles Taylor felt troubled by the denial which liberalism harboured toward the principle of group identity. He saw a moral affront in the denial position. (Taylor and Gutmann 1992) As a consequence, he argued for the recognition of difference on a moral basis common to both individualism and communalism. On the one hand, he maintained that conscience is the source of man's moral sense, a view, which retains the integrity of individual autonomy. To balance this position, he argued that the self-image of the individual is socially created. In effect, while seeing an autonomous moral being in the individual, Taylor admits that the individual is nevertheless defined socially as a member of a community, whose conscience is inextricably linked to his social existence. The individual's *moral sense*, in Taylor's view, is a natural endowment, but his *social identity* is formed by outside actors. According to that logic, "the other" becomes responsible for the self-images of the individual and of the community. To deny a community's status or identity in a commonwealth is to demean its members, and by so doing inflict moral harm upon it. Thus denial of community status is a violation of a moral principle.

The "harm principle" is a classical moral position of liberalism, which Taylor has successfully invested in the service of the reconciliation of liberalism to the spirit of the times. He has made sure that the integrity of the individual is preserved, while at the same time giving recognition to communal identities as fundamental features of society. Taylor opened the door for liberalism to become applicable to a broader range of analysis and societies. He provided a philosophical basis for the recognition of communal diversity in strife ridden pluralist societies, such as Canada and Lebanon.

Though ingenious, Taylor's position is inevitably bound with the Christian idea of an innate moral conscience. For those who are non-religious thinkers, Taylor's moralist position fits awkwardly with their normative sensibilities. Nevertheless, the contribution he has made toward opening liberalism to contemporary realities and concerns remains undeniable.

The Phenomenological Approach to Multicultural Democracy

For liberals, or democrats, who do not share Taylor's Christian fundamentals, a sociological outlook should prove more acceptable. It establishes a communally pluralist view of society free from unsettled moral trappings.

Though it shares basic liberal values, the phenomenological approach advanced in this essay is free from the need for establishing inviolable moral foundations. It also rejects the liberal-national symbiosis that has plagued democracy for such a long time. The liberal-national alliance nurtures ethnic and religious discrimination, tolerates deprivation, and undermines peace in the global arena (Harik 1994; Harik 2001 (2); Harik 2002).

Taylor has struggled with the paradox of grafting equality on the principle of dignity. That effort, however, does not settle concerns for the recognition of comparable legitimacy in the public arena for all value systems entertained by various citizens, especially in a multicultural setting. Citizens bring a very wide range of values into the political arena, some of which rest on almost unrelated cultures. Since every single group of citizens has equal right to express its preferences and most have a hierarchy of values of their own, a way must be found to a meeting ground for their irreconcilable cultures. A phenomenological perspective reconciles ideological authenticity and security of cultural groups with intellectual selectivity and pluralism in the interest of political and social co-existence.

A hierarchy of moral objects is fully understandable when it is a product of deliberation and consent across the board in a democratic social order. However, when the hierarchy rests on authority derived from a sacred or irreproachable source external to democratic procedures, then it becomes a hindrance to social understanding and peace. A sacred or inviolable authority is an act of faith relevant to the particular individual, who possesses it, and may serve as the supreme rule in the privacy of his/her life. An irreproachable authority, however, is ill-suited as a medium of exchange, or as a social imperative in the public sphere. Any claim for the authority of norms solely on the strength of an irreproachable and infallible source, be that divinity or reason, is exclusionary, discriminatory and oppressive.

As simple humans, we have no means to discern sacred or transcendental objects, and therefore cannot legitimately bring demands for sacred status into the public arena. The reason is simple: we have no established methods by means of which we can settle differences over such claims. Moreover, being exclusive and discriminatory, sacred attributes cannot serve as material of exchange in a democratic arena. Finally, they lack the qualities of making co-existence among diverse people possible in a fair and democratic manner. Mobility across social borders is an essential prerequisite of a pluralist polity, a condition that cannot be served by rigid ideological positions.

But is that a call for banning religion and/or metaphysics from politics? Not necessarily, democracy is open to all views, but then "all views" are subject to scrutiny by everybody in a free spirit of deliberation. That is the inevitable logic of a democratic public sphere. Since norms are inseparable from the concept of authority, it becomes imperative that only an authority open to man-made scruples can be admissible in the political arena.

An actor whose beliefs rest on what to him is an irreproachable source will have to submit to the supreme democratic rule of leaving his sacred gods at home, otherwise they would become a fair target for deliberation and criticism in the political arena. It is doubtful that the religious would tolerate or want such scrutiny. The alternative to deliberation in a public sphere is authoritarianism, the use of force, and of counter-force. That is not a democratic option.

It is up to citizens to decide whether they prefer to pay the price for democracy, or for authoritarianism.

To opt for democracy is a weighty measure; it means to accept vulnerability and submit to the slings and arrows of public debate. If the protagonist chooses to make the source of his claims a public issue, the "sacred" or "inviolable" loses its protective shield and becomes a fair game in a rough terrain. While such an eventuality is possible, it does not veer in a democratic direction. A democratic direction makes a positive contribution toward mutual understanding helpful in preparing the grounds for resolution of conflict and peaceful co-existence. Public debate of sacred and metaphysical objects cannot result in resolution of differences or in a *modus vivendi;* it arouses emotions to a boiling point.

Being functional, democratic debate ultimately seeks to facilitate the making of public decisions. Pragmatic actors tend to agree to set aside any source of authority claimed to be irreproachable or inviolable and focus on the merits of the proposition regardless of where it is derived from. Thus, if issues such as abortion or the death penalty are under consideration in a legislative process, appeals to the Scriptures would not do; it cuts off debate and imposes a categorical imperative. On the other hand, it serves no purpose to deny a political actor from adopting the Scriptures view on these issues, as long as he/she claims no privileged position to that source.

Where there is diversity of beliefs and no recognition of privileged positions, an appeal to the Scriptures may become vulnerable to fierce attack with impunity. What is privately sacred may in the public arena become profane. Those who cannot take the heat of having their sacred gods subjected to the discourtesies of public debate should leave their sacred objects at home, or leave democracy to its adherents.

There is of course a democratic alternative to bringing your sacred objects with you to the forum. Since different parties have different gods, one feasible way in a pluralist society is to consider the sacredly derived propositions but only as objects detached from their sources. Rules of conduct are more amenable to deliberation and modification than are the sources from which they are derived. Still, those who bring their religiously derived claims to the public arena should be prepared to see their propositions modified and/or rejected. But there is also the promise that they may be accepted on their own merit. In a multicultural society, one cannot afford to put one's gods to the test.

No democratic system can justify the prohibition of advocacy of a belief-system held in good faith, religious or otherwise. In the same spirit, no religiously minded citizen, can justify the authoritarian claim of infallibility or a privileged position for his/her views in the public arena. For those who choose to make their gods the object of contention in a pluralist society can legitimately do so, but should at the same time weigh the consequences of such a step.

Is this distinction between divine sources and the norms that are derived from them an exclusionary clause? Not in the phenomenological approach, for here it is acknowledged that public claims come from numerous sources of conflicting authorities, some of which are held as inviolable and some are not. Just as the democratic system is color blind, so it is blind to the origins of citizens' beliefs, but not to their concerns. Norms are everybody's concern and are subject to discussion under the means equally available to ordinary human beings; inviolable sources are not. To preserve the sacredness of private faith and at the same time participate in the public arena, a citizen must come to terms with the need to cross a major ideological divide from one dimensional to multidimensional vectors. Under such a perspective, every view is considered as equally legitimate a platform for open and free discussion as every other view. The debate takes the form of a relentless struggle under conditions of open, free, and equal access.

In a democracy, the public arena is a harsh contestation ground, yet shorn of violence. It is peaceful, but energized by a sense of shared well-being and uninhibited free debate. By irreverence, it is made immune from complacency and folly; by respect it is shielded from transgression. Clearly, the political arena is not a hospitable environment for spiritual discourse.

Am I unwittingly legislating here for others, i. e. claiming what I have denied to others, namely authority to unilaterally set up rules? The answer is unequivocally no. The rules in question are procedural: the right of a citizen to hold and live by any belief he/she chooses, so long as its practices are not in violation of state law; the exclusion of privileged sources of authority from the democratic arena; the rights of citizens to derive norms and policy propositions from any sources including privileged ones; the subjection of all normative claims and propositions in the public arena to equal discourtesy; and finally the legitimacy to modify and/or reject any proposition presented for legislation purposes.

The principles just outlined are not authored by any one person, or persons in particular. They are a logical consequence of a democratic point of departure. Democratic procedures, which are based on equality before the law and on free consent logically preclude *a priori* claims for privileged positions in the public arena. Similarly, freedom of expression is mandatory, not a discretionary option in a democracy. No political proposition therefore can be excluded from deliberation or from competing in the public arena on the grounds that it is derived from what an inviolable source, so long as it stands on its own free from any claim to a privileged position.

Religious ideas are just as legitimate as so-called "secular" ideas, when presented without a claim to a privileged consideration. Democratically, this is the only defensible position, not the so-called secular position, which in certain cases excludes religious ideas and the religious from participating in the political arena. If presented as unprivileged propositions for discussion on their own merit, religiously derived norms may be legitimate subject for legislation purposes.

Secularism in the Lebanese Context

Free communal interaction in the public sphere, politically and otherwise, has been a common feature of the Lebanese polity since the inception of the republic, though not credited as a form of secularism by Lebanese intellectuals or by scholars in general. To most, the standard of secularism has been the rigid Franco-American model with its thorough adherence to complete separation of religion and politics.

Dissimulation and Sublimation

To give an adequate picture of the issue of secularism in Lebanon, let us first have a brief review of the history of identity in this country (Hudson 1968; Johnson 1986; Khalaf 1987; Hanf 1993; Messarra 1994; El-Khazen 2000; Khalaf 2001; Khalaf 2002).

It has been clear for a long time that every Lebanese is a carrier in his/her own person of multiple identities, though the religious sect stands out as the signature one. It may thus sound curious that while the Lebanese are convinced that communal pluralism is an undeniable fact of life in their society, most of them openly decry the Republic's political and juridical recognition of communalism. Hardly any of them admits openly subscribing to it. The pretence is always that it is the "other" who is the true adherent to communalism. Much as I have tried, I have never been able to find the "other" in this case. The Lebanese seem to have been engaged in a dissimulating behaviour. Each individual and group, in effect, avails itself of a secular identity veil to cover up its adherence to communal identification.

The dissimulation tendency in Lebanon is a social complex resulting from the rigid conceptual supposition that secularism is a replacement identity rather than an adjunctive one. Thus rather than appear as a self-centred sectarian, each Lebanese pretends that his/her own communal identity is something else. Some clever observers have satirically expressed the tendency in this form: the sectarianism of a Maronite is projected as Lebanese nationalism, of the Sunni Muslim it is Arab nationalism, of the Druze progressivism, of the Orthodox Christian secularism, of the Shiite egalitarianism! Is this some kind of duplicity, a *takiya* that inflicts Lebanese minds? Not necessarily, given that all is said and done in the open. *Takiya* is practiced where one cannot speak out.

The Lebanese attitude on communalism may well be considered as a form of sublimation of group preferences. The sublimation phenomenon may also be summed up as a commercial attitude in a merchant republic, an "*emballage*" of political products. The "*emballage*" phenomenon though is practiced heavily in non-commercial countries too, such as Egypt, for instance, where official spokesmen talk of "raised consumer prices" in such euphemistic terms as: "the movement of prices." But while in Egypt the euphemism is intended to soften the shock of unpleasant news, in Lebanon it is an expression of a preferred self-image. In the last resort it is an indication that a Lebanese is not willing to submit to the base line preferring some higher grounds. This is a kind of a transcendence of the narrow and exclusive sectarian identification, the politically degenerate form of communalism.

The sublimation phenomenon has been part of an expressive culture whose people are used to high notes. They are at home with the practice of basic freedoms, and like most cosmopolitan societies, at ease with several social currencies. It is what makes the Lebanese villager, who is able to live in a Mexican style house[9] remain a *baladi* in the local community. This perceptual mobility, this empathy, may be something propitious of a new understanding of secularism as a mode of behaviour, an additional not a replacement identity.

Sublimation is also a reflection of the feeling that the line separating communalism from sectarianism is blurred, which makes the phenomenon wanting in legitimacy. Communalism is aggravating to many people, especially among progressive activists who are stymied by the pettiness and waste caused by narrow concerns to be found in most partisan relationships.

---

9 See below

Whatever the reasons, and they are many, the unease felt *vis-à-vis* communalism is synonymous with distrust of pluralism, especially by nationalists and intellectuals given to abstract, yet passionate habits of thought.

In the last resort, it is clear from the persistence of communalism that the Lebanese are locked into it. Why? Obviously, they do not seem to know how to get over it. Having made up their minds that it is an evil in need of eradication, they manoeuvred themselves into an intractable position. The persistence may also be seen as a tacit awareness that the management of communalism is functional and cannot be bypassed easily, especially the way events have been unfolding regionally in the last fifty years. Others feel, on the contrary, that recognition of political communalism nourishes the phenomenon and, in effect, it becomes self-perpetuating. (For communal management as a moderating factor, see (Harik 1972 (1); Harik 1972 (2); Harik 1980).

Lebanese Democratic Secularism and National Identity

As an attitude and a mode of behaviour, secularism in Lebanon has for a long time been one colour in the multicultural panorama. Its origin can be traced back to the latter part of the nineteenth century, especially as it was clearly and forcefully articulated by Butrus al-Bustani (Abu-Manneh 1980; Makdisi 2002), a Maronite scholar and educator influenced by the sorrows of the communal civil war of 1860 and, curiously, by contact with Protestant missionaries. Bustani's view of secularism was a harbinger of the Franco-American rigid prototype (Harik 2002), namely as a replacement identity in alliance with nationalism. Like many in Lebanon today, he thought that his secular perspective was also a call to social peace (*silm ahli*) as a replacement of communal dissension. Little did he think that communalism itself appeared in Lebanon of the nineteenth century as a replacement to the *iqta' ismiya* identity and as a modernizing and revolutionary force in the logic of the time. No surprise that it generated social and political turmoil from the 1820s to the 1860s (Harik 1968). In the same logic, Bustani's call for national secularism was a revolutionary idea ahead of its time and prone to generate socio-political turmoil and conflict with the strongly entrenched cultural patterns. The record of the organized secular parties that are heirs to Bustani's secular perspective, such as the Syrian Social Nationalist Party and the Communist Party has clearly pointed to those turbulent effects.

The national identity, seen as a possible outlet freeing the Lebanese from narrow communal perspectives, has come along in a protracted, almost imperceptible manner as a product of political events and modernizing forces[10]. At present, no observer can deny that there is an overarching sense of Lebanese identity, after all, the republic is three quarters of a century old now, and it has had the advantage of starting out with some sort of a Lebanese identity predating the modern state (Binder 1966; Hourani 1966;

---

10 In the sense used by Karl Deutsch, Deutsch, K. W., *Nationalism and Social Communication: An Inquiry into the Foundations of Nationality* (Cambridge, Mass.: M. I. T. Press, 1966).

Harik 1968). By the early twentieth century, Lebanese identity started to take on a dimension of civic nature amounting to association with a state constitutionally defined. Being subject to the same laws and obligations, along with a common language and a historical habit of free expression, were the most common denominators among the members of the new state. As in most other state-building cases, the Lebanese communities were brought together by forces, in which they were only partial participants. They tried to make do and adjust to what they had at hand in as a creative way as they could.

I can detect five sources of inspiration for the formation of an overarching Lebanese state constitutional identity.

1. Political Culture of the Founding Fathers

First, there is the perception entertained by the Lebanese participants in the founding of the state (1920-1943). By the founding fathers, I mean primarily key legislators and public figures during the formative years of the modern Republic.[11] They envisaged a commonwealth of multicultural communities who were bound by common language, a degree of mixed residential areas, urbanism, and a limited degree of shared history. The founders compensated for the communal diversity by propounding (a) a perspective of tolerance toward all spiritual families, (b) designating a public sphere tailored for commonly conceded grounds, and (c) stressing a comparatively reasonable degree of liberty, (culturally, socially and economically). In crafting the state institutions together with a democratic foreign sponsor, known as the mandatory power, they preserved the religious zone in personal law as they had found it and promoted political participation and various political and civic freedoms.

In addition, the founders were very deliberate about putting in place a design with an underlying idea of political justice based on proportional representation. This is the original meaning of the communal quota system, which initially provided (1) a protective shield for small communities from the possible tyranny of the majority community, or from a majority made up of a coalition of communities, and (2) security for all sects in whichever constituency they happened to vote. Fixed proportionality meant that no cutthroat electoral competition would deprive any of the communities of its rightful place in the government.

The Lebanese image of themselves as members of a representative and democratic system has been strongly imprinted in their minds. In contrast, the sense of justice implied in proportional communal representation, however, has been a subject of contention, with supporters and detractors equally divided, and hardly successful in by-passing the object of their differences.

---

11 Habib Pacha al Sa'd, Mousa Nammour, Maronite Patriarch Ilyas Huwayyik, Shibl Dammous, Ibrahim Talhuq, Shaykh Muhammad al-Jisr, Yusuf al-Khazin, Charles Debbas, Fuad Arslan, Emile Edde, Michel Shiha, Fuad Junblat, Bshara al-Khury, 'Umar al-Daouq, 'Umar Bayhum, and Riyad al Sulh.

2. The Ottoman Reform Legacy

The second source of inspiration came from the Ottoman and European legacies. Most important was the Ottoman Reform tradition of the nineteenth century as it was manifested institutionally in the special status of the Mutasarrifiyah of Mount Lebanon (1861-1914). As the first formal system of government known to Lebanon, the Mutasarrifiyah institutions included constitutionalism, representation on communal basis, and a wide array of rudimentary political and economic freedoms (Baaklini 1976). Religious communalism, which had emerged as a widespread social phenomenon a few decades earlier, was institutionalized for the first time in that new political structure.

There are two things that ought not to be overlooked about communalism in Lebanon: it was a modern phenomenon,[12] going back only to the first decade of the nineteenth century and not given a formal status until the 1860s. Second, but not less important, it was indigenous (Harik 1968; Fuad Khuri 1972; Harik 1972 (1)).

Constitutionalism and formal representation were ideas and institutions of European origins first transferred to Lebanon by the Ottoman government in the form of the Mutasarrifiyah. Then the process was developed further in the *Republic of Grand Liban* installed by the French under the League of Nations mandate in the 1920s. The constitution of the new Republic adopted legal features and ideas from the constitution of Third French Republic, which for the framers of the new Lebanon served as a reference point rather than as a model to be replicated.

The Lebanese Republic, which emerged from the French mandate, was altogether a different animal from the French Third Republic (1871-1940). It took shape in what may be described as "build as you go" process. Whatever the origin, the structure that emerged was a presidential system,[13] which by the forties became increasingly a system of *co-habitation*,[14] a combined presidential-cabinet system with a privileged presidential role. In the post-Taif republic, the system of *co-habitation* became three-headed, a *troika*, to use the favourite term in Lebanese parlance, with the privileged position passing informally to the Syrian government.

At any rate, by 1947, the Lebanese Republic showed very few recognizable political features comparable to those in the constitution of the French Third Republic.

---

12 Sectarianism as a recent phenomenon was first manifested in Mt. Lebanon at the outset of the nineteenth century as a successor to the feudal bond of ismiyah, as I show in Politics and Change in a Traditional Society. A more recent wave of communalism is the one that emerged among the Shiites in the first half of the twentieth century in association with urbanism, as it has been shown by Fuad Khuri in his book, *From Village to Suburb*, and in his article, "Sectarian Loyalty Among Rural Migrants in Two Lebanese Suburbs," in Richard Antoun and Iliya Harik (eds.) *Rural Politics and Social Change in the Middle East* (Bloomington: Indiana University Press 1972).

13 Unlike the French prototype, which was a cabinet system, not presidential.

14 It may be interesting to note that the French Fifth Republic with its cohabitation arrangement may have copied the Lebanese system of the Second Republic, 1943-1975. This may not be so surprising considering that the top engineer of the Fifth Republic was Charles De Gaulle, a statesman who spent some time in Lebanon and was quite familiar with the nature of the Lebanese system. In the last resort, presidentialism simply suited his temperament, while the office of premier as reflective of parliamentary distribution of power was a strong French tradition.

3. The European Legal Tradition

The third source of inspiration for the state constitutional identity came from a European legal tradition. This tradition entered Lebanon through Saint Joseph University and the Lebanese émigré intellectual and merchant communities residing in Europe and Egypt before the 1920s. The legalistic tradition is reflected in the operating laws and courts of the land, the separation of powers, and the principle that a deputy represents the nation, not his own local constitutency. It is also reflected in the formal educational system introduced during the Mandate and expanded subsequently.

4. Arab Nationalism

The fourth factor in the formation of a Lebanese political identity was the addition of an Arab face to what was basically a Western oriented local outlook of the original two communities, Christians and Druze. The Arab feature of the new state developed at the outset of independence in the National Pact of 1943, and in Lebanon's role as a founding member of the League of Arab States in 1945. This last phase transformed the idea of Lebanon as "the land of minorities" to one of membership in the dominant national culture of the region, *al-uruba*.

The League of Arab States was the perfect fit for most Arab regimes, each one of which, like Lebanon, had a strong local character while sharing in the larger Arab cultural community. This marriage of the particular and the universal was not "a made in Britain" product, but a regional response to an urgent local need expressed by a native voice. Like an arranged marriage, there was an implicit bargain in the deal for each country. In Lebanon, the Christians expressed the bargain by raising their hat in recognition of regionalism. The Muslim expression came as recognition of the integrity of localism. The former subscribed to *al-'uruba*, and the latter to an independent Lebanese state. The Muslim new commitment partially reflected their attraction to the rudimentary democracy then prevalent in Mt. Lebanon and in the city of Beirut. Beirut was then the most progressive and educated city in the Ottoman State and its population entertained, in addition to national ideas, a democratic orientation, which brings us to our next point.

5. Beirut

The fifth inspiration and perhaps the least recognized is the emergence of Beirut as a primate city, major nexus between the people of Mt. Lebanon (*al-jabal*) and the people of the coast (*al-sahil*), even before the Lebanese Republic came into being. The city that had emerged first as a port town in the early nineteenth century grew into a satellite population centre with a constellation of villages and towns revolving in its sphere.

As a port town and locus of government, Beirut became a centre of employment, commerce and education. The role of the port town as a progenitor of a domestic market and as a population magnet was at the heart of the rise of national states in the Middle East and elsewhere (Harik 1972(3)). Beirut was only one of those instances.

The influx of Christian mountain people into what was basically Sunni Beirut as of the nineteenth century for business or to partake in education turned the city into a hub for the surrounding highland areas and further into the interior. The merging of the people of *al-jabal* and the people of *al-sahil* was an event consecrated with blood in 1916 on the hanging posts of the fading Ottoman power. It was also completed with Shiite emigration into greater Beirut mainly after independence in 1943.

The population influx and the rise of Beirut as the national focus never abated until 1975, a catastrophic date. But up to that time, a "nation state" had been shaped under the impetus of a primate city. By 1975, most Lebanese were Beirutis in one form or another: commuting from their satellite towns, residing in the city while maintaining a family home in villages and towns, working, or carrying on business enterprises. Hardly any business, trade, finance, official matter, education, health, or entertainment could be undertaken without Beirut being involved one way or another

Every Lebanese experiences his national self first via being Beiruti. Like the coming of age ritual, we become Lebanese by passing first through the gates of Beirut. Beirut is the nexus that links us all to one another and to the world. The national consciousness that emerges as a result of the frequency and intensity of interaction within a geographic location (Deutsch 1966), tends to give way among analysts now to image and formal ideology. It is a tendency that led to the ready understanding and popularity of the idea of the nation as an object of imagining (Anderson 1983), a view that leaves out more than it includes.

The two civil wars have obviously been the major arguments in the arsenal of sceptical observers who believe that the emergence of a Lebanese identity has proven untenable. I find myself on the side of some hard-nosed believers, on the opposite side of the argument. Not to be distracted though from the sequence of my thesis, I shall limit myself to one argument in support of the notion that an overarching Lebanese identity has been forged as an adjunct entity cementing without replacing the other identities.

One argument in support of an overarching Lebanese identity is durability. A brutal and protracted war, which had led to the intrusion of external powers, has failed to result in the dissolution of the Lebanese state. The resolution of the bitter war of civil and regional dimensions has reproduced the system in its entirety, with constitutional adjustments that could have been made without war. Lebanon now is an entity that is weakened and more dependent than it had been before, but in all other respects is much the same.

The staying power of the founders' perception of the Lebanese identity has been sustained by a number of factors reflecting vested interests of most inhabitants. The social elite improved their chances for occupying formal political leadership positions without closing access to others. Second, almost every Lebanese group, corporate or primordial, has found a vested interest in the democratic arrangement of communal co-existence. Economic growth made it possible for most citizens to have a share of the pie, and precluded the bitterness, which is usually attendant with a zero-sum game. Above all, the population was free from the political oppression and violence witnessed in other regimes of the region. Those advantages made up for the numerous other drawbacks, which characterized the political process in Lebanon.

In the last resort, a Lebanese saw himself/herself as a citizen of a relatively democratic and advanced state, educated, free and better off economically than neighbouring countries, though lagging behind the industrially advanced nations. Those conditions reduced the chances of regional integration and raised the height of the wall separating Lebanon from other Arab states. Arab nationalism continued though to be experienced, for some as an autonomous cultural expression, regardless of political plans.

On the whole, the last forty years have seen the vitiation of both regional loyalties as well as those of centrifugal nature. The rise of religious revivalism among the Shiites has not shown itself to be universalistic in orientation. However, the jury is still out on the issue of Lebanese future survival and may not be resolved while the conditions of unabated regional turmoil prevail.

The Tag Identity

The emergence of an overarching Lebanese identity among disparate groups who were brought together by social and economic accidents has been advanced by what I shall call the tag identity, for lack of a better term. I am referring here in part to what psychologists call the power of suggestion. Give an individual or a group a name and it will stick. In my school, we were divided every year into two competing sports groups: "Sanin" and "al Arze", after the snow covered mountain, which we could all see from the school yard, and an ancient cedar tree overlooking the tennis court on the school campus. Sharing a name with others is appealing, because it amounts to an extension of the self beyond its own boundaries and at the same time appropriating "the other", an act of enlarging the self. That is how group obligations become readily accepted.

State vs. Nation

The state is clearly an identity granting agency whose impact on its members is tangible and strong. A state may thus be a major cause behind the forging of a community with a national character. In modern times, it is the most common cause. The concept of "nation", in contrast, is indefinite and often overlaps with other ascriptive social attachments

I shall make the contention here that the Lebanese national political community is the child of an organized authority, not the reverse. This is how it started centuries ago and this is how it is at present. Before a nucleus authority was formed some centuries ago, there was no history, no name, and no culturally distinctive people. An authority structure became somehow institutionalized early in the sixteenth century creating a land base, loyal subjects, and diverse "fiefs" tied tenuously to one overlord. The geographic terrain expanded in proportion to the expansion of the authority structure. In time, the object became known as Lebanon, a state and a people.

Whether it is the Lebanese state, the Kenyan, or the French, there is a name, a flag, and a formal structure and a function. Membership generates a sense of identification with the organization, a sense of interest representation and of honour. One fights on behalf of his/her organization for resources, clients, justice, turf, all at the expense of other organizations. The organization sheds its character on its members and gives them a name and a place of their own. It is in that sense that most new states are progenitors of new societies, new identities.[15] Suddenly the tag assumes tangible features of growing significance. It distributes and allocates resources, security, privilege, obligation, constraint and need for cooperation.

The idea of the state as a formal organization creating a national society (Harik 1972 (2); Harik 1987; Harik 1972 (3); Harik 1999; Zubaida 2002) has turned the nationalist argument on its head. Nationalists argue that because they form a nation, they ought to have a state corresponding to the national group. The nation, in their perspective, precedes the state and is its *raison d'être*.

In contrast, the thesis that the state is the progenitor of the "nation" assigns to culture a secondary role, while placing political power and civic relations in the front seat. The state is a definite concept, outlined with the precisions of legal language.

As a subjective notion, the nation is of a tenuous and ambiguous nature whose object expands or contracts according to the perceptions of the actor. There are no precision or fixed boundaries in the idea of a nation, which is a sociological observation and/or a plain normative proposition. The sociologist simply brings to attention the multiplicity of subjective perceptions among people and the conflicting claims regarding the boundaries and membership of the national group. The sociological observation itself is not necessarily subjective, whereas the perception by the nationalists is. Membership in a nation is highly ambiguous.

The nation is an elastic term that arbitrarily includes categories of people and excludes other, depending on selective criteria. The inclusion or the exclusion, moreover, is not based on the consent of the concerned parties, who are hardly ever asked for their opinion.

The irony is that nationalists claim the unformed and amorphous object to be the progenitor of the formed and definite: the nation the mother of the state.

On the normative side, deriving political obligations from the fact that people have the same language, colour, or religion, is totally arbitrary. The relevance of a fact, such as speaking a particular language, to one's legal rights and obligations is imperceptible and a *non sequitor*. There is no necessary connection.

---

15 The term "old societies," which was made in the famous book, *Old Societies and New States*, was not meant to refer to "nations" but to highlight developed social traditions in Africa and Asia. The term societies was never intended to refer to fully formed political societies, i. e. nations. C. Geertz., *Old Societies and New States. The Quest for Modernity in Asia and Africa* (New York: Free Press of Glencoe, 1963).

In contrast, there is simplicity and elegance in the concept of the state as a progenitor. People become identified by formal membership and the rules by which they live together. As political participation and awareness are widespread in our modern era, the state project stands a better chance of survival. Crafting the rules together and becoming subject to them willingly have a formative effect on the personality and behaviour of citizens. In earlier eras, the will and power of a potentate, or a dominant solidarity group, was enough to create a state of inchoate mass, after which act, a national community was forged.

In the service of their cause, nationalists can do better than force a connection between a cultural object and political obligation. They can argue more effectively from the fact that an observable solidarity is a force to reckon with in the process of crafting a nation-state. The making of the state in that case would be affected by the *force* inherent in a social solidarity, not by a *logical connection* of a common feature or political obligation.

The Dissipation of Territoriality

Lebanon in the twenty-first century is in as a curious a situation as it has ever been. It is caught between two contradictory tendencies: a hardening of the particularistic perspectives of identities, and a new form of cosmopolitanism. Curiously enough, both tendencies have been the product of the protracted civil war.

The political significance of the new cosmopolitanism drew my attention recently during a walk in a small mountain village. Passing through the main street, I could see that not a single house looked like the other! Some were in the Mexican style, others decidedly French, a third looked like a Byzantine church next to a traditional eastern Mediterranean house. A step further I could see a house adorned with a pagoda! Could these be expressions of rural self-images?! Whatever, the spectacle obviously demonstrates the presence of an empathy, which transfers its bearer beyond the native and authentic self to new acquisitions of the imagination, to a cosmopolitan image.

Where is the true Lebanese in that small town? Most of the owners are at home also in Mexico, France, Russia, Thailand and God knows where else!

An out of proportion demographic sea change has swept over us since the war "was lost and won" in this small country. We are no longer exclusively a resident nation. The homeland seen as a people exclusively rooted in a congested space is no longer an adequate description for the Lebanese who now are a footloose population dispersed in a worldwide space. Those wanderers pay tribute, emotionally and economically, to a homeland, alias a "port town" state. Like "airborne" passengers, they live with the times but not in a fixed space. Old Lebanon is but a reference point with which they are still engaged.

The people one encounters at present on the streets of, say Beirut, have been away, may be going back, are linked to people far away, or have plans to go away. They are on the move, and most no longer have a fixation over the knot by which they are bound to the land. The younger generation may even be aspiring for a final territory elsewhere. The university system in Lebanon is no longer circumscribed to the production of a working force for the indigenous labour market, but prepares graduates with skills adequate for living and working in the world at large.

The fact that a major section of the footloose population remains in the region, in particular the Gulf States, makes it unlikely that the naval cord will be cut off for good. Territorial Lebanon will remain but only as a port for this new trans-national identity. What will it all eventually amount to is anybody's guess. For now, the trans-national aspect of the population has a pressing presence.

The enigmatic question is how will this fact of dissipating territoriality play out with its closest and most influential neighbour Syria, which is unable to move with the times? Syrian political hegemony may one day go, but demographically there is a population replacement provided by Syria, which may have a more lasting effect on the country. It is a major aspect of this population flow, and a key reason why the Lebanese now should be concerned with Syrian affairs.

The civil war has contributed in no mean terms to this demographic development, which came at a time ripe for coalescence with globalization trends. Those Lebanese with skills and resources pulled out to resume their careers and businesses outside the country but not to sever relations. Some of those who were sent away as children, returned to stay permanently, to attend to undetached concerns, or to answer to a cultural drive as occasional visitors. Financially, their impact has been most noticeable in the form of spending lavishly, maintaining business, or sending remittances. Thus, what could have been an economic disaster during and after the war was averted.

Culturally, the migrant press has been the most impressive in adapting to the new worldwide community of footloose Lebanese, adding in the process migrant Arabs to their readership. Qualitatively, the press, whether in print or visual, has acquired new cosmopolitan talents and its outreach is co-extensive with the far-flung footloose population.

Resident or footloose, are all part of the new Lebanon whose self-image is becoming increasingly one of an "airborne" people, in which politics may be taking a back seat. The overarching cosmopolitan identity is shared by all sectarian groups, and may leave the politics of identity for something else that is more auspicious and fruitful. There is reason to believe that in that impending future, centrifugal forces will be vitiated, while Arab regionalism becomes more functional than political. We need, of course, to have up-to-date research to enable us to confirm such trends, in particular, new surveys, which would include the footloose population. The most recent surveys were taken five to ten years ago right after the war (El-Amine 1997; Qa'i 2000), and were limited to the resident population, which reflect the hardening attitudes of that tense period.

Some of the top decision-makers in the country today belong to the new transnational identity of footloose Lebanese. Their impact shows putative signs of cosmopolitanism, which mixes poorly with the bogged down influential Arab neighbour, a cause for a continually tiresome relationship. The new leaders have shown patience and faith that in the long run they will be free from the coercive arm of Syria, which finds it hard to cope with the restless and multifaceted footloose population, if for nothing else, but to keep the Lebanese away from politically contaminating the Syrian population. Up to this point, though, the Syrians have been able to resuscitate parochial sectarian sentiments in the interest of their continued hegemony.

Is trans-nationalism something unique to the Lebanese? Maybe not, but it definitely has dimensions of its own: low key political interest, suspended primordial and national attitudes, and facile relations with host societies. The Lebanese in the diaspora do not live or act as social blocs, and in no way can they be described as a refugee community, worker enclaves, or estranged from the old country. In that sense, they differ from Kurdish (Cizre 2001), Turkish, or North African migrants in Europe. The Lebanese represent themselves as single persons, or nuclear families, playing the game on their own in the host countries, a fact which makes them take to the cosmopolitan features much faster than bloc communities do.

Disguised underneath this gigantic struggle in solitude is appreciation by the migrants of the might of their host and of their dependency. The paradox is that while tough enough to stand alone, the Lebanese develop a tendency common to the "small man" mentality, namely to see oneself as an accommodating "salesman" playing a private role. It is a role of compromise, of pleasing, of mimicking, and of distancing oneself from the public sphere. Curiously, this attitude is in many ways comparable to the "small man's" role played by Lebanon as a state *vis-à-vis* the bigger and more assertive neighbours.

Conclusion

The focus on the politics of identity in this essay should not make us lose perspective or exaggerate its centrality in the discipline. Identity is not a new discovery, nor a new approach revealing the hidden secrets of the political phenomenon. It is rather an old political tendency that has reclaimed its place in the political arena and in the scholarly halls of deliberation. Suffice it to say here that the diverse aspects of politics will be manifest in the variety of other studies published in this book.

The ambiguous sense toward territoriality has re-enforced the habit of separate Lebanese communities to forge external dependency relations, which is as old as the state itself. No matter how one rationalizes this tendency, the selling of one's services and the active pursuit of external links to shore up one's domestic position against its rivals remain a disturbing feature of Lebanese politics, and a proof of the limited relevance of identity as an expression of freedom and independence.

In the course of this discussion, we have noted that the politics of identity is not a Lebanese peculiarity, or a phenomenon limited to less developed countries, but is an increasingly felt problem the world over. No longer seen as an attribute of traditional societies, the politics of recognition has been receiving considerable attention in advanced industrial societies, which tended in the past to push identity issues under the rug or reject them on ideological grounds.

The politics of identity has in Lebanon been an open and acknowledged feature of the public space since its inception in the nineteenth century and has been undergoing modifications, adjustments and invention of new forms. It has also been subject to a recycling, or a pattern of repetition manifested in the injection of new and large segments of population into the state during different periods of its history.

The recycling of basically the same patterns of identity for over a century now has made the political process tedious and increasingly unwelcome, but the spirit of the country retained its dynamism unperturbed. This is important because the hope that the Lebanese are not stuck ideologically in stagnant waters rests on this dynamism. They redefine the way they see them selves, reinvent their mythologies, and are miraculously transformed while remaining the same, shaking the earth beneath them in the process.

The fact that a citizen can imagine him/herself in several roles and in a multiplicity of colours allows him/her to move easily across social and political borders of porous and overlapping nature.

This versatility of social mobility skills is what we have termed here as secularism. The way secularism has been perceived in this essay constitutes a departure from the classical view, which conceives secularism as a substantive ideological position. It is seen here as rather a mode of behaviour in the public space. To be a Maronite running on the same electoral ticket with a Sunni Muslim candidate and campaigning in Muslim quarters is a secular activity, one that tolerates differences as a feature of the landscape. In contrast, prohibiting an ethnic or religious community from seeking representation and self-protection in a democracy is a partisan, not a secular activity. It pits up one cultural preference against another. Neither communalism nor nationalism are to be considered secular, but different world-views.

The new perspective acknowledges religious identity and the social attributes that go with it, while the classical view acknowledges individual or national identity only; it tends to be exclusive. In contrast, the distinctive feature of secularism is the ability of the individual or group to be inclusive, interactive, and spatially mobile. Under this perspective, we can see that a Soviet citizen was less secular than a citizen in so-called sectarian Lebanon and India during that same period.

As a substantive doctrine, communalism may be considered as a rival nationalism of a local form, not as a sectarian versus secular phenomenon. The same may be said of the Muslim dress code for women, which is a rival symbol of identity. Its prohibition in France or Turkey is a partisan behaviour, not a secular act. The French and Turkish republicans who prohibit the Islamic dress code in the name of secularism are in fact acting in ideologically partisan manner in violation of secularism.

Viewing secularism as a mode of behaviour means that the passing of a religiously inspired law in a free process, which involves deliberation, criticism, and opposition in accordance with established legislative procedures is in fact a secular activity. If the same law is, however, passed without due process of deliberation and the freedom to consider the matter as a fair game for disagreement and criticism, then the act would be religiously partisan, not a secular act.

Secularism is the freedom of the individual or group to move in and out across social borders in a process of interaction, which does not obliterate distinctive identities nor uses them as a pretext to exclude others. Given the definition of a citizen in multicultural terms, a person's behaviour is not always bound to the same identity; on the contrary, one or the other of diverse identities borne by one and the same citizen come up to the surface under different contexts. Does this mean that a secular citizen is everything to everybody? Not at all.

The diverse identities of a citizen, which facilitate intercourse in a pluralist society, are not all active at one and the same time. The context determines which identity takes the front position, depending on the nature of the provocation. "When the chips are down", a citizen rallies to the identity most threatened, not necessarily to a signature identity, as the old proverb implies. There is no ultimate identity toward which a person falls back. What emerges is contextual, which means it may not be the same under a different type of provocation.

The multiplicity of identification and its contextual variability is the label of the modern man, and mostly of the citizen in a democratic society. This tendency may also be the deep reason behind the decline of political parties in the advanced industrial societies today.

References

Abu-Manneh, B., "The Christians Between Ottomanism and Syrian Nationalism: the Ideas of Butrus al Bustani", in *International Journal of Middle East Studies* 11 (May 1980)3.

Amine, A. El, and Muhammad Faour, *al-Tullaab al-Jaami'iyun fi Lubnan wa Ittijaahaatihim: Irth al-Inqisaamaat* (Beirut: al-Hay'ah al-Lubnaaniyah lil-Ulum al-Tarbawiyah, 1997).

Anderson, B. R. O. G., *Imagined Communities: Reflections on the Origin and Spread of Nationalism* (London: Verso, 1983).

Antoun, R. T. and I. F. Harik, *Rural Politics and Social Change in the Middle East* (Bloomington: Indiana University Press, 1972).

Baaklini, A. I., *Legislative and Political Development: Lebanon, 1842-1972.* (Durham, N. C.: Duke University Press, 1976).

Barry, B. M., *Culture and Equality: An Egalitarian Critique of Multiculturalism.* (Cambridge, Mass.: Harvard University Press, 2001)

Binder, L. (ed.), *Politics in Lebanon* (New York: Wiley, 1966).

Bradbury, M. L. and J. B. Gilbert, *Transforming Faith: The Sacred and Secular in Modern American History* (New York: Greenwood Press, 1989).

Cizre, U., "Turkey's Kurdish Problem: Borders, Identity, and Hegemony," in Brendan O'Leary et al. (eds.), *Right-Sizing the State: The Politics of Moving Borders* (Oxford University Press, 2001).

Deutsch, K. W., *Nationalism and Social Communication. An Inquiry into the Foundations of Nationality* (Cambridge, Mass.: M. I. T. Press, 1966).
Dworkin, R. M., *Sovereign Virtue: The Theory and Practice of Equality* (Cambridge, Mass.: Harvard University Press, 2000).
Khazen, F., El, *The Breakdown of the State in Lebanon, 1967-1976* (Cambridge, Mass.: Harvard University Press, 2000).
Khuri, Fuad, "Sectarian Loyalty Among Rural Migrants in Two Lebanese Suburbs: A Stage Between Family and National Allegiance", in R. T. Antoun and I. F. Harik, *Rural Politics and Social Change in the Middle East* (Bloomington: Indiana University Press, 1972).
Geertz, C., *Old Societies and New States. The Quest for Modernity in Asia and Africa* (New York: Free Press of Glencoe, 1963).
Hanf, Th. et al., *La société de concordance. Approche comparative* (Beirut: Publications de l'Université Libanaise, XI, 1986).
Hanf, Th., *Coexistence in Wartime Lebanon: Decline of a State and Rise of a Nation* (Oxford and London: Centre for Lebanese Studies in association with I. B. Tauris, 1993).
Harik, I. F. (2), "The Ethnic Revolution and Political Integration in the Middle East", in *International Journal of Middle East Studies*, Vol. 3 (July 1972)3: pp. 303-323.
Harik, I. F. (3), "The Impact of the Domestic Market on Rural-Urban Relations in the Middle East", in *Rural Politics and Social Change in the Middle East* (Bloomington: Indiana University Press, 1972).
Harik, I. F., "The Origins of the Arab state System", in G. Salame (ed.) *The Foundation of the Arab State* (London: Croom Helm, 1987).
Harik, I. F. (2), "Individualism, Communalism and the Quest for Democracy", in Hazim Saghie (ed.) *The Predicament of the Individual in the Middle East* (London: Saqi Books, 2001).
Harik, I. F., *Al-Dimuqratiyah wa Tahaddiyaat al Hadaatha: Bayna al- Sharq wa al-Gharb* (London and Beirut: Dar al-Saqi, 2002).
Harik, I. F., *Politics and change in a traditional society; Lebanon, 1711-1845* (Princeton, N.J.: Princeton University Press, 1968).
Harik, I. F. (1), *Mann Yahkum Lubnan?* (Beirut: Dar al-Nahar, 1972).
Harik, I. F., "Voting Behavior: Lebanon", in Jacob M. Landau, Ergun Ozbudun and Frank Tachau (eds.) *Electoral Politics in the Middle East* (London: Croom Helm, 1980)
Harik, I. F., "al-Qawmiyah al-'Arabiyah fi al-Mizan", in *Al Bahith* 17 (1981)5.
Harik, I. F., *Economic policy reform in Egypt* (Gainesville, Fl.: University Press of Florida, 1997).
Harik, I. F., "Citizenship and Civic Values with Special Reference to Lebanon" (in Arabic), in Walid Mubarak, Antoine Messarra, and Suad Joseph (eds.) *Bina' al-Muwaatiniyah fi Lubnan* (Beirut: A. L. A.U. Publication, 1999).
Harik, I. F., "Democratic Thought in the Arab World: An Alternative to the Patron State," in Charles Butterworth and I. William Zartman (eds.) *Between the State and Islam* (Cambridge University Press, 2001).
Hourani, A., "Lebanon: The Development of a Political Society", in Leonard Binder *Politics in Lebanon* (New York: Wiley 1966).
Hudson, M. C., *The Precarious Republic. Political Modernization in Lebanon* (New York: Random House, 1968).

Johnson, M., *Class & Client in Beirut: The Sunni Muslim Community and the Lebanese State, 1840-1985* (New York, Ithaca Press, 1986).
Khalaf, S., *Lebanon's Predicament* (New York: Columbia University Press, 1987).
Khalaf, S., *Cultural Resistance: Global and Local Encounters in the Middle East* (London: Saqi, 2001).
Khalaf, S., *Civil and Uncivil Violence in Lebanon: A History of the Internationalization of Communal Contact* (New York: Columbia University Press, 2002).
Khuri, F., *From Village to Suburb: Order and Change in Greater Beirut* (Chicago: University of Chicago Press, 1975).
Makdisi, U., "After 1860: Debating Religion, Reform, and Nationalism in the Ottoman Empire", in *International Journal of Middle East Studies* 34 (2002)4.
Marty, M. E., *The Modern Schism. Three Paths to the Secular* (New York: Harper & Row, 1969).
Messarra, A. N., "Theorie générale du système politique libanais" (Paris: Cariscript, 1994).
Qa'i, A., "Nadhrat al-Lubnaaniyin ila al-Masaar al-Dimuqrati", in A. Messarra (ed.) *Marsad al-Dimuqratiyah fi Lubnan* (Beirut: Markaz al-Silm al-Ahli, 2000).
Rawls, J., *A Theory of Justice* (Cambridge, Mass.: Belknap Press of Harvard University Press, 1971).
Rawls, J. and E. Kelly, *Justice as Fairness: A Restatement* (Cambridge, Mass.: Harvard University Press, 2001).
Taylor, C. and A. Gutmann, *Multiculturalism and the Politics of Recognition: An Essay* (Princeton, N.J.: Princeton University Press, 1992).
Van Ness, P. H., *Spirituality and the Secular Quest* (New York: Crossroad, 1996)
Zubaida, S., "The Fragments Imagine the Nation: The Case of Iraq", in *International Journal of Middle East Studies* 34 (2002)2.

Taif Revisited

NAWAF SALAM

The war that broke out in 1975 in Lebanon reflected the brittleness of the consensus among the various Lebanese sects (*Wifaq*) as well as the failure of the Lebanese power-sharing formula (*Sigha*) to accommodate the social and demographic changes that the country witnessed in the 1960s and 1970s. But it is impossible to fully comprehend the course of this protracted crisis and the attempts to resolve it without taking into account Lebanon's turbulent environment and the role of external factors in its conflict.[1]

The role external factors played in the conflict is reflected in the deadly dialectic of Lebanese protagonists' search for outside support to strengthen their domestic positions against local rivals and of foreign actors' exploitation of Lebanon's internal divisions to enhance their regional power. Lebanon was thus gradually transformed into a battlefield of regional and international rivalries. Besides the fall-out from the Arab-Israeli conflict, Syrian-Egyptian, Iraqi-Syrian, and Syrian-Palestinian quarrels were fought out on Lebanese territory by Lebanese proxies. Moreover, between 1982 and 1985 Lebanon became a warm spot of superpower competition. This is not to mention how internal disputes of foreign countries were also played out in Beirut in the late 1980s, e. g. that between "extremist" and "moderate" factions in the Iranian government.

At the same time, external factors could be seen to bear on the possible solution and/or containment of the conflict as of its early stages. Thus, the general hostilities in 1975–76 were ended by resolutions of the 1976 Arab summits of Riyadh and Cairo, which formalized a Saudi-sponsored Syrian-Egyptian reconciliation and provided a framework for deploying an Arab Deterrent Force in Lebanon.

---

1 On the origins, course and interpretations of the war, see Theodor Hanf, *Coexistence in Wartime Lebanon. Decline of a State and Rise of a Nation* (Oxford and London: Centre for Lebanese Studies and Tauris 1993); Samir Kassir, *La guerre du Liban. De la dissension nationale au conflit régional (1975-1982)* (Paris: Karthala 1994); Walid Khalidi, *Conflict and Violence in Lebanon: Confrontation in the Middle East* (Cambridge: Center for International Affairs, 1979); Farid El-Khazen, *The Breakdown of the State in Lebanon, 1967-1976* (London: Tauris, 2000); Elizabeth Picard, *Lebanon, a Shattered Country: Myths and Realities of the Wars in Lebanon* (New York: Holmes & Meier, 1996); and Kamal Salibi, *Crossroads to Civil War. Lebanon 1958-1976* (Delmar, N.Y.: Caravan, 1976).

The Taif accord, or Document of National Entente,[2] adopted by the Lebanese deputies meeting in Saudi Arabia in 1989 is striking evidence of how intertwined the internal and external dimensions of the Lebanese conflict had become. Although domestic reforms are the cornerstone of the Taif agreement, the agreement would never have seen light had it not included clauses regulating Lebanese-Syrian relations and provisions on policies to end Israel's occupation of South Lebanon.

The agreement was, indeed, predicated on the readiness of the Lebanese adversaries – exhausted and finally aware that none of them could achieve a decisive victory – to compromise. Moreover, with the failure to elect a new president to succeed Amin Gemayel, Lebanon faced, for the first time since 1975, constitutional deadlock with two rival governments. But Taif was also made possible by the concurrence of a series of favorable external changes.

First, Palestinian influence in Lebanon had been weakened by the Israeli invasion of 1982, which drove the bulk of PLO armed forces out of Beirut and the South, the confrontation between the remaining Palestinian troops and the Syrian army in the north and the Bekaa valley, and the "battle of the camps" between the Palestinians and the Amal movement.

Second, Israel scaled back its objectives owing to the failure of the 17 May 1983 accord with Lebanon and, after 1987, the need to focus on the Palestinian *Intifada*.

Third, Syria's position in Lebanon had been reinforced; in particular, its army was back in Beirut after having had to pull out in the wake of the Israeli invasion of 1982. However, Syria now had to compete with an Iraq seeking, after its war with Iran, to develop a power base in Lebanon by supporting the Lebanese Forces and the Awn government, which had declared a "war of liberation" against Syria. This facilitated Syria's acceptance at the 1989 Casablanca Arab Summit of the formation of the Higher Arab Tripartite Committee consisting of Saudi Arabia, Algeria, and Morocco, which was entrusted with finding a solution to the Lebanese crisis.

Last but not least, the radically new policies adopted by the Soviet Union under Gorbachev reduced superpower tensions in the Middle East.[3]

Owing to these external changes, the Taif Agreement was able to modify the rules of the internal game in Lebanon. First and foremost, it permitted the silencing of the guns. It also initiated a political process that helped rescue the constitutional institutions by ena-

---

2 On the Taif accord, see Al-M arkaz al-Lubnani lil-dirasat (collective work), *Wathiqat al-wifaq al-watani. Muraja'a naqdiyya wataniyya* (Beirut 2001); Arif al-Abid, *Lubnan wa-l Taif, Taqatu' tarikhi wa masar ghayr muktamil* (Beirut 2001); Judith Palmer Harik, "Democracy (Again) Derailed: Lebanon's Ta'if Paradox", in Bahgat Korany, Rex Brynen and Paul Noble, *Political Liberalization & Democratization in the Arab World,* Vol. 2 (Comparative Experiences) (Boulder: Rienner, 1998); Hassan Krayyem, "The Lebanese Civil War and the Taif Agreement", in Paul Salem (ed.), *Conflict Resolution in the Arab World: Selected Essays* (Beirut: American University of Beirut, 1997); Joseph Maila, *The Document of National Understanding: A Commentary* (Oxford: Centre for Lebanese Studies, 1992); and Paul Salem (translator and annotator) "The New Constitution of Lebanon and the Taif Agreement", in *The Beirut Review,* Vol. 1, No. 1 (Spring 1991).

3 See Arif al-Abid, op. cit., pp. 132-141 and 193-217; and Hassan Krayyem, op. cit., pp. 418- 421.

bling parliament to meet and formally endorse the text of the Agreement, which was the precondition for presidential elections and the formation of a unitary government. The army was also reunified and the militias disbanded – though this did not apply to Hizballah, which benefited from a "special treatment" due to the Israeli occupation of parts of southern Lebanon. As a result, the major obstacles that had hindered for years the free movement of the Lebanese within their country and had virtually divided its territory were removed.

However, the restoration of full state authority was still predicated on external conditions since Taif called for the unconditional withdrawal of Israeli forces from Israel's self-declared "security zone" in South Lebanon through the implementation of UN Security Council resolution 425.[4]

The agreement also provided for the redeployment of Syrian troops in Lebanon to the Bekaa Valley, and "if necessary, to other locations to be agreed upon by a joint Lebanese-Syrian military committee" within a period not exceeding two years from the formation of a government of National Reconciliation and the passing of constitutional reforms.[5] No reference was made to the withdrawal of Syrian troops, only to the fact that their "size and duration" in Lebanon is a matter that will have to be agreed upon between the governments of the two countries. As a translation of "Lebanon's Arab identity and affiliation", Lebanese Syrian relations are considered "privileged" and based on the "principle of cooperation and coordination" that should materialize in the conclusion of bilateral agreement in "all domains".[6]

Regarding the presence of Palestinian refugees, the rejection of their permanent resettlement in Lebanon was elevated to a constitutional provision.[7]

Obviously, fulfillment of these preconditions for restoring the full authority of the state as well as territorial sovereignty was not in Lebanese hands. It was contingent upon external factors and developments related mainly to the Arab-Israeli conflict, but also to other elements of the broader regional balance of power, such as the role of Iran. Hence, without significant progress in the Middle East peace process, the authority of the Lebanese state would not be fully restored or the internal reforms agreed to in Taif fully implemented. Moreover, such implementation depended increasingly on Syria's growing influence in Lebanon, especially after the US-Syrian rapprochement that followed Syria's support for the anti-Iraq coalition in the Gulf War and its agreement to take part in the Madrid Peace Conference and subsequent bilateral negotiations.

It is also important to note here that the deputies meeting in Taif were unable to amend to these sections of the Accord – unlike those dealing with domestic reforms. They were the outcome of international and regional negotiations primarily between Syria and the members of the Arab Tripartite Committee. The Lebanese deputies had

---

4 See *Wathiqat al-wifaq al-watani al-lubnani,* Beirut 1990, Section 3.
5 Idem, Section 2.
6 Idem, Section 4.
7 Idem, Section 1, Part 1, paragraph I.

the choice between adopting them word for word and jeopardizing the whole agreement.

In addition to the price of remaining in a "suspended sovereignty" condition, proceeding with the Taif deal had required a domestic cost as well. To persuade the Lebanese warlords to accept the agreement, they had to be granted a substantial slice of the new political pie. Hence, Taif's provision empowering the government, contrary to all basic democratic principles, to appoint deputies to the vacant parliamentary seats of deceased members and to new seats created to establish parity between Christians and Muslims.[8] One cannot but note here that since 1976 all attempts to end the Lebanese war that did not offer the militia chieftains a substantial stake in the projected postwar order or ignored Syria's interests in Lebanon failed dramatically and paved the way for another round of violence.[9]

Inasmuch as Taif was an expression of the interrelation between the external and internal dimensions of the conflict, the section on domestic reforms – a result of a give and take process of compromise – was itself a "package deal". Its subsections are mutually dependent and only make sense in the context of their broader framework, based on the principle of measure for measure. Moreover, certain articles of the Accord, such as those in the preamble, stand out as expressions of the same underlying logic of symmetry and reciprocity.

As to the contents of the accord, most of its provisions could be found in preceding documents. As a matter of fact, Taif incorporates many compromise formulae already drawn up in previous texts such as the Constitutional Document (1976), the Principles of Entente (1980), the Lausanne Paper (1984), the Policy Statement of the National Unity Government (1984), and the Tripartite Agreement (1985).

The Accord is a reworking of the blueprint submitted to the deputies meeting in Taif by the Higher Arab Tripartite committee (1989). The latter, for its part, drew heavily on the following four reform drafts: the "Main Principles for Solving the Lebanese Crisis" agreed on in the Salem – Shar' Discussions in Damascus (1987), the Hariri Working Paper that elaborated on the latter (1987), the U.S. "Non-Paper" of April Glaspie (1988), and the joint Husseini-Hoss Proposal (1989).[10]

Therefore, while the crucial "package deal" approach to the Taif Agreement is innovative, the reform elements of that package, as Joseph Maila pertinently points out in his early commentary on the agreement,[11] are not. Moreover, at an ideological level, Taif has been criticized and rejected by many Lebanese for falling short of their ideal model of political organization and/or their perception of the reforms needed for Lebanon.

---

8 Idem, Section 1, Part 2, Article A, paragraph 6.
9 See Hani A. Faris, "The Failure of Peacemaking in Lebanon, 1975-1989", in Deidre Collings (ed.), *Peace for Lebanon? From War to Reconstruction* (Boulder: Rienner, 1994).
10 See Arif al-Abid, op. cit., pp. 163-192.
11 Joseph Maila, op. cit., p. 3.

For example, Taif satisfied neither those who had pleaded for a federal solution for Lebanon nor the advocates of the principle of "one person, one vote". On the other hand, as it was a compromise reached under a given domestic and regional balance of power, none of the Lebanese parties could, by definition, identify fully with its terms.

It remains that Taif constitutes a major political turning point in the history of independent Lebanon because of the importance of changes it introduced in the Lebanese political system through constitutional reforms. And just as the internal aspects of Taif cannot be comprehended in isolation from the external dimensions of the conflict, so the relevance of Taif's constitutional reforms cannot be grasped from a pure legal perspective. They need to be understood in the context of the underlying sectarian balance of power and interpreted in accordance with the prevailing sectarian political culture.

In fact, the relationship between the executive, the legislative, and the judiciary, the respective prerogatives and the powers enjoyed by the respective officeholders, and the structures and functions of the main institutions and agencies of state are less an expression of general constitutional principles than a reflection of the distribution of power among the various sects, the identity and strength of the parties by whom they are represented, and the alliances they make, whether inside or outside Lebanon. Yet, given the fact that such equations and relationship are taken into account when constitutional rules are drafted and no less when it comes to how they are applied – witness the sectarian allocation of the three highest offices of state –, it is still a useful exercise to analyse the post-Taif constitutional amendments. Four points warrant special attention.

First, the highly controversial issue of Lebanon's identity which had much divided the Lebanese and inflamed many ideological debates as of the inception of modern Lebanon finds a "consensual" recast in Articles (a) and (b) of the preamble to the amended constitution. The new formula is based on balanced parallelism. While Lebanon is declared "a final homeland for all its sons", its "Arab identity and affiliation" is also confirmed. By virtue of this definition, Muslims are deemed committed to Lebanon *per se*, not as a transient entity pending the establishment of a single pan-Arab state or the unification of the Islamic *Umma*. Similarly, Christians are presumed to accept that the Lebanese state be bound in its policies and obligations by the requirements of a shared Arab destiny.[12]

Second, Taif operates a "novation" of the confessional political system. It maintains the same old game, but updates its rules. On the one hand, Taif affirms the religious sects as the basic constituent units of the system; the legitimizing principle of the repub-

---

12 For the "historical" dimension of the identity debate in Lebanon and a commentary on the Taif preamble, cf. Edmond Rabbath, "'Wathiqat al-wifaq al-watani' wa ta'dil al-dustur", in *Proche-Orient. Etudes Juridiques*, No. 45-46 (1993). On the general question of identity in Lebanon, cf. in particular, Ahmad Beydoun, *Identité confessionnelle et temps social chez les historiens libanais contemporains* (Beirut: Publications de l'Université Libanaise, 1984); Ghassan Salame, *Lebanon's Injured Identities. Who Represents Whom During a Civil War* (Oxford: Centre for Lebanse Studies, 1986); and Kamal Salibi, *A House of Many Mansions. The History of Lebanon Reconsidered* (London: Tauris, 1988).

lic remains, as in the unwritten Pact of 1943,[13] that of a communal "social contract". However, this is now solemnly enshrined in Article "j" of the preamble to the amended constitution, which reads: "Constitutional legitimacy shall not be extended to any authority that contradicts the pact of coexistence". On the other hand, Taif purports – often indirectly – to redefine confessional representation and prerogatives in all the main institutions of state with the objective of achieving a more balanced and equitable formula for confessional power-sharing.

Paradoxical though it may seem, to enhance the stability of the new confessional formula, Taif provides for an institutional process to deal with the controversial issue of deconfessionalization by calling on the first parliament to be elected to form a "National Committee" to "study and propose the means to ensure the abolition of confessionalism".[14] In reality, this essentially means adjourning the issue of deconfessionalization *"ad Calendas Libanicas"*, as Theodor Hanf elegantly remarks,[15] for neither an agenda nor a time frame for said committee has been set.

Third, the main features of the new power-sharing formula can be summarized as follows. Executive powers formerly constitutionally vested in their entirety in the president of the republic, but in fact substantially restricted by tradition, are transferred to the council of ministers as a collegial body[16] in which confessional groups are to be "represented in an equitable manner" pursuant to Article 95 of the constitution.

The principle of confessional collegiality is further reinforced by the new provisions of Article 65 of the constitution, which specify that "the legal quorum for a Council (of ministers) meeting shall be a two-thirds majority of its members. It shall make its decisions by consensus. If that is not possible, it shall make its decisions by vote of the majority of attending members. Fundamental issues shall require the approval of two-thirds of the government named in the decree of formation".[17]

The president, by tradition a Maronite Christian, acting now as a head of state, retained, however, considerable powers of quasi-arbitration. He can still veto a bill passed by parliament and request its reconsideration. In this case, he is not required to promulgate it as law until it "has been discussed again and approved by an absolute majority of

---

13 On the 1943 Pact, see Bassim al-Jisr, *Mithaq 1943. Limadha Kan? Wa hal Saqat?* (Beirut 1978); and Farid el-Khazen, *The Communal Pact of National Identities. The Making and Politics of the 1943 National Pact* (Oxford: Centre for Lebanese Studies, 1991).
14 Article 95 of the Lebanese Constitution, as amended in 1990. (All references are to an English translation of the constitution, with all amendments since 1926, published by the Lebanese Ministry of Justice in 1995).
15 Theodor Hanf, op. cit., p. 588.
16 Cf. Article 65 of the Lebanese Constitution, op. cit..
17 Issues deemed "fundamental" are listed in Article 65 as follows: "Amendments to the constitution, the declaration of a state of emergency and its termination, war and peace, general mobilization, international agreements, the annual government budget, long-term comprehensive development plans, the appointment of employees of grade one and its equivalent, the reconsideration of administrative divisions, the dissolution of the Chamber of Deputies, electoral law, nationality law, personal status laws, and the dismissal of ministers."

all the members legally composing the Chamber".[18] Even in this case, the president has the right to submit the matter to the scrutiny of the Constitutional Council.[19] Although not a member of the council of ministers, he may nevertheless attend and preside over its meetings, participate in its deliberations – but without the right to vote – and submit to it any "urgent matter" that is not on its agenda.[20] Bound to promulgate and publish the decrees taken by the council of ministers within a period of 15 days, he may nonetheless ask the latter to reconsider its decision, but once upheld he can no longer block its entry into force.[21] Although the president is now bound by the results of parliamentary consultations in designating the president of the council of ministers,[22] he plays a crucial role in the composition of the latter, since the promulgation of the decree for its formation requires the "agreement" of both the designated president of the council and the president of the republic.[23] Finally, the moral authority of the president, as head of state, allows him to provide critical guidance, as he may "address, when necessary, messages to the Chamber of Deputies".[24]

In sum, the President's powers have been reduced, but his remaining powers are certainly not "inconsequential". Nor has he been "completely cornered", left without "even the choice of putting up or shutting up".[25] Similarly, it would go too far to describe his functions as "largely ceremonial".[26]

As noted earlier, powers have been transferred from the president of the republic to the council of ministers as a *collegium*, not to its president. Yet, the latter's position, traditionally held by a Sunni Muslim, is strengthened by virtue of the fact that he now presides over an institution vested with executive powers. By comparison, under the pre-Taif constitution, whenever the cabinet used to convene under the chairmanship of the prime minister, it did so as a ministerial council *(majlis wizari)*, which could not act in even routine matters, but only prepare the meeting of the council of ministers, which was presided over by the president of the republic and as such did constitute an organ empowered to make decisions. In the words of Edmond Rabbath, the former, i. e., the *majlis wizari*, was but "a form of reunion", not an institution.[27]

The position of the president of the council of ministers has also been strengthened by the Taif Agreement which gives constitutional force to the prerogatives he had previously exercised by force of tradition. In addition, and most importantly, he now sets

---

18 Article 57 of the Lebanese Constitution, op. cit.
19 Cf. Article 19 of the Lebanese Constitution, op. cit.
20 Cf. Article 53 of the Lebanese Constitution, op. cit.
21 Cf. Article 56 of the Lebanese Constitution, op. cit.
22 Cf. Article 53, paragraph 2 of the Lebanese Constitution, op. cit.
23 Cf. Article 53, paragraph 4 of the Lebanese Constitution, op. cit.
24 Cf. Article 53, paragraph 10 of the Lebanese Constitution, op. cit.
25 Joseph Maila, op. cit., pp. 58 and 59.
26 Paul Salem, "Two years of Living Dangerously: General Awn and the Precarious Rise of Lebanon's 'Second Republic'", in *The Beirut Review*, Vol. 1, No 1 (Spring 1996): p. 78.
27 Edmond Rabbath, *La constitution libanaise: Origines, textes et commentaires* (Beirut: Libr. Orientale, 1982): p. 365.

the agenda of meetings and is responsible for supervising the implementation of decisions of the council of ministers.[28]

The position of speaker of parliament – traditionally a Shi'i – has been considerably enhanced as well. His mandate has been extended from one to four years. It cannot be terminated but once at the end of the second year by a two-thirds majority of the Chamber.[29] Enjoying greater security of office, the speaker now presides over a parliament whose stability has also been enhanced, as the executive can no longer dissolve it, except in four unlikely instances.[30]

In the pre-Taif era, the balance between the executive and the legislative powers was tipped in favor of the former. Taif reversed this situation – rather than established equilibrium. As a matter of fact, it is an established principle of constitutional theory that in parliamentary regimes the government's answerability to parliament and the latter's capacity to bring it down by a vote of no confidence are counterbalanced by the executive's ability to dissolve parliament. In French jurisprudence this principle is known as that of *"moyens d'action réciproques entre gouvernement et parlement"*.

The prerogatives of parliament have been strengthened as well. As already noted, the president of the republic has become bound by the result of his consultation with members of parliament on whom to nominate as president of the council of ministers. The president of the republic is also required to inform the speaker of this result and to consult with him on the matter.[31] Likewise, the legislative role of parliament is reinforced through an amendment to Article 58 of the constitution, whereby bills that the council of ministers deems "urgent" can no longer be put in to effect by decree 40 days after being sent to parliament if parliament has not acted upon them, unless they are placed on its agenda and read in a public session.

Taif also provided for a change in the composition of parliament from a 6 to 5 ratio in favor of Christians to parity between Muslims and Christians and for a new electoral law in which the territorially larger and confessionally mixed *Muhafazats* (or governorates) serve as electoral districts.[32]

Fourth, and finally, Taif provided for the strengthening of the independence of the judiciary,[33] administrative decentralization,[34] and the creation of a Constitutional Council[35] and a Socio-Economic Council.[36]

Taif's implementation was delayed mainly because of General Awn's radical opposition to the Accord. However, in the wake of the Gulf Crisis, Syrian troops backed by

---

28 Cf. Article 64 of the Lebanese Constitution, op. cit.
29 Cf. Article 44 of the Lebanese Constitution, op. cit.
30 Cf. Article 65, paragraph 4 and Article 77 of the Lebanese Constitution, op. cit.
31 Cf. Article 52, paragraph 2 of the Lebanese Constitution, op. cit.
32 See *Wathiqat al-wifaq* ... op. cit., Section 1, Part 2, Article A, paragraphs 4 and 5; and Section 1, Part 3, Article C.
33 Idem, Section 1, Part 3, Article B, paragraph 3 (C).
34 Idem, Section 1, Part 3, Article A.
35 Idem, Section 1, Part 3, Article B, paragraphs 2, 3 and 4.
36 Idem, Section 1, Part 3, Article D.

Lebanese army units removed him from the presidential palace in Baabda. The regional effects of the Gulf crisis and the changes in the domestic balance of power after Awn's ouster could not but affect the course of Taif's implementation.[37]

"Implementation" is perhaps a misnomer. Although the Taif reforms were translated into 31 constitutional amendments, which were approved by parliament in August 1990, many have still not entered into force. This has undermined the nature of the Accord as a "package deal". Other reforms have been either twisted at the implementation stage or later distorted in practice.

Key reforms that have not been implemented include:
- the decentralization of administration,
- the strengthening of the independence of the judiciary,
- the formation of the National Committee entrusted with the task to "study and propose the means to ensure the abolition of confessionalism", and,
- most importantly, the promulgation of a new electoral law in which electoral districts coincide with *Muhafazats*.

The last point demonstrates how twisted a fundamental Taif provision has become once implemented as well as how detrimental its effects could accordingly be.

The 1992 parliament, the first elected after Taif, reflected the agreed change in communal representation from a 6 to 5 ratio in favor of the Christians to parity between Christian and Muslim deputies. While this necessarily implied an increase in the number of seats from 99 to 108 pursuant to the provisions of Taif,[38] the electoral law governing these elections raised the figure further to 128. This was clearly designed to enable a greater number of representatives of the war and postwar new "elite" to enter parliament. And whereas Taif had called for elections to be held at the regional level of the *Muhafazat*, hoping that this would encourage coalitions across local and sectarian boundaries and hence foster national reconciliation, the 1992 electoral law adopted a hybrid system; in the predominantly Shi'i South two *Muhafazat*(s) were combined to form one electoral district, while in the predominantly Christian *Muhafazat* of Mount Lebanon, the *qada*(s), districts at the subgovernorate level, served as electoral districts. Apportionment was even less uniform in the *Muhafazat* of the Bekaa Valley: one electoral district was based on a *qada*, while the others were made up of two *qadas*. Only in Beirut and in North Lebanon was the *Muhafazat* adopted as the defining electoral unit.[39]

As is well known, such anomalies led to the boycott of these elections by a large – and predominantly, though not solely Christian – segment of the population. Participation was estimated at 30.34%, the lowest level ever in Lebanese parliamentary elec-

---

[37] Regarding the ouster of the Awn Government, cf. generally Carole Dagher, *Les Paris du Général* (Beirut 1992); Annie Laurent, "A War Between Brothers: The Army – Lebanese Forces Showdown in East Beirut", in *The Beirut Review*, Vol. 1, No. 1 (Spring 1991); and Sarkis Na'um, *Michael Awn: Hilm am wahm* (Beirut 1992).

[38] See *Wathiqat al-wifaq* ... op. cit., Section 1, Part 2, Article A, paragraph 6.

[39] For a detailed appraisal of the 1992 legislative elections, see Farid El-Khazen and Paul Salem (eds.), *Al-intikhabat al-'ula fi Lubnan ma ba'd al-harb. Al-arqam wa-l waqai' wa-l dalalat* (Beirut: Dar al-Nahar, 1993).

tions.[40] The genuine representativeness of this first post-Taif parliament was thereby in doubt from the day of its election.

The obvious need to redress such a situation was, however, frustrated by the self-serving interests of the 1992 deputies, combined with Syria's regional concern in asserting its influence in Lebanon, especially after Likud's Netanyahu victory in Israel.

As it turned out, the old/new 1996 electoral law maintained the same hybrid pattern of electoral districting as that of 1992. Mount Lebanon voted in *qada*-based electoral districts, which divided the predominantly Christian electorate and helped to secure the reelection of the Druze leader, Walid Joumblat, and his candidates. The two *Muhafazats* of South Lebanon were again treated as one electoral district, thus favoring the alliance of Amal's leader, Speaker Nabih Berri, and Hizbullah over its Shi'i opponents.[41]

The Constitutional Council declared the law unconstitutional because it violated the principle of equality among Lebanese. The government, however, responded by insisting that the law would be implemented as initially presented. But it did add a clause stating that exceptions to the rule of uniform electoral districts based on *Muhafazats* were "for this one time only". The 2000 electoral law, however, was no less hybrid than that of 1996, and therefore still in violation of the constitution. Significantly, in the 1996 parliament it proved impossible to find the ten deputies required to bring the matter before the Constitutional Council.

Evaluating the results of the post-Taif elections in Lebanon in terms of the functions generally attributed by political scientists to legislative elections in democratic regimes, we come to the following conclusions.

First, with regard to the key function of legitimizing the system and its participants, the Lebanese elections failed rather than succeeded:
– they were held under unconstitutional electoral laws;
– significant segments of the population continued to boycott them, though decreasing in size with each election; and
– the government was accused by a number of leading civil society organizations and respected columnists, not to mention candidates, of blatantly ignoring the norms and requirements of neutrality and independence.

Second, the elections failed to improve political stability. Excluding the opposition from state institutions or only allowing opposition forces minimal representation within these institutions has nowhere proved to be a good recipe for stability in the long run. There is nothing to suggest that Lebanon will prove an exception to this golden rule.

Third, elections are supposed to offer citizens the possibility of choosing change in the form of different people and policies. This is only true if elections are genuinely competitive, but this is not the case if candidacies and electoral alliances are subject to limits and ceilings, which deprive the voters or any real choice, as happened in many districts

---

40 Idem, p. 72.
41 For a detailed appraisal of the 1996 legislative elections, cf. Al-Markaz al-Lubnani lil-dirasat (collective work), *Al-intikhabat al-niyabiyya 1996 wa 'azmat al-dimuqratiyya fi lubnan* (Beirut 1998).

in all three elections, in 1992, 1996 and 2000. Elite circulation was thus seriously impeded and the possibility of change frustrated.

Finally, if the goal of elections is to represent the views of the voters as closely as possible, an electoral system based on simple majorities in large multimember districts (up to 28 seats in the *Muhafazat* of North Lebanon) is inadequate for this purpose.

In fact, the greater the number of seats per district, the more likely that plurality systems will distort results.[42] (This is why in e.g. senate elections French electoral law provides for a shift from simple majority to proportional representation when the number of seats in any district exceeds five.)

As to how reforms which were "implemented" have been distorted by ensuing practices, the case is best illustrated by the dysfunctions of the council of ministers as a *collegium*. The underlying objective in transferring executive powers to the council of ministers was to offer an equitable solution to the question of confessional power-sharing. But while Taif's fine-tuning of the sectarian balance helped contain sectarian violence, it could not at the same time temper sectarian jealousies because what was at stake was but a new division of the sectarian pie. More than ever before, ministers felt obliged to act as guardians of the particular interests of their communities or at least to appear to be doing so before their respective communal constituencies. They could not form a team capable of formulating a common policy or of carrying it out, whenever it seemed as if they were able to do so.

Some ten years before the outbreak of war in 1975, Malcolm Kerr observed that governments in Lebanon were "not made to create public policy ... but to reflect faithfully and adjust the competing interests of various groups".[43] He judiciously added that "Lebanese politics exists only in Lasswell's limited sense of 'who gets what, when, and how', as a competition for the honors and spoils of office. Within that sense its existence is a thriving one; but there is no room for politics in the more full-blooded sense of the competition for power to create and impose new policies".[44] More than ten years after the end of the war, it is difficult to find better words to describe the nature of government or the scope of politics in Lebanon, in spite of the radical Taif constitutional amendments regarding the prerogatives and role of government.

Furthermore, engaged in fierce competition for patronage and benefits, ministers seldom feel bound by the constitutional principle of "collective responsibility". As a matter of fact, in the post-Taif era there have been numerous instances of ministers publicly criticizing the composition of the cabinet to which they belong, condemning positions taken by their colleagues, disapproving of the actions of the president of the council of ministers, denouncing the general orientation of the cabinet, or even boycotting cabinet

---

[42] For a discussion of such distortions and a critique of the Lebanese electoral system, cf. Nawaf Salam, *Ab'ad min al-Taif, Maqalat fi al-dawla wa-l 'islah* (Beirut: Dar al-Gadid, 1998), Chaps. 6 and 8.
[43] Malcom Kerr, "Political Decision Making in a Confessional Democracy", in Leonard Binder, *Politics in Lebanon* (New York: Wiley, 1966), p. 190.
[44] Idem.

meetings for certain periods of time without feeling the need to resign or being forced to do so.

In brief, the council of ministers as a constitutional *collegium* has been incapable of becoming a policy-making – or even a decision-making – body. In practice its functions have often been assumed by a non-constitutional power-sharing "troika" of the three presidents, i.e. the president of the republic, the president of the council of ministers and the speaker of parliament, acting simultaneously as representatives of their respective communities and as holders of constitutional office. But it has been still difficult for this "troika" to rule effectively, as its members were constantly quarrelling over their respective shares of the pie, particularly in matters of civil service appointments and public appropriations. To function, the system often needed external arbitration, and no party was better prepared or had a greater vested interest in assuming – or continuing to exercise – this role than Syria.

Based on his experience as minister of defense and of information, respectively, in the first two post-Taif cabinets, former deputy Albert Mansour writes in his *Al-inqilab 'ala al-Taif* (Coup against Taif):

"All important and fundamental decisions were made outside the council of ministers, and later presented to it for ratification. As a matter of fact, decisions were not only made outside the council of ministers, but in place of it."[45]

Moreover, let us note here that the same factors that have determined Lebanese politics and hampered the functioning of government as a *collegium* have also prevented members of the opposition from forming national – as opposed to sectarian – alliances and formulating concrete programs of action.

Implemented in an eclectic and twisted manner, Taif itself became a source of new imbalances that could not but further increase sectarian suspicions. This is reflected not only – though perhaps most clearly – in the Christian so-called *ihbat*, a negative attitude based more on frustration with the Taif process than mere disenchantment with its outcome. It is the result of the cumulative effects of Awn's forced exile, Dany Chamoun's assassination, Samir Geagea's trial, obstacles and delays in the return of displaced people, the lack of transparency in the criteria of the massive grant of Lebanese citizenship by decree, the conditions surrounding the 1992 elections, and, above all, the non-redeployment of Syrian troops in 1992.[46]

Though it is true that the position of the president of the council of ministers has been substantially strengthened, Sunni leaders remain greatly concerned about the fact that the president of the republic appears reluctant to come to terms with his new role as head of state and continues to attend, and hence to preside over, most cabinet meetings. They fear that such a recurrent practice may with time turn into a new custom. Their sectarian jealousies were further aroused first by President Hrawi's call in 1996 for new constitutional amendments and later by President Lahoud's controversial style and his

---

45 Albert Mansour, *Al-Inqilab 'ala al-Taif* (Beirut 1993): pp. 188-189.
46 Generally see, George Sa'ada, *Qissati ma' al-Taif* (Beirut 1998).

creation of a special unit at the presidential palace to monitor the day-to-day management of affairs in the various ministries. The result was a Sunni *malaise*, which was the main reason for the dramatic defeat of Salim Hoss, the president of the council of ministers, in the 2000 legislative elections, the first time in modern Lebanese history that an incumbent prime minister has failed to win a parliamentary seat.

Hopes that the redefinition of the prerogatives of parliament and its speaker, and the greater stability granted to both, would satisfy Shi'i's demands have not been borne out. Shi'i leaders continue to demand for their community a quasi-executive position with veto power comparable to that of the Maronite head of state and the Sunni president of the council of ministers, i.e., the post of minister of finance, as the latter's signature is mandatory for almost all decrees. This is not to mention Hizbullah's rejection of the whole confessional system as such for "ideological" reasons.

Besides heightening the sectarian suspicions of the three main sects, the dialectic of confessional jealousies generated by the Taif process has created a situation in which three other smaller sects are no longer satisfied with their constitutionally guaranteed participation in the council of ministers, in spite of the fact that Taif had vested the latter as a *collegium* with all executive power. Each of these three sects has thus been asking for its own turf. Hence, the Greek Orthodox demand that the prerogatives of the vice-president of the council of ministers be defined in law, and the Greek Catholics demand the permanent presidency of the Socio-Economic Council. And long before Taif the Druze had been demanding the creation of a senate, in which they would hold the presidency.

In his critique of Lijphart's revised model of consociational democracy, renamed consensus democracy, Sartori warned:

"By facilitating something you make it happen. The more you give in, the more you are asked to give. And what is not discouraged becomes in fact encouraged. If you reward divisions and divisiveness (...) you increase and eventually heighten divisions and divisiveness. In the end then, Lijphart's machinery may well engender more consensus-breaking than consensus-making".[47]

In the case of Lebanon, the danger is that the Taif model, which was meant to neutralize "the centrifugal forces of society", might instead have put Lebanon on "a one-way slope that leads to a self-reinforcing system" of confessional appetites.[48]

Taif succeeded in containing sectarian violence, but it has also reinforced sectarianism. Designed to rebalance Lebanon's power-sharing formula, its implementation has kept Lebanon off balance. Furthermore, post-Taif no less than pre-Taif, Lebanon's future appears predicated on external factors.

Remarkable though Taif was in silencing the guns, a distorted, partially implemented Taif failed to put Lebanon on track to build a state. In view of the experience of the past decade, it is doubtful whether this can now be achieved just by putting Taif back on track.

---

47 Giovanni Sartori, *Comparative Constitutional Engineering. An Inquiry into Structures, Incentives, and Outcomes* (New York: New York University Press, ^{2}1997): p. 72.
48 In analogy to Sartori's "minority appetites"; idem.

The Postwar Political Process: Authoritarianism by Diffusion

FARID EL KHAZEN

Whether before or after Lebanon's fifteen-year war (1975-1990), the political system in Lebanon has stood in striking contrast to political systems in the region, both at the level of the state and the political order it generated, and at the level of state-society relations. Notwithstanding its shortcomings, Lebanon's consociational democracy in the prewar period functioned relatively well. Over a period of three decades, from independence in 1943 to the outbreak of war in 1975, Lebanon has experienced political pluralism, competitive elections, and orderly regime change.[1] More important, political liberalisation was a cumulative process. This was clearly apparent in the electoral process. Held on a regular basis every four years, especially since 1960, parliamentary elections were increasingly competitive and government conduct in the elections continued to improve.

Despite occasional crises, presidential elections have resulted in regime change. At a time when Syria, for example, which gained independence roughly at the same time as Lebanon, was in its third military regime in the early 1950s, Lebanon held an orderly presidential election and was able to surmount the political crisis that led to the resignation of Lebanon's first president after independence in 1952. Similarly, the six-month armed conflict in 1958 ended with the election of president Fouad Chehab. Under Chehab's leadership, Lebanon witnessed unprecedented political and administrative reforms and economic development. In the presidential election of 1970 – the last held before the outbreak of war – the opposition scored a significant victory.

In the same vein, Lebanon's civil society, liberal economic system, and large private sector differed from state-controlled economies in many developing countries.[2] By the standards of the 1950s and 1960s, Lebanon's free wheeling economy was the exception

---

[1] On the political system in the prewar period, see, for example, Leonard Binder (ed.), *Politics in Lebanon* (New York: John Wiley, 1966); Michael Hudson, *The Precarious Republic. Political Modernization in Lebanon* (New York: Random House, 1968); David Smock and Audrey Smock, *The Politics of Pluralism: A comparative Study of Lebanon and Ghana* (New York: Elsevier, 1975).

[2] See Albert Dagher, *L'Etat et l'économie au Liban: Action gouvernementale et finances publiques de l'indépendance à 1975* (Beirut: Centre d'Etudes et de Recherches sur le Moyen-Orient Contemporain, 1995); Iliya Harik, "The Economic and Social Factors of the Lebanese Crisis", in *Journal of Arab Affairs* I (April 1982): pp. 209-44.

to the norm of command economies and the socialist model. By contrast, Lebanon's regional order, notably in the Arab East, was controlled by authoritarian regimes, ranging from one-party rule to regimes dominated by the military. In fact, as the Lebanese state became more democratic and civil society more vibrant and open in the 1960s and 1970s, Arab regimes became more authoritarian and society increasingly closed.[3] This pattern dominated Arab politics until the 1990s, when political "infitah", paving the way for "ta'adudiyya" – as opposed to economic "infitah" which began earlier[4] – was visible in some Arab countries and has influenced the political process and broadened political liberalisation. But the process as a whole remains in the hands of the authoritarian state and its ruling elites who opted for various forms of "guided" or "defensive" political liberalisation either to adapt to growing domestic demands or to neutralise external political and/or economic pressure.

In wartime Lebanon, the political system was crippled. Government institutions were paralysed, the Lebanese army was factionalised, and several armed groups dominated the decision-making process. From beginning to end, the war involved a large number of internal and external state and non-state actors, notably the PLO, Syria, Israel and, subsequently, Iran.[5] Only on rare occasions were military confrontations confined either to Lebanese or to non-Lebanese groups. Conflict was at once internal and regional. It unfolded in phases and underwent several mutations both in its nature and in the objectives of the protagonists.

As conflict continued and military confrontations escalated the internal divide deepened and the war system was institutionalised. Although the war did not alter the nature of the economic system, it led to large scale damage in virtually all sectors of the economy and to the destruction of much of the country's infrastructure.[6] By the time hostilities ended in 1990 Lebanon was more divided than before, not only along confessional lines (that is, between Christians and Muslims) but also more along sectarian lines within each confessional group, particularly within Muslim communities.

Postwar Lebanon

Unlike the ending of armed conflicts involving internal and external parties, most recently in the former Yugoslavia, Cambodia, Angola and Sri Lanka, the war in Lebanon did not end following a negotiated settlement accepted by all the warring parties, or with

---

3 Farid el Khazen, *The Breakdown of the State in Lebanon, 1967-1976* (Cambridge: Harvard University Press, 2000): pp. 89-122.
4 See Nazih N. Ayubi, *Over-Stating the Arab State. Politics and Society in the Middle East* (London: I. B. Tauris, 1995): pp. 329-395.
5 On the war years, see Theodor Hanf's comprehensive work, *Coexistence in Wartime Lebanon. Decline of a State and Rise of a Nation* (Oxford and London: Centre for Lebanese Studies and I. B.Tauris, 1993). See also William Harris, *Faces of Lebanon: Sects, Wars, and Global Extensions* (Princeton: Markus Wiener Publishers, 1997).
6 On the war damage, see Boutros Labaki and Khalil Abou Rjeily, *Bilan des guerres du Liban, 1975-1990* (Paris: Editions l'Harmattan, 1993).

a peace conference sponsored by the United Nations and/or by the direct involvement of major powers. And contrary to protracted armed conflicts both before and after the Cold War, the war in Lebanon did not involve any sustained military and political interventions by one or several major powers. Apart from the brief American intervention in the aftermath of the Israeli invasion in 1982-83, the war in Lebanon remained essentially a local and regional affair. It served the conflicting interests of regional actors and was very much linked to the ups and downs of the Arab-Israeli-Palestinian conflict.

Nor did the ending of war involve an orderly interim period that could have facilitated transition from war to peace, one that could be conducive to democratic reconstruction in the aftermath of conflict.[7] War ended with another act of war, when Syrian forces joined units of the Lebanese army to oust an interim premier General Michel Aoun from office. And unlike the ending of a previous armed conflict in Lebanon in 1958, when military confrontations ended in 1990, several thousand foreign troops were present on Lebanese soil: over 30000 Syrian troops in various parts of the country and Israeli troops in the south.[8] Whatever political settlement was reached between Lebanese groups, it was embodied in the Document of National Understanding, commonly called the Ta'if Agreement, signed by the Lebanese deputies in the Saudi city of Ta'if on October 22, 1989.[9]

Beginning in 1990, the political process was reactivated: three parliamentary elections were held, two presidents were elected, and eight cabinets were formed, most recently in October 2000. Lebanon seemed to have regained the necessary conditions for a return to the political liberties and competitive politics. In reality, however, that was not the case. At a time when other countries in the region are moving toward a more open and competitive political process, such as Jordan, Kuwait, and Morocco,[10] Lebanon's political process has moved in another direction. But movement is neither in the direction of classic authoritarianism nor in the direction of a functioning democratic order. How can we explain this state of affairs, and how does it manifest itself in the political process?

This essay seeks to explain the causes and nature of Lebanon's emerging authoritarianism since the end of the war. Authoritarianism in postwar Lebanon is neither "from below" nor "from above". It does not involve a zero-sum confrontation between state and society, nor is the state facing new modes of communication and external political and economic pressure, as in other countries in the region. Unlike, for example, the process of "political deliberalisation" in Egypt[11] and Tunis, Lebanon's process of "politi-

---

7 On interim governments, see Yossi Shain and Juan J. Linz, *Between States: Interim Governments and Democratic Transitions* (New York: Cambridge University Press, 1995): pp. 3-27 and pp. 92-102.
8 Israeli troops withdrew from South Lebanon in May 2000.
9 On the last phases of the war, see William Harris, *Faces of Lebanon: Sects, Wars, and Global Extensions* (Princeton: Markus Wiener Publications, 1997): pp. 243-326.
10 See Abdo Baaklini, Guilain Denoeux, Robert Springborg, *Legislative Politics in the Arab World. The Resurgence of Democratic Institutions* (Boulder: Lynne Rienner, 1999).
11 See Eberhard Kienle, "More than a Response to Islamism: The Political Delieralization of Egypt", in *The Middle East Journal* 52 (Spring 1998): pp. 219-235.

cal deliberalisation" is measured against a "domestic" benchmark, that of the political liberties and democratic process that prevailed prior to the war.

From Armed Conflict to Political Conflict

In recent years, several armed conflicts (a total of 101 fought between 1989 and 1996) were ended through negotiated settlements or by the use of force.[12] Of these, 68 had come to an end as armed conflicts during the period. Only 19 ended in a peace agreement and in 23 there was victory to one side or another, and some other outcome obtained in the remaining 24 terminated conflicts.[13] In many of these cases, violence ended but political conflict remained or the potential for conflict was there.[14]

Lebanon, in this regard, was no exception; its multiple wars ended in the late 1990s but political conflict has continued. Two instruments were used to end armed conflict: the use of force and political settlement. Force was used to defeat militarily the party that engaged in military confrontations against Syrian forces in Lebanon and to impose a settlement disputed on political and legal grounds. But unlike the ending of other armed conflicts, particularly since the end of the Cold War, which would not have been possible without the active involvement of third parties, Lebanon's conflict was ended with the partial involvement of a third party: the Arab Tripartite Committee, established in May 1989 at the Arab summit meeting in Morocco and composed of heads of states of Saudi Arabia, Morocco, and Algeria.

Following its initial recommendation, blaming Syria for obstructing settlement, the Arab Tripartite Committee suspended its work for nearly two months.[15] It then resumed its mediation in early September 1989 but only after it espoused Syria's position regarding the withdrawal of Syrian troops from Lebanon[16] and, in the process, it lost partiality and effectiveness. This was compounded by the fact that the United States, which was in a position to influence the decisions of the Arab Tripartite Committee, favored the Syrian position and sought a quick ending of conflict to neutralise General Michel Aoun, Syria's main opponent in Lebanon.[17] Although Aoun did not object to the political reforms in the Ta'if Agreement nor did he give them priority in his dealings with the

---

12 See P. Wallensteen and M. Sollenberg, "Armed Conflicts, Conflict Termination and Peace Agreements 1989-96", in *Journal of Peace Research*, 34 (3) (1997): p. 357.
13 Ibid., pp. 243-257.
14 See Roy Licklider, "The Consequences of Negotiated Settlements in Civil Wars" 1945-1993, in *American Political Science Review*, vol. 89, no. 3 (September 1995): pp. 681-690; Hugh Miall, Oliver Ramsbotham, Tom Woodhouse, *Contemporary Conflict Resolution. The prevention, Management and Transformation of Deadly Conflicts* (Cambridge: Polity Press, 1999): pp. 152-215.
15 See report of the Arab Tripartite Committee, in *Cahiers de l'Orient*, no. 15 (1989): pp. 61-82.
16 See Albert Mansour, *Al-Inqilab ala al-Ta'if* (Beirut: Dar al-Jadid, 1993): pp. 279-282.
17 Barbara M. Gregory, "US Relations with Lebanon: A Troubled Course", in *American-Arab Affairs* (Winter 1991): pp. 72-75.

Arab Tripartite Committee, his opposition to the Ta'if Agreement was mainly due to the lack of an enforceable timetable for the withdrawal of the Syrian army from Lebanon.[18]

The Ta'if Agreement consisted of two components: one dealt with political reforms, the other addressed sovereignty by defining Lebanon's external relations, notably with Syria, and called for the withdrawal of Israeli forces from the south in accordance with United Nations resolutions 425 and 426.[19] Ta'if's central internal feature concerned the distribution of power within the executive and between the latter and the legislative. Although Ta'if preserved the custom of the Maronite presidency, the Sunni premiership, and the Shia speakership, it greatly diminished the power of the president and enhanced the power of the prime minister, the council of ministers, and that of the speaker.[20] The broad lines of reforms were initially agreed upon in the Constitutional Document of February 1976 and were elaborated in the mid-1980s to include the restructuring of power in the executive.

Although Ta'if called for the establishment of "privileged relations" (al-alaqat al-mumayyaza) between Lebanon and Syria, sovereignty in the 1980s meant the ending of the Syrian military presence. This was the most divisive issue both before and during the meeting of Lebanese deputies in the city of Ta'if. The Ta'if Agreement called for the relocation of Syrian troops to the Beqa region in the eastern part of the country, two years after the constitutional amendments based on the Ta'if Agreement went into effect in September 1990. This meant that Syrian troops were supposed to withdraw from Beirut and other parts of the country and relocate in specified areas in September 1992. This first phase of withdrawal would then be followed by an agreement on final withdrawal between the Lebanese and Syrian governments though without indicating any timetable for either agreement or withdrawal. Neither phase, however, was implemented, and public reference to these issues has become a taboo in the political discourse.

Twelve years have passed and the Ta'if Agreement has not been fully implemented. Reforms were introduced in the constitution, particularly in relation to the distribution of power within the executive and between the legislative and executive branches of government, but Syrian troops have stayed.[21] What is more, Syrian influence has continued to increase. It has been institutionalised de jure through the signing of several bilateral agreements beginning in May 1991[22] and de facto through the exercise of hegem-

---

18 See Sarkis, Naoum, *General Wa Rihan* (Beirut: n. p. 1992): pp. 62-76. On the meetings of Lebanese deputies in Ta'if, see also George Saadé, *Qissati Ma' al Ta'if* (Beirut: n. p., 1998): pp. 71-138.
19 For an analytical assessment of the Ta'if Agreement, see Joseph Maila, *The Document of National Understanding. A Commentary* (Oxford: Centre for Lebanese Studies, 1992). See also Bechara Menassa, *Bayn al-Ta'if wa al-Tawa'if* (Beirut: Dar al-Jadid, 1994): pp. 40-112.
20 See Elie Salem, al-Khayarat al-Sa'ba, *Diblomasiyyat al-Bahth An Makhraj* (Beirut: Shariqat al Matbu'at Liltawzi' wa al-Nashr, 1993): pp. 423-460.
21 On the selective implementation of reforms, see Nawaf Salam, *Ab'ad Min al-Ta'if* (Beirut: Dar al-Jadid, 1998): pp. 13-27 and Issam Suleiman, *Al-Jumhuriya al Thaniya Bayn al Nusus wa al Mumarasa* (Beirut: n. p., 1998): pp. 17-90.
22 Over 30 bilateral agreements have been signed since May 1991. See the recent collective work *Al-Alaqat al-Lubnaniyya al-Suriyya: Muhawala Taqwimiyya* (Antelias: al-Haraka al-Thaqafiyya, 2000).

ony over the decision-making process in domestic and foreign policy.[23] Syria, in the other words, has had since 1990 unhindered access to Lebanon's political, security, and military establishments. And on issues that Syria considers to be of importance for whatever reason, political or otherwise, final decisions are made in Damascus and not in Beirut.

Democratic Transition in Crisis

The question that concerns us here is to situate the political system that emerged since the end of the war in comparison with that of other countries which have undergone transition to a democratic regime, particularly in the post-Cold War period. Two types of transitions can be singled out: transition following the collapse of an authoritarian regime dominated by the military, as in Southern Europe in the mid-1970s and in South America in the 1980s; and transition to democracy following the collapse of communist regimes in the late 1980s as in countries of Central and Eastern Europe.[24]

Unlike countries that have witnessed transition from non-democratic to democratic rule, Lebanon prior to the eruption of warfare in the mid-1970s had a competitive political system, which compared positively with political systems in many developing countries. In comparison with the prewar period, how has the political system fared since the early 1990s? Two aspects of the transition are significant: political liberalisation as a prerequisite for democratisation followed by democratic consolidation.[25] Two arenas of the transition process will be examined in this paper: parliamentary and presidential elections.

The starting point for our analysis is the political environment that prevailed at the time of the ending of the war and the process by which war was brought to a close. Initially, the Ta'if Agreement was rejected not only by General Aoun but also by the leaders of Lebanon's largest militias: the Christian Lebanese forces, the Shia Amal, and the Druze Progressive Socialist Party. Militias, which greatly benefited from the war, both politically and financially, stood to lose from the termination of hostilities; their interests were at stake not only because their power would be constrained in the postwar period but also because under the Ta'if Agreement militias would have to be dissolved. But for various reasons, militia leaders ended up accepting Ta'if, partly because they had no choice, as was the case with Lebanese Forces leader Samir Geagea who clashed with Aoun over the Ta'if Agreement and the control of East Beirut, and partly because they were integrated in the political process, as in the case of the other militias.

---

23 See Augustus Richard Norton, "Lebanon's Malaise", in *Survival*, vol. 42, (Winter 2000-2001): pp. 35-50; Habib C. Malik, *Between Damascus and Jerusalem. Lebanon and Middle East Peace* (Washington, D.C.: The Washington Institute for Near East Policy, 1997): pp. 25-45.
24 See Juan J. Linz and Alfred Stepan, *Problems of Democratic Transition and Consolidation. Southern Europe, South America, and Post-Communist Europe* (Baltimore: The Johns Hopkins University Press, 1996): pp. 3-83.
25 Ibid., pp. 3-15.

Missing in the transition process from war to peace was national reconciliation. The abrupt ending of war left no time for national reconciliation; nor was there a possibility for such reconciliation when conflict involved Lebanese and non-Lebanese parties, with Syria capable of vetoing any settlement or attempts at reconciliation that would be detrimental to its interests. As a substitute for the absence of such reconciliation at the time of the ending of war, supporters of Ta'if expected that national reconciliation will follow in the aftermath of Ta'if, if not formally, but at least through the proper implementation of the terms of the agreement. Such implementation, some believed, will generate a postwar consensus on Ta'if and, as a result, will help narrow the gap between critics and supporters of Ta'if. In other words, the merits of the settlement of Ta'if would then be appreciated through political practice, and this in turn would give Ta'if whatever popular support and legitimacy it lacked at the time of its making. But that did not materialise and Ta'if has been fundamentally derailed. A key architect of Ta'if, former speaker Hussein al-Husayni, saw little resemblance between the original text of Ta'if and the reality that emerged few years later.[26] Similarly, a former defence minister in the first cabinet after Ta'if, Albert Mansour, called government action since 1990 a "coup against Ta'if".[27]

Rather than forming national unity cabinets, as called for in the Ta'if Agreement, cabinets formed since 1990 have not representative. Lebanese authorities acted on the assumption that the power equation rested on winners and losers: Christians lost the war while Muslims won. This ran counter to the notion of confessional coexistence (al-'aysh al-mushtarak) embodied initially in the National Pact at the time of independence in 1943[28] and revived in the Ta'if Agreement and in the 1990 constitution. In reality, however, the winner was the party that exercised ultimate political and military power: Syria commanding more power than both Muslims and Christians, and the former exercising more influence than the latter. Nominal power was that of the Lebanese government, but real power was in Syria's hands.

This brings us to the most divisive issue regarding the Ta'if Agreement and its implementation: the absence of a definite and enforceable timetable for the withdrawal of Syrian forces from Lebanon. The problem here has to do with Syria's objectives both at the level of bilateral relations with Lebanon and as a regional power. Syria was involved in Lebanon's wars since the mid-1970s in all their phases and had as much interests at stake in Lebanon as the Lebanese themselves. But apart from the troubled course of Syrian-Lebanese relations ever since the two countries became independent in the mid-1940s, Syria's main target in Lebanon since the early phases of the war was the PLO armed in Lebanon. A powerful PLO led by Yasser Arafat in Lebanon in 1975-76 was the kind of military and security threat that Syria's Alawite regime could not tolerate.

---

26 *An-nahar*, November 7, 1994.
27 Albert Manour, al-Inqilab..., op. cit., pp. 143-129.
28 On the National Pact, see Farid el Khazen, *The Communal Pact of National Identities. The Making and Politics of the 1943 National Pact* (Oxford: Centre for Lebanese Studies, 1991).

Gradually, Lebanon was turned into an open battlefield for Syria's friends and foes alike, both in Lebanon and the region.

Prior to 1990, Syria was asked to withdraw its troops from Lebanon by two Lebanese presidents in 1982, but these requests went unheeded.[29] Similarly, the 1982 United Nations Resolution 520 called for the withdrawal of all foreign forces from Lebanon. And in 1989, when the Arab Tripartite Committee put its finger on what it considered as the main obstacle to reach a settlement in Lebanon – namely, Syria's unwillingness to show any flexibility on the withdrawal of its army from Lebanon – it abandoned its mediating role immediately after the signing of the Ta'if Agreement.

While armed conflict was ended and militias were dissolved in the early 1990s, one armed group was given a new lease on life: Shia-based Party of God (Hizbollah). Armed and funded by Iran and supported by Syria, Hizbollah received also the backing of the Lebanese government to engage in guerrilla warfare in areas occupied by Israel in south Lebanon.[30] Warfare in the 1990s had a well-defined agenda for it was linked to the unfolding phases of the peace talks between Israel and Arab countries since the launching of peace process in October 1991. And that was a more unpredictable war than Lebanon's previous wars because it was a function of Syria's (and Iran's) agenda in the Arab-Israeli peace talks and in their relations and interests with the United States. Conflict gained additional strategic significance as south Lebanon was in fact the only active war zone between Israel and its Arab neighbours. For the Lebanese government, contradictions in policy could not be more striking: reconstruction in Beirut and open warfare in the south. Prime Minister Rafiq Hariri sought to market Lebanon in Arab and Western capitals, as a land of opportunity for business "market" while the south was the scene of war over which the Lebanese government had little control.

Confrontations in south Lebanon led to massive Israeli attacks (in 1993, 1996, 1999 and 2000) targeting civilians and destroying infrastructure.[31] Even after Israeli withdrawal in accordance with the 1978 United Nations Security Council resolution 425 in May 2000, armed conflict continues. This is because for the Lebanese government, part of Lebanese territory (the Shebaa farms) is still under Israeli occupation. Therefore, Lebanon would not deploy the Lebanese army in the south and Hizbollah's military operations against Israel would not cease until Israel withdraws from that disputed territory. But for the United Nations and Israel, UN resolution 425 was fully implemented

---

29 President Elias Sarkis before leaving office in July 1982 and president Amin Gemayel following his election in September 1982.
30 On Hizbollah's origins and politics, see Waddah Sharara, *Dawlat Hizbollah. Lubnan Mujtama'n Islamiyyan* (Beirut: Dar al-Nahar, 1996). See also Augustus Richard Norton, *Hizbollah of Lebanon: Extremist Ideals vs. Mundane Politics* (New York: Council on Foreign Relations, 1999); Amal Saad-Ghorayeb, *Hizbu'llah: Politics and Religions* (London: Pluto Press, 2002).
31 On the 1996 Israeli attack, see Rosemary Hollis and Nadim Shehadi (eds.), *Lebanon on Hold. Implications for Middle East Peace* (London: The Royal Institute for International Affairs, 1996).

since the Shebaa farms were occupied by Israel in 1967 when they were under Syrian control, and Lebanon never claimed these territories until recently.[32]

The inclusion of militia leaders in the political process was another problematic aspect of the transition. This led to the institutionalisation of the war system in the postwar political order. Almost overnight militia leaders, whose entire career was linked to political violence and the abuse of power during the war, turned now into peace-makers and were the custodians of the political process in post-conflict Lebanon. Amal leader Nabih Berri was elected speaker of Parliament in 1992; Druze leader Walid Jumblatt was deputy and minister in most cabinets formed since 1990; and several members of former militias-turned-political parties were influential members of parliament and cabinet ministers. Nearly 24 percent of the numbers of the first parliament elected after the war in 1992 represented parties involved in the war.[33] One exception to this pattern was the Lebanese Forces and its leader Samir Geagea. Although acquitted from the bombing of a church north of Beirut, the cause of his initial arrest in 1994, Geagea had been in detention since that time and the Lebanese Forces have been dissolved. As Lebanese government officials have indicated, Geagea's detention and the successive death sentences he has received are politically motivated.[34] Geagea, who was instrumental in backing in implementing the Ta'if Agreement, was never on good terms with Syria both before and after the end of war.

Another missing element for a successful transition to democracy after the termination of hostilities is the lack of a sovereign state.[35] Here rests Lebanon's intractable problem in the postwar period: how can democracy be exercised when the decision-making process is a function of the domestic priorities and foreign policy agenda of another state, Syria, with which Lebanon has little in common. Apart from being two neighboring countries facing a "common enemy", Israel, Syria and Lebanon have been at odds ever since the two countries parted ways immediately after independence. With radically different political and economic systems, Lebanon and Syria have had divergent priorities and objectives in domestic and regional politics.

After over twenty five years of its military presence in Lebanon and twelve years after the Ta'if Agreement, it has become clear that Syria has no intention either to withdraw its troops from Lebanon or to refrain from meddling in its domestic affairs. This state of affairs has served the interests of several parties, notably the United States, the main architect of the Syrian military intervention in Lebanon since the mid-1970s.[36]

---

32 See Asher Kaufman, "Who Owns the Shebaa Farms? Chronicle of a Territorial Dispute", in *The Middle East Journal*, vol. 56, No. 4 (Autumn 2002): pp. 576-596.
33 Farid el Khazen, *Lebanon's First Postwar Parliamentary Election: An Imposed Choice* (Oxford: Centre for Lebanese Studies, 1998): p. 58.
34 Statements made by Lebanese officials to that effect, notably by president Elias Hrawi, *al-Hayat*, October 5, 1995.
35 Linz and Stepan, *Problems of Democratic...*, op. cit., pp. 17-19.
36 See Henry Kissinger, *Years of Renewal* (New York: Simon and Schuler, 1999): pp. 1019-1058. See also 'Abdallah Bu Habib, *al-Daw' al-Asfar* (Beirut: Shariqat al-Matbu'at Liltawzi' wa al-Nashr, 1991): pp. 107-163.

Washington's priority since the launching of the Arab-Israeli peace process has been the Syrian-Israeli track in the peace talks rather than the course of Syrian-Lebanese relations. In fact, the predominant view in Washington has been that a comfortable Syria in Lebanon would make Hafez Assad more forthcoming and flexible in the peace talks with Israel.

In light of the problems encountered in the transition from war to peace, how has the political system evolved to enhance democratic reconstruction since the end of the war? One way to address these questions is to analyse the electoral process since 1992.

The Electoral Process Since 1992

The benchmark for the assessment of Lebanon's electoral process since the end of the war is neither the non-competitive elections held in authoritarian regimes[37] nor elections in democratic systems, but elections in prewar Lebanon. Over a period of three decades, Lebanon held nine parliamentary elections and six presidential elections. Except for two parliamentary and presidential elections (in 1952/3 and in 1960), elections were held at regular intervals.[38] Electoral laws were changed in the 1940s and 1950s, particularly in relation to the size of constituencies, thus practicing gerrymandering for the purpose of influencing the outcome of elections by government authorities. Gerrymandering peaked in the two elections held during the presidency of Camille Chamoun in 1953 and 1957. But since 1960, the electoral law was stabilised and on the basis of which four elections were held (in 1960, 1964, 1968, 1972) before the outbreak of war in 1975.

Elections in the 1940s and 1950s involved extensive government meddling on election day and, as a result, elections were neither free nor fair, particularly in 1947 and 1957. But government conduct in parliamentary elections after 1960 improved; elections became more competitive and government authorities were not in a position to intervene in elections in the same way as in previous elections. The 1968 parliamentary elections resulted in a victory for the opposition, at a time when Lebanon was ruled by what was likened to a "military regime" dominated by army officers loyal to president Fouad Chehab. The freest and most competitive election since independence was that of 1972, the last held before the war. It was an election in which all parties and political currents active in the country took part, and it resulted in a truly representative parliament.

Despite their shortcomings, elections in Lebanon did produce change. It was in fact the outcome of the parliamentary elections in 1943 that produced a parliament controlled by a majority that abolished the French mandate, thus proclaiming independ-

---

37 Guy Hermet, "State-Controlled Elections: A Framework", in Rose and Rouquiné Hermet (eds.) *Elections Without Choice* (London: Macmillan Press, 1978): pp. 1-18.
38 On parliaments and parliamentary elections since 1920, see Antoine Messarra, *La structure sociale du Parlement Libanais, 1920-1976* (Beirut: Publications de l'Université Libanaise, 1977).

ence.[39] As for elections that involved government pressure and vote rigging, they led to political crises that brought together the opposition against the government. This in turn helped to constrain the regime and hastened its downfall, as in the 1952 crisis that led to the resignation of president Bechara al-Khoury and, subsequently in 1958, when president Camille Chamoun was unable to seek reelection for a second term.

Parliamentary elections have also enhanced the performance of the political system and contributed to its development, as explained by Michael Hudson and Iliya Harik.[40] So did parliament, which has enhanced the performance of the political system.[41] Elections have also resulted in high elite circulation, as shown in table 1. As for party representation in Parliament, it has continued to increase until it peaked in 1968, as shown in table 2. In sum, elections in the 1950s were more orderly and representative than in the 1940s, while elections in the 1960s were freer and more competitive than in the 1950s. And the 1972 elections scored better on all counts than all previous elections and compared favourably even with elections in democratic countries.

Table 1: New Entrants* in Parliament, 1960-1972

Year	1960	1964	1968	1972
Percentage	52.5	29.3	32.3	39.4

* New entrants are deputies who entered parliament for the first time
Source: M. Hudson (1966:176) and A. Baaklini (1976:173).

Table 2: Party Representation in Parliament, 1964-1972

Year	1964	1968	1972
Percentage	28	36	30

Source: A. Baaklini (1976:187)

Presidential elections in prewar Lebanon followed a similar pattern to that of parliamentary elections. According to the Lebanese constitution, members of parliament elect presidents every six years. An electoral pattern was institutionalised: as parliamentary elections became orderly and competitive, so did presidential elections. While in the 1940s and 1950s presidential elections were greatly influenced by the incumbent re-

---

39 On the 1943 elections, see Eyal Zisser, *Lebanon: The Challenge of Independence* (London: I. B. Tauris, 2000): pp. 41-67.
40 See Michael Hudson "The Electoral Process and Political Development in Lebanon", in *The Middle East Journal* 20 (Spring 1966): pp. 173-186. Iliya Harik, *Mann Yahkum Lubnan* (Beirut: Dar al-Nahar, 1972).
41 On the role of parliament in prewar Lebanon, see Abdo Baaklini, *Legislative and Political Development: Lebanon, 1842-1972* (Durham: Duke University Press, 1976). See also Ralph E. Crow, "Parliament in the Lebanese Political System", in Allen Kornberg and L. D. Muslof (eds.), *Legislatures in Developmental Perspective* (Durham: Duke University Press, 1970): pp. 273-302.

gime, they became more competitive in the 1960s. The last presidential election held before the war in 1970 was no doubt the most competitive reflecting the rivalry between government and opposition. It resulted in the election of the opposition candidate, Suleiman Frangieh, by a margin of one vote, and this outcome ended a regime that had been in power for two consecutive terms over a period of twelve years.

How do parliamentary and presidential elections held since the end of the war compare with prewar elections? The three parliamentary elections in 1992, 1996 and, more recently, in 2000 differ from prewar elections in at least four ways.

First, neither the Lebanese government nor the political actors are the sole decision-makers in political matters, electoral and otherwise. The closest analogy to the present state of affairs is that of the French mandate period (1920-1943). Under French rule, opposition politics, was effective both in and outside Parliament. In fact, many of the vocal critics of French rule were political elites from within the system, including several members of parliament. Despite the power they exercised, the French generally sought to abide by the rules of the game set by the 1926 constitution and were under scrutiny by the League of Nations. They were also challenged by the British who yielded more power than the French in the region, particularly since the early 1940s following the German occupation of France in the second World War. Such balancing factors to French power in pre-independence mandate politics are not present in postwar Lebanon.

Second, elections prior to the war led to political change in government and in policy objectives, both domestic and foreign, as well as in the power structure in the country, particularly at the level of the elites.[42] Elections were also a political event that mobilised people from all communities and political persuasions. By contrast, elections since war ended have been largely detached from the political process and have helped to institutionalise the status quo since 1990. Postwar elections have largely become a social event devoid of political substance.

Third, one constant practice in postwar Lebanon has been the instability of the electoral law. Each parliamentary election since 1992 has had its own electoral law and this has become a "normal" practice, contrary to the stable electoral law in the decade and a half preceding the outbreak of war. Instability has created a situation of permanent uncertainty for all parties concerned: deputies, candidates, and voters. This has also increased the dependency of all parties on the makers of electoral laws in Lebanon and, more importantly, in Syria. As former prime minister Salim al-Hoss described in a recent book covering the period of his premiership in 1998-2000. After calling upon the public to submit proposals for a new electoral law and forming a special ministerial committee to look into over 45 proposals submitted by politicians, political parties, and experts, here is what premier Hoss had to say: " I was informed by president Lahoud that the Syrian brothers favored the division of the Muhafazat into districts, including Beirut, and then we received a project [for an electoral law] delivered to me and to

---

42 See Samir Khalaf, *Lebanon's Predicament* (New York: Columbia University Press, 1987): pp. 121-145.

president Lahoud by the minister of the interior Michel al-Murr. And it was well known that General Jamil al-Sayyed, the director of General Security, played a role in brokering the project in coordination with the Syrian 'marja'iyya' in Anjar [that is, General Ghazi Kanaan]".[43] Hoss then explained that he was opposed to the project but went along with the decision of the cabinet to adopt the Syrian-proposed electoral law.[44]

Fourth, boycott of elections by political parties and leaders was exercised twice: during the French mandate and in the last three elections since 1992. Although boycott was practiced in these two instances for different reasons and under internal and regional circumstances which differed from those of the 1990s, boycott, as an act of protest used by political elites and counter-elites in nondemocratic regimes, was not practiced in prewar Lebanon. Even political parties that were officially banned by government in the 1950s and 1960s were allowed to operate and to take part in parliamentary elections, particularly the Lebanese Communist Party and the Syrian Social Nationalist Party.[45]

One common feature of elections since 1992 was the boycott exercised by voters and candidates. Boycott was largest in 1992 with the lowest level of voter turnout since independence: 30.34 percent, compared with the post-1960 percentages of above 50 percent. While boycott was exercised in all constituencies, more Christian voters boycotted the elections than Muslim voters. For example, in the constituency of Jbeil in Mount Lebanon, the two Maronite candidates received 130 and 41 votes each, or 181 out of the district's total of 63,878. Similarly, all major Christian-based political parties and several established Christian politicians did not participate in the elections while a fewer number of Muslim politicians boycotted the elections. Boycott in 1996 continued but was more limited in scope and impact than in 1992. It was mainly confined to Christian voters and candidates, although some of the Christian politicians who boycotted the 1992 elections ran in 1996. Voter turnout in 1996 and 2000 was about 45 percent, up by 15 percent from 1992. But it declined in the 2000 elections by about 5 percent (see table 3) and boycott was confined to the three major Christian-based parties: the Lebanese Forces, the political movement led by General Michel Aoun, and the National Liberal Party headed by Dory Chamoun.

Table 3: Voter Turnout in Elections, 1968-2000

Year	1968	1972	1992	1996	2000
Percentage	52.80	52.50	30.34	44.98	40.51

---

43 Salim al-Hoss, *Lilhaqiqa wa al-Tarikh: Tajarib al-Hukm ma bayn 1998 wa 2000* (Beirut: Shariqat al-Matbu'at Liltawzi wa al-Nashr, 2001): p. 61.
44 Ibid.
45 On political parties in the prewar period, see Michael Suleiman, *Political Parties in Lebanon: The Challenge of a Fragmented Political Culture* (Ithaca: Cornell University Press, 1967).

The more problematic aspect of postwar elections concerned the electoral law – the instrument that was most effectively used by government authorities to influence the outcome of elections. Two components of the electoral law are significant: the number of seats in parliament and the size of the constituencies (see table 4). Only four weeks prior to the 1992 elections government elevated the number of seats from 108 to 128. This was in violation of the Ta'if Agreement which stipulated an increase in the number of seats from 99 to 108 to provide parity in representation between Christians and Muslims. In fact, the increase in parliamentary seats to 128 (that is, by 18.5%) was a Syrian demand in the Ta'if meetings in October 1989, but was opposed by the majority of Lebanese deputies.[46] Having at the time other pressing concerns, Damascus dropped its demand following mediation by Saudi Foreign Minister Saud al-Faisal. Clearly, these additional seats could not be justified either on political or demographic grounds, nor did they enhance representation. The real undeclared objective, however, was to distribute seats arbitrarily in certain constituencies to favor the election of candidates close to Syria, particularly in the north and Beqa regions.

Table 4: Distribution of Seats by Sect, 1943-92

	1943-47	1951	1953	1957	1960-72	1992
Maronite	18	23	13	20	30	34
Greek Orthodox	6	8	5	7	11	14
Greek Catholic	3	5	3	4	6	8
Armenian Orthodox	2	3	1	3	4	5
Armenian Catholic	-	1	1	1	1	1
Protestant	-	1	-	-	1	1
Minorities	1	1	1	1	1	1
Sunni	11	16	9	14	20	27
Shi'a	10	14	8	12	19	27
Druze	4	5	3	4	6	8
Alawite	-	-	-	-	-	2
Total	55	77	44	66	99	128

The other aspect of the electoral law relating to the size of the constituencies was even more problematic. Both the number of seats in constituencies and the number of voters in the three electoral laws since 1992 were highly uneven: the largest was 28 seats, the smallest 3 seats (See table 5). The Constitutional Council, established in 1993, declared the 1996 electoral law unconstitutional, but parliament passed it with the justification

---

46 Albert Mansour, *Al-Inqilab...*, op. cit., pp. 57-59.

that it will be adopted only once due to "exceptional" circumstances. The 2000 electoral law was equally uneven but deputies, unlike in 1996, were not willing to challenge it on legal grounds by petitioning the Constitutional Council, as is required by law. In Lebanon's simple plurality system, as opposed to small constituencies or to the proportional system, large constituencies of 28, 23, or 17 seats are likely to produce non-competitive elections and to give government authorities and Syria room to influence the making of electoral alliances and to tamper with vote counting on election day.

Table 5
Discrepancies in the Distribution of Seats, 1972-2000

	1960-1972*	1992	1996	2000
Smallest Constituency	1	3	3	6
Largest Constituency	8	28	28	17
Discrepancy	7	25	25	11

* Same electoral law in four elections.

Electoral districts were gerrymandered to suit the political interests of all communities except the Christians. In 1992, 1996 and 2000, Speaker Nabih Berri demanded and received the combination of two southern provinces in one constituency. Likewise, Beirut was one constituency in 1992 and 1996, to the benefit of Sunni leaders running in Beirut, especially Prime Minister Rafiq Hariri. Beirut was then divided in three districts in 2000 to cater to the electoral interests of Prime Minister Salim al-Hoss. In 1992 and 1996, Mount Lebanon hosted six constituencies, as demanded by Druze leader Walid Jumblatt to preserve his hold over his traditional Druze power base concentrated in the districts of Shuf and Aley.

In reality, the electoral laws of 1992 and 1996 and, to a lesser extent, in 2000 have marginalised the impact of Christian voters upon the election of Christian deputies. In Lebanon's confessional system, parliamentary seats are allocated on a sectarian basis, but people vote for candidates irrespective of the sect. In a simple plurality electoral system like Lebanon's, the decisive factor in influencing the outcome of elections is the size of the electoral district, that is, the number of Christian and Muslim voters in each constituency. In regions with a Muslim majority, large constituencies (19 to 28 seats) were adopted, while small constituencies were adopted (3 to 8 seats) where Christians are a majority. In effect, Muslims influenced the election of Christian deputies in far greater proportions than Christians impacting the outcome of Muslim districts so that the elected Christian leadership often did not represent the view of a majority of Christians.[47] In 1992, Muslim voters elected 35 percent of Christian deputies[48] and none of

---

47 Farid el Khazen, *Lebanon's First Postwar...*: pp. 25-28.
48 Ibid, p. 27.

the fourteen deputies representing the Greek Orthodox community was actually elected by decisive Greek Orthodox vote. Similarly, in 1996, neither the Greek Orthodox nor Greek Catholic voters had decisive influence in choosing their twenty two deputies. This was not the case with most Muslim deputies whose elections were decided by voters from their respective sects. The 2000 elections differed little from the two previous elections, particularly in the north and the south.

Lebanese authorities and Syria exercised influence in another way in all three postwar elections through the making and unmaking of electoral alliances before election day. This was the most effective instrument to influence the outcome of elections in most constituencies next to the electoral law. In practice, political parties and politicians ran on one electoral list despite their staunch rivalry, for under different circumstances they would be running against each other. One notable example was the two rival Shia parties, Amal and Hizbollah. In 1996, only few days before Hizbollah was about to announce an electoral list in the south opposed to Amal in alliance with independent candidates also opposed to Amal, Hizbollah suddenly opted for an alliance with Amal at the request of Syrian officials.[49] Similar practices were recorded in the 2000 elections, particularly in the Beqa and the north, where Syria has much greater control and influence in local politics and where the Syrian military presence dates back to the mid-1970s. Even President Assad had a hand in the making of electoral lists, as stated by Walid Jumblatt.[50]

Government conduct on election day was the worst in 1992. An official report on the 1992 elections leaked to the press described in detail the infringements that occurred on election day: breaking and stealing of ballot boxes, the disappearance and concealment of voter registration lists, vote tabulations unsigned by government officials, and tampering.[51] The 1996 elections were less chaotic, though in some districts, especially in the north and the Beqa, vote rigging was widely practiced.[52] The notable development in 1996 and, more so in 2000, was the large amount of money spent on elections whether in campaigns or in "buying" votes on election day. There are no laws in Lebanon which regulate the spending of money in elections.

Parliament and Political Parties

Another pattern common to postwar elections concerns parliament. Elections have produced parliaments with a similar predominant political colouring. While in parliamen-

---

49 This and similar accounts of the making of electoral alliances are described in Nqula Nassif and Rosanna Bou Monsif, *Al-Masrah wa al-Kawalees: Intikhabat 96 fi Fusuliha* (Beirut: Dar al-Nahar, 1996): pp. 167-196.
50 *An-Nahar*, April 10, 2000.
51 *An-Nahar*, September 2, 1992.
52 See Ziad Majid, "Qira'at fi al-intihakat wa 'Amaliyyat al-Tazweer al-Murafiqa Lilintikhabat al-Niyabiyya", in *Al-Intikhabat al-Niyabiyya 1996 wa Azwat al-Dimuqratiyya fi Lubnan*, collective work (Beirut: Al-Markza al-Lubnani Lildirasat, 1998): pp. 255-268.

Authoritarianism by Diffusion 69

tary debates deputies in and outside political parties are at odds on various domestic issues, ranging from government policy on reconstruction to the national debt, they are in agreement on the nature of "privileged relations" between Lebanon and Syria. From 1990 to 2000, Syrian military presence and government failure to implement the Ta'if Agreement did not figure in parliamentary debates, nor was there any critical assessment by deputies of foreign policy issues and specifically Lebanon's absence in the peace talks since 1993 at a time when Syria negotiated with Israel and the two countries were about to reach an agreement on at least two occasions in 1996 and, especially, in 2000.[53] Much of the heated exchanges between government and opposition in parliament concerned issues detached from policies that have political substance.[54]

The first time a taboo issue was raised in parliament since the end of the war was in October 2000. Veteran politician Albert Mokheiber called for the withdrawal of the Syrian army from Lebanon and for the establishment of diplomatic relations between the two countries. Walid Jumblatt, Syria's longtime ally, also called for the relocation of Syrian troops in accordance with the Ta'if Agreement and for the reassessment of Syrian-Lebanese relations. While Mokheiber's position regarding Syria's presence in Lebanon was well-known prior to his election in 2000, Jumblatt's position drew a strong reaction from Syria and its allies in Lebanon. He was attacked in parliament by deputies close to Syria and one Baathist deputy, 'Assem Qanso, accused him of collaborating with Israel. Damascus also responded by banning Jumblatt and members of his party in parliament and in the cabinet entry to Syria for a few months.[55]

The other important dimension of the depoliticisation of parliament concerns the role of political parties represented in parliament. Owing to their organisation, ideology, and representation both at the regional and communal levels, parties constitute traditionally the most politicised group of deputies in parliament when compared with deputies with no political affiliation who are likely to cater to local interests. This was particularly the case of political parties and party leaders in the prewar period who were active in legislation and in the initiation of policies in all political, economic, and social domains.

Today, by contrast, parties have been most "active" in political inaction, that is, in the preservation of the status quo that emerged since 1990 to insure their largely predetermined share in parliament. They all support the prevailing political order and do not contest any of the political issues that have become taboos in recent years (See tables 6 and 7). Whether for political or ideological reasons, political parties have been the most effective supporters of Syria's military presence in Lebanon. Although the dependence and/or allegiance to Syria varies between parties, some owe much of their representation

---

53 See Itamar Rabinovich, *The Brink of Peace, The Israeli-Syrian Negotiations* (Princeton: Princeton University Press, 1998): pp. 235-264.
54 See Fares Sassin, *Al-Tamthil wa al-Sulta, Majlis Nuwwab 1992-1996* (Beirut: al-Markaz al-Lubnani Lildirasat, 1997): pp. 51-86.
54 Beginning in spring 2002, Jumblatt has reversed his position regarding the redeployment of Syrian troops and became one of the most vocal critics of the Qornet Chehwan gathering, the Christian-based alliance close to Maronite Patriarch Nasrallah Sfeir.

in parliament and cabinet to Syrian backing, particularly the Baath Party and the Syrian Social Nationalist Party. As for politicians not affiliated with parties, over 80 percent in the 1992 and 1996 parliaments have close ties with Syria or are dependent on Syrian backing, directly or indirectly, for their election. Although in the 2000 parliament, a larger number of deputies are critical of Syria's hegemony over Lebanon, particularly deputies belonging to the Qornet Chehwan gathering, were unable to alter the status quo. In short, with the exception of few deputies, particularly in the 2000 parliament, postwar parliaments have been solidly pro-Syrian.

Table 6
Members of Political Parties in Parliament, 1992-2000

	1992	1996	2000
Number	36	34	32
Percentage	28.12	26.56	25

Table 7
Political Parties in Parliament, 1992-2000

	1992	1996	2000
Hizbollah	8	7	9
Amal	5	8	7
SSNP	6	5	4
Progressive Socialist Party	5	5	5
Baath Party	2	2	3
Wa'ad Party	2	2	-
Islamic Jama'a	3	1	-
Al-Ahbash	1	-	-
Kataeb Party	-	-	2
Tashnag*	1	1	1
Hinshag*	1	1	-
Ramgavar*	-	1	1
Total	34	33	32

* Armenian Parties

Another political outcome of parliamentary elections is reflected in the presidential elections since members of parliaments elect presidents. In the prewar period, politicians competed in parliamentary elections, particularly those that preceded presidential elections with an eye to the upcoming presidential election. Indeed, much of the electoral alliances were structured with the presidential election in mind. In the 1947 elections, a parliamentary majority loyal to president Khoury was secured to amend the constitution to allow for his reelection for a second term. Similarly, parliamentary elections in 1957 were intended to produce a majority loyal to president Chamoun. Elections in 1964 brought a majority in parliament loyal to president Chehab which insured the election of a Chehabist candidate, president Charles Helou. In 1968, the opposition joined ranks in the parliamentary elections and scored a victory which was decisive in the outcome of the presidential election in 1970.

In postwar elections, by contrast, presidential elections were dissociated from parliamentary elections since the outcome of one has no political bearing on the other. The election of deputy René Moawad in October 1989 – the first president after the Ta'if Agreement – took place in an army base in northern Lebanon at a time of intense conflict. Two weeks after his election Moawad was assassinated in a massive explosion that ripped his car in Syrian-controlled West Beirut. Two days later deputies held a hasty session of parliament in a hotel in the Syrian-controlled Beqa and elected deputy Elias Hrawi.

Hrawi's six-year term was renewed for three more years in 1995 after amending the constitution. The decision to renew Hrawi's term was announced by Syrian president Assad in an interview to the Egyptian daily al-Ahram, despite opposition to Hrawi by several influential politicians from all communities, including parliament speaker Nabih Berri.[56] Following Assad's statement in support for Hrawi, parliament amended the constitution and voted for Hrawi. Only 11 deputies voted against constitutional amendment. More recently, the election of Lebanese army commander General Emile Lahoud in November 1998 was no different. Lahoud, who had no power base of his own either in or outside parliament, was Syria's candidate for the presidency.[57]

Authoritarianism by Diffusion

What can we conclude from the functioning of Lebanon's political system over the last twelve years? A pattern of inaction can be discerned: elections are intended to produce parliaments with a uniform political colouring; parliaments in turn have legitimised these non-competitive elections and the prevailing status quo; and members of parliament, both party and non-party based, engage in all issues except those that have a bearing on the Syrian backed structure of power in the country and the decision-making process.

---

56 Sassin, *Al-Tamthil*, op. cit., p. 65. According to president Elias Hrawi, president Assad suggested that Hrawi's term should be renewed for three years in April 1995, that is, seven months prior to the end of his term. Elias Hrawi, *Awdat el-Jumhuriyya Min al-Duwaylat Ila al-Dawla* (Beirut: Dar al-Nahar): pp. 402-403.
57 Elias Hrawi, *Awdat el-Jumhuriyya...*, ibid., pp. 603-605.

This has produced an unprecedented phenomenon: the dismemberment of the political process since the electoral process has been largely detached from the making of the power structure in the political system: in the executive branch of government and in the relationship between the legislative and the executive. Presidents, prime ministers, and many cabinet members have reached office irrespective of the outcome of parliamentary elections and the power equation in parliament between a majority supporting government and a minority in the opposition, as is the case in a functioning parliamentary system and as was the case prior to the war, particularly in the 1960s and 1970s. In other words, real power in present-day Lebanon is not generated by the outcome of the electoral process. In fact, elections have performed functions that are largely similar to those performed by authoritarian regimes to support the system and to make people comply and adjust to the anomalies of the political process. Therefore, "whatever voters may think about the elections, their participation in it is an act of compliance".[58]

Another pattern of dismemberment is manifested in the absence of the concept of a regime or administration (al'Ahd) bringing together the president and the prime minister at the centre of power in the executive and the speaker in the legislative. In prewar Lebanon, elections generated the separating line between government and opposition at all levels of government: the Maronite president in alliance with the Sunni premier and the Shia speaker. Electoral alliances bringing together politicians from all three communities were formed so that all three would come to power after defeating the incumbent regime with its three top posts in the country. This concept of alternating power between "teams" in power and in the opposition has been broken in postwar Lebanon.

The link that ties the centres of power together and the electoral process to government institutions is provided by Syria and is, therefore, under its control. This has served not only to legitimise Syria's role in the country but also to make it a necessity. This state of affairs was most apparent between 1992 and 1998, when the so-called "Troika" system emerged between president Hrawi, prime minister Hariri, and speaker Berri. When the three "presidents" were in agreement over a particular issue, they bypassed government institutions and when they were at odds they depended on Syria to sort out the problem and to preserve their share of rewards in the system.

Contrary to the widely-held belief in the early 1990s that Lebanon's political pluralism and openness would end up influencing Syria, both politically and economically, Lebanon's political system and practices have been "syrianised". The increasing influence of the security apparatus and practices such as the banning of politicians, the detention of political prisoners, and the presence of political exiles were alien to political practice in prewar Lebanon, when it was possible for politicians to defeat rivals even in rigged elections and when no politician could ban opponents from engaging in politics. Internal political equilibrium in prewar Lebanon was homegrown, while equilibrium to-

---

58 Martin Harrop and William L. Miller, *Elections and Voters: A Comparative Introduction* (London: Macmillan Press, 1987): p. 28.

day is insured by an external party whose power exceeds that of any of Lebanon's most popular and/or influential politicians.

This raises the question of political liberalisation as a prerequisite for democracy. Lebanon today is less liberal and less open than prior to the war. Its press, although the freest and the most diversified in the Arab world today, has had to adjust to the shrinking margin of tolerance since the early 1990s. So has Lebanon's legal system which has become increasingly an instrument of control by government authorities and has lost whatever independence it has had even during the war.[59] Perhaps the deepest problem at present concerns the gradual erosion of the two tenets on which Lebanon's political system has rested and from which it has derived legitimacy: compromise and pluralism, which can only flourish in an environment of political liberalisation.

The decline of political liberalisation has paved the way for the institutionalisation of non-democratic practices in the political process. Consequently, this has given Lebanon many of the traits of an authoritarian regime. Authoritarian practices have been integrated in the system, as demonstrated by the non-competitive electoral process, even though Lebanon is not yet a full-fledged authoritarian state. While Lebanon has no police state similar to that of other countries in the region, it is not capable of shielding itself from creeping non-democratic practices despite the political activism of its civil society.

The case that the postwar Lebanese state presents is rather unusual. This is because authoritarian practices are not necessarily for the benefit of the state itself, as is usually the case in authoritarian states. Nor are its ruling elites the sole beneficiaries of authoritarianism as was the case, for example, in the Soviet-controlled regimes in Eastern and Central Europe. The ultimate beneficiary is Syria with its authoritarian power structure and government institutions dominating economy and society. Using the analogy of the autonomy of state from society, the state in postwar Lebanon exercises a significant degree of autonomy from society, exceeding that of the postwar state, but it is really the Syrian state that exercises autonomy from both state and society in Lebanon.

Since the end of the Cold War, several countries have been experimenting with different forms of political liberalisation and democracy. Middle Eastern countries have failed to keep pace with this sweeping change. This is no doubt detrimental to an open and vulnerable country like Lebanon. The fundamental problem that Lebanon faces today is neither linked to the take-off phase for democratic transition nor to the adjustment necessary after years of non-democratic rule. Needless to say, the transition will not be smooth after fifteen years of violence, but the problem is that the cumulative outcome of change since 1990 has been in the opposite direction of the cumulative process of liberalisation and democracy that characterised the prewar period.

No democratisation was possible in the former Soviet bloc countries except only after the lifting of the veto by the regional hegemon. Democracy can take place "by

---

59 See the revealing interview given by Nasri Lahoud, former head of the Supreme Council of the Judiciary and former military Prosecutor General for several years, in *al-Safir*, November 14, 2002.

diffusion" in a favourable regional and international environment or even "by trespassing", as argued by Giuseppe di Palma.[60] In Lebanon, neither mode of democratic transition applies. The consequences of the Syrian presence and influence in Lebanon have been in the opposite direction. They have produced a new mode of authoritarianism: by diffusion immediately after the ending of war and by trespassing from then on. While it is true that democracy does not happen in an international vacuum, the regional vacuum is clearly more relevant in the case of Lebanon. And it is far from being filled not only in Lebanon's immediate neighbourhood in the Arab East but also in the larger Middle East.

---

60 Giuseppe di Palma, *To Craft Democracies. An Essay on Democratic Transitions* (Berkeley: University of California Press, 1990): pp. 183-199.

A Note on Confessionalism

AHMAD BEYDOUN

Confessionalism, the usual translation of the Arabic word *taifiya* – communalism would better express its use in Lebanon – has a range of meanings that gives it a certain vagueness and allows for all sorts of ambiguities. It may refer to the politico-administrative system of government, the social reality of multicommunalism, the institutional organization – in the widest sense – of a community, a collective or individual attitude tending to involve communal institutions in the global organization and management of society, the rather exclusive, or at least privileged, identification with a religious community, affiliation with an institution or even a way of communal thinking, acting or living, etc. In the following, we use this term in the subjective and objective sense of collective identification and its institutional expression in global society.

Consequently, in the context of the contemporary Lebanese state we define confessionalism as an unequally accepted and diversely interpreted contract between the confessional communities that constitute Lebanese society: a contract that stipulates the preservation of a minimal public space that all communities expect will ensure the exercise of the internal functions and the international privileges of the state. The space in question compensates at these two levels for the deficiencies of each community, but allows each community to evolve in the direction of greater social and political autarky, which may include the direct involvement of the community in international, political and other networks. As we know, in times of great tension certain communities pushed the call for autarky as far as acquiring military wings and claiming the status of quasi-state, as accredited diplomats in Beirut were more willing to negotiate with the communal systems than the central government. At the same time, this public space has always been somewhat porous. Each community strives to establish zones of influence for itself (often known as "strongholds", in other words, public services it takes as much advantage of as possible). At the same time, each strives to carve out an increasingly large share of the state manna, which the Lebanese, good francophones that they are, sometimes call "cake" and sometimes call "cheese".

Clearly, to speak of "communities" in this regard is rather simplistic. More often than not, a "stronghold" is controlled not by a community, but by a leader in the community. As a rule, he shuts the doors of his "stronghold" to competitors in his own community, rather than competitors representing other communities. Nonetheless, it is the communal system itself that allows and maintains this phenomenon of monopoly.

Even more striking is the fact that struggles for influence in large communities are a vital necessity in the confessional state. An important community that became a political monolith (highly improbable, in times of peace), would, if it boycotted the institutions of state, deprive the central government of alternatives. If the system were globally threatened, the government would be forced to heed even excessive demands of the dissident block: fatal conduct, because it would almost surely provoke other communities to similarly refuse unless their own, possibly even more excessive claims were met. Unconsciously trying to follow the trend, these other communities would also try to establish unanimity. While constantly deplored by communal leaders, the endemic disunity of the communities is, in fact, a condition for the survival of the country.

To conclude this introduction, allow me to add that contemporary confessionalism is fundamentally different than the intercommunal environments of pre- or proto-state Lebanon. It is an insult to people's intelligence (and unfortunately one accepted frequently and willingly), but also a serious mistake of political perception to treat the last Lebanese war as the continuation of the series of conflicts that marked the history of intercommunal relations between the early 17th and mid-19th century. After 1920, the territory, even more the city, and the government emerged as theatres of compromise as well as of conflict between communities.

Making up for Lost Time in Confessionalisation: The Case of the Shiites

That said, one very important historic fact needs to be mentioned, since it continues to influence the present. At the time Lebanese government emerged, our communities were not equally confessional, or even confessionalist for that matter. Let us consider the case of the Shiites in Lebanon. They were divided into two regional collectives that were not very open to one another: one in Jabal Amel and the other in the northern Bekaa. Each practised a system of solidarity, and familial or tribal competitiveness divided almost every village into two competing alliances of families. The leadership of each region was in the hands of so-called political families. The most influential of these had controlled the affairs of their region for centuries. Other competing families owed their rise to their positions as civil servants in the last half-century of Ottoman rule, to fortunes founded on trade, or, in individual cases, to modern education. Sometimes, two or more of these factors coincided. In the villages and the sub-regions, the great zaims were supported by other smaller ones. Also, the body of the ulemas had practically very little institutional hierarchy. The great mujtahids certainly had moral influence over the less prestigious ulemas as well as the zaims, with which they maintained often ambiguous relations. Some mujtahids played a direct political role and strove for direct representation in the political arena. After the Mandate authorities created Jaafarite tribunals (which did not exist under the Ottomans), the cadis swiftly acquired a certain importance, as their role and their prestige came to symbolize Shiite communal aspirations. Compared to the wealth of other communities, the waqf assets were rather modest. Only after an enormous effort to mobilize support among Shiite emigrants in Africa did a deputy and a mujtahid succeed in opening two communal secondary schools in Beirut and Tyre.

Communal grievances were intermittently aired in parliament as well as in the local press (for a long time just a single magazine published in Sidon). But these odd outbreaks were inconsistent and ineffective. The communalism of the marching wing, made up of modernizing intellectuals – the most important of which were ulemas – went hand in hand with an Arabic nationalism that ended up smothering it after 1948. In short, the aforementioned binary system of familial solidarity, a system often called Arabic, effectively managed to contain the vague communal desires. The maturing of Shiite communalism continued slowly until 1967. By that time, the regional situation began to directly threatening the future of the Lebanese Shiites and the country.

It would go beyond the scope of this paper to trace the Shiites' communalization, from the birth of the Moussa Sadr's movement, through the mutations of the war years, to the present. Let us term this immense transformation: institutionalization.

Nowadays, Lebanon's Shiites have a central communal body that wields considerable secular and religious authority. Nonetheless, a large part of the ulemas practically eludes the authority of this body. Most of them are integrated into other "spheres of influence" that owe their coherence to a common political affiliation or the prestige of a great ulema. Consequently, we find a level of structuring unknown before the war, one which exhibits clear parallels to Christian religious orders. There has also been a remarkable concentration of financial and institutional resources. Nowadays, the ulema body manages substantial waqf assets that support a complex system of social activities. Many important establishments (schools, hospitals, etc.) depend on communal associations. The most important establishment networks are controlled by political organizations that emerged during the years of war and resistance, or by great ulemas. These organizations (the Amal movement and Hizbullah) put an end to the scattered politicization of Shiite youth between diverse pre-war secular parties and movements, whether nationalist, left-wing or even Palestinian. They have ousted the old political families or taken them under their wing. Together they control almost all of the community's parliamentary representation, whereby the Amal movement practically monopolizes the management of the Shiite "share" of the civil service and public institutions. Owing to its mission of resisting the Israeli occupation (the regional factor has ensured it virtual exclusivity), Hizbullah maintains a dreadful military machinery, whereas the Amal movement is only sporadically and marginally active in this field.

To build up an impressive network of institutions, the Shiites made use of their own internal evolution, i. e., their demographic growth, their increasing economic clout and their greater skills due to massive progress in education.

They have also benefited from solid regional alliances and international relations. As the war ultimately beneficial to this reversal in their situation, in the 1980s the community succeeded in acquiring a favourable crucial revision of the terms of the intercommunal partnership that runs the country.

Regardless of undoubted differences in particular circumstances or style, in terms of content the Shiites were inspired with regards to the content by the pure tradition of Lebanese confessionalism. They followed in others' footsteps in that civil war or international crisis, latent or open, and thus outside intervention, brought the advantages of their internal evolution to the fore and enabled them to carve out the place for themselves. Alas, it was not the virtues of dialogue, negotiation and compromise – often shamelessly attributed to a confessionalist system – that won them their place, but the reserves of violence generated by the fundamental lack of adaptation, which, for those who have eyes to see, this system favours. It took the Maronites World War I and Gouraud, Maysaloun and the occupation of Damascus to get the Greater Lebanon they wanted. The Sunnites owed their position of second partner to nothing less than World War II, Spears, the 1956 crisis and Eisenhower, the 1958 crisis and Nasser, not to forget the Saudi contacts. The Shiites had to wait till the war of 1967. They needed Syria and Iran, and – in the midst of the Lebanese war – one war against Palestinians and another one against Israel. If one were to make another observation about the tendency of Lebanese communities to opt for institutionalization it is that even though the Maronites suffered, as we often hear, considerable losses at the end of the last war, long before the war their historic role as an organized community had been adopted by all partners in Lebanon as the ideal type of organization.

The Legacy of War

Important signs of generalized confessionalisation since the war include the following:
1) The reinforcement of the influence of religious authorities, or simply of religious people who now occupy key political positions. Thanks to their material resources, the influence of these authorities has also spread to various aspects of social life, marginalizing the role of the state as well as secular forces. Together with their growing influence in all communities, the spontaneous confessional orientation of social activities run by these authorities (particularly educational establishments) tends to widen the communal cleavages in the country.
2) The greater influence of this effect, because it is no longer compensated by other factors that traditionally promoted the intercommunal mix. Fewer mixed residential areas, the repartition and ghettoisation of several institutions and public services, the decentralization of markets, the duplication of all sorts of agencies, etc. all curtail possibilities of contact between Lebanese from different communities. Some of these phenomena are the result of a normal evolution, others, however, are the legacy of war.
3) The confirmation of the rural bias in the Lebanese political system regime. This characteristic is reinforced by the electoral law. At its heart is the fact that certain large communities identify closely with their geographic and historical origins, either a region of the Mountain or peripheral areas, and desire to associate the main elements of their political representation with these origins. Other communities have

traditionally been concentrated in the cities. Willingly taking advantage of the backward-looking motivations of others, which they actually share, they reduce the cities, the representation of which they practically monopolize, to a political status worthy of large villages. As waves of voters return at election time to their places of origin, cities become plagued by the logic of origins, a logic which necessarily favours the criteria of familial and confessional affiliation. Yet, it is the mix of people migrating to and mingling in cities that makes them what they are. They are the salt of urbanity, and, following the logic of urbanity, they entrust to the city the reins of modernization. To let half-empty villages capture the bulk of political representation means holding the city hostage to trivial problems raised with members of parliament by individuals who often live in the city, but whose vote may serve as an access card to the deputy of their region of origin. In turn, the serious problems of the cities overwhelm the political representation of their elected representatives. The ability to address these problems is monopolized by the central nucleus of the government. It is the logic of origins, not life. As mentioned before, citizens' votes and representation are largely confined not to where they live, but to where they will be buried, as we mentioned elsewhere.

4) The evolution of the system towards a narrower communal control of individuals. We are witnessing an unprecedented collectivization of cultual practices. In some communities, occasions that might call for collective commemoration have become the object of a new census. Anniversaries that once passed unnoticed have seen their profile hyped in order to lengthen the list of days on which the common confessional affiliation is reintroduced to the target audience. There is a tendency to multiply occasions at which, during a celebration, the throng is asked to repeat in unison formulas or emblematic gestures. Improvements in audio techniques have made it easy to broadcast ceremonies, calls for prayer or recitations elsewhere besides normal cult places. This is really offensive to people of other beliefs (as well as for less active members of the same rite). It is not surprising that non-conformists feel like renegades. They must be secretive about their thoughts and their way of life, and they find that the spaces where they can express these are constantly growing smaller. Clearly, the pressure is more acute – intellectuals in some quarters of Beirut tend to forget that – in villages, in the suburbs and in the monocommunal quarters of the cities. The boundaries of fairly public spaces have grown tighter since the beginning of the war. These boundaries remains endlessly problematic for individuals who have broken with their community and take refuge in these places, which are also a haven for somewhat pluralist press bodies, liberal publishing houses, institutions preoccupied with preserving a certain independence, etc. Observers have often underlined the fact that confessionalism reduces the ambitions of individuals to the confines of their community. Members of 14 out of 18 communities cannot normally hope to attain a rank higher than that of minister. We have mentioned the two world wars: it would need supernatural intervention to enable a Greek Catholic to head one of our three famous presidencies. At another level, there is no chance for 17 communities

out of 18 that one of theirs will one day be the commander-in-chief of the Lebanese army, governor of the central bank, rector of the Lebanese University, etc. Even if it is true that these exclusivities perpetuate collective frustrations, you can bet, however, that, taken individually, they kill no one. In fact, by limiting competition, they are an insult to common sense, and cause greater harm to the functions themselves than to the individuals they apparently intimidate. Rather, it is at another level, in the state of siege in which they live and in the mobilization they are subjected to, that one must seek the impediments to the creation of independent citizens. It is not surprising, either, to see these impediments often turned into voluntary servitude. What we are living does not lack for followers. Since the war, confessionalism has enjoyed immense popularity. Critics of confessionalism, on the other hand, have little support. So little, that it is legitimate to ask - at the risk of offending some people – if there is any significant demand for true democracy in this country.

Is it Paramount to Overcome Confessionalism?

At the national level, there was no need to reject confessionalism because in the past many Lebanese politicians and experts in public law had described it as "unbearable". It could have been possible to disregard its structural predisposition towards corruption, aided by general clientelism, an inevitable outcome of the practice of strongholds and quotas, and the presence behind the civil servant of a benefactor that could, if need be, become a protector.

Confessionalism could also have been forgiven for making appear the separation of powers (once almost unnecessary due to the constitutional as well as communal imbalance between these same powers) as an attempt to square the circle.

Could it have been any different? By reason of their position, each of the members of the troika is held to two standards, one institutional, the other communal, and hence must obey two masters whose wishes are frequently opposed. In particular, how can the speaker of house be convinced to act differently when, as occupant of one of the leading offices of state by virtue of the constitution, he believes that he has a mandate under the National Pact to protect the interests of his community?

Admittedly, at present it would be very difficult to stop each – inextricably personal and communal – stronghold from inflating public spending as it strives to increase the share of its community and, hence, our enormous public debt. It would also be difficult to maintain that because of confessionalism, one or more external powers have always (though more candidly: since the end of the war) assumed the role of a tutor or co-tutor not for the country's doctoral students, but for the country itself. It is hard to criticize the trustee for playing, as far as his resources will allow, a game in which he uses carefully dosed exploitation of communal imbalances to generate almost daily conflicts, which he manipulates as a master. He is only exploiting to his advantage the power game he had a crucial role in installing, but whose foundations (as successive elections have shown) are very real. He exploits his Lebanese partners' limits as well as assets by guaranteeing their power and, at the same time, their powerlessness. Given the qualified importance of their respective assets, he counts on their incapability to single-handedly manage the balance of power.

Confessionalism would not necessarily be objectionable if it were merely an impediment to the country's modernization. Non-modern or inelegant choices would be acceptable if shown to be the price of the country's survival. The objections to confessionalism lie elsewhere.

They lie in the medium- and long-term failure of confessionalism to run the country reasonably and to ensure a viable national peace. We have already mentioned the reputation of flexibility that the system continues to enjoy unduly, thanks to the beneficiaries. The system's ability to compromise is much lauded, yet the compromises it does manage to make in practice are concerned only with details, and even these are worked out so laboriously that solutions often come too late or are paid for dearly. Major problems must wait for major upheavals.

On the Verge of Going Under?

Does Lebanon stand any real chance at ridding itself of the confessionalist burden that periodically threatens to overwhelm it? If so many Lebanese continue to consider their own interests, which they always confuse with the multicommunal reality, as being their country's raison d'être, the answer is No. If they continue to regard as a trait of national genius what is but a vague desire to commit national suicide, the answer is No. If so many Lebanese continue to exonerate the system by imputing all their quandaries to the people in power, instead of admitting that it is through the system itself that they make their choices and act politically, the answer is No. If these Lebanese continue to believe that a tweaking the system will be able to enough to effectively combat clientelism, to permanently curb corruption, to stop the merry race towards financial disaster caused by wasting public resources and, last but not least, to restore genuine political independence, the answer is No. If so many Lebanese continue to regard as civil democracy what looks a lot more like a straitjacket cut according to the cloth of origin, the answer is No. Finally, if so many Lebanese continue to think that lasting civil peace can be achieved if only the "others" agree to let them handle their own affairs on the basis of sovereignty, the answer is No. Any condition that is so dependent on the good will of "others" is not much of a guarantee. The "others" will take pleasure whenever they can in hindering the achievement of this goal. It is not the confessional communities, torn as they are between the imperatives of their respective futures and the immutability of the existing socio-political system, that are the obstacle to this aspiration.

In short, the answer is No. Any hope that the Lebanese will rid themselves, before it is too late, of the many wrong perceptions that have prejudiced their mental outlook presumes immoderate optimism. These perceptions are buttressed by ancestral fears revived by the last war and by a web of particular interests that, thanks to their increased symmetry, are mutually support. Nonetheless, as the clock approaches midnight, does the Lebanese nation have any choice but to go under? Are there any subjective and objective guarantees for those Lebanese who, in desperation, would even go so far as to prefer the worst, rather than watch their country reach a new shore one day? With such lust for life, at other levels, and with such ability to adapt to the most unprecedented situations, are our people willing to pay the mental price to successfully overcome the crisis of the system, whose jolts are costing us increasingly dearly?

Outline of an Announced Reform

In theory, overcoming confessionalism was a key to the consensus that emerged to end our last war. Relative though it may be, this asset should not be sacrificed. While keeping a critical distance – the necessity of which is underlined by our experience of the past decade – it is still possible to build on the Taef Accord. The application of the Accord – as it has repeatedly been emphasized – has been exceedingly selective and biased. Without excluding a revision of the text – indeed, the experience of the past dozen years shows this to be desirable –, the coherence of the document and the complementarity and equilibrium of its principal provisions need to be restored. In particular, deconfessionalisation of the government should no longer be brandished as a threat every time the departure of the Syrian troops is requested; on the contrary, this departure should be treated as the initial condition for a move to deconfessionalisation. Other conditions will be necessary to ensure that deconfessionalisation serves to rescue the country, and is not the beginning of the end of the Lebanese Idea. In the absence of certain guarantees and cautionary measures, deconfessionalisation could easily turn into a national catastrophe. All communities must have substantial and legitimate representation in all progress towards a secular future. All talks should preferably take place under the auspices of the UN and the Arab League. Syria will have a place in the foreground, of course, but not dominant, let alone exclusive. Supranational sponsorship will ensure that the measures adopted are internationally respected. The Taef Accord makes provision for an institutional process to set up a National Committee to deal with the question of deconfessionalisation. Issues to be discussed include the following.

a) A new nationality law. Lebanese emigrants who meet certain requirements (born, having lived a certain number of years, or maintaining a residence in Lebanon, etc.) and wish to regain their Lebanese nationality will be able to apply. Cases dealt with under the 1990 decrees will be examined to verify compliance with the laws in force at the time. In a break with the past, it is time to end a scandal (unique in today's world) that has lasted for almost three quarters of a century and conduct a proper general census.

b) The law on optional personal status under civil law. Every citizen must – without prejudice to his personal religious beliefs – have the freedom to legally belong to a community under public law. The draft bill to provide the legal framework for such a community and for its organization must be revised and completed, and the bill submitted to parliament.

c) A new administrative division of the country, almost doubling the number of existing departments. The communal mix must as far as possible be preserved, and large communities must be granted regional seats, making it impossible for deconfessionalisation to mutate into camouflaged discrimination of certain communities by others. Although contradictory in theory, in practice these two requirements should not be very difficult to combine: the proportion of a community will not be the same in a new department as it was in the old one, but generally the communal mix will be preserved.

d) A new electoral law that does not apportion seats by confession. Constituencies will coincide with the new departments. The system of proportional representation (whose functional modalities and their implications for the political organization of society must be defined) will be applied at the level of the caza, introducing some qualification requirements such as attaining a minimum quota of votes at the lower level. Voters will have the option of registering according to their effective place of residence. By having an electoral roll separate from the Civil Status Register, it will no longer be necessary to use the latter. All candidates will be guaranteed equal access to the media. There will be a ceiling on election spending, and mechanisms to monitor it. Specialized NGOs will be authorized to monitor all the aspects of the election, and their reports will be made public. The right to appeal to the constitutional council will remain in force. Lebanese emigrants who have retained their nationality will be able to cast their votes at the nearest Lebanese consulate. Before each election, the apportionment of seats to each constituency will be reappraised on the basis of the number of registered voters. Finally, a law will determine the composition and method of electing a senate in which, in compliance with the Taef Accord, the communities will have proportional representation.

e) Deconfessionalising the three presidencies and the ministerial positions, but leaving executive power in the cabinet. As a complement to this measure, the term of office of the speaker of the house will have to be shortened, and the conditions under which the cabinet can dissolve parliament will have to be eased. Possible questions for discussion include electing the president of the republic in a joint session of both houses of parliament, and of granting the senate the right to reject parliament's choice if it is judged to be dangerously sectarian. Taken in conjunction with reforms to ensure the independence, and hence the deconfessionalisation, of the judiciary, these measures will provide a basis for eliminating the dual (constitutional and extra-constitutional) definition of powers, and give the separation of powers real meaning.

f) Adopting measures for effective deconfessionalisation of the civil service, including the judiciary. One must anticipate that the Christians, who still enjoy a comparative, though narrowing, advantage in quality of education, would run a rather small risk of being sidelined for positions filled by examination. Nonetheless, deconfessionalisation must extend to top civil service positions. These (and other managerial positions) must be filled by public competition. Submitted documents will be made accessible to the public via the media and specialized NGOs. The candidates will be as-

sessed by independent juries of experts. The cabinet must publicly justify any departure from the jury's recommendation.
g) Socio-political efforts to enhance national bonds. Politically, we must break the deadlock on the reflection on the War (1975–1990) as well as its implications. Such reflection is necessary for true national reconciliation. A new law will have to be promulgated regulating political parties and allowing for the creation of non-communal parties. Most importantly, we must restrict the interference in government of political organizations exploiting confessionalism in the form of clientelism and communal quotas in state employment. The finances of political organizations must be strictly controlled, mainly to suppress foreign interference in society's political structure and behaviour. As far as culturally or socially active NGOs are concerned, the government should adopt measures to encourage the intercommunal mix and to control their financial resources. The same principles of conviviality will guide the development and reform of public education (unsegregated schools, appointment of teachers regardless of communal affiliation, deghettoisation of the Lebanese University, etc.). The same goes for the government policies on housing, information, culture, etc.

Reform Without Reformists?

Deplorably, these measures, which have long been imperative, have few supporters among the Lebanese. The Lebanese – we must repeat again and again – are caught in a system of symmetrical fears, protected impotence and very real, but very narrow, interests. So far, they have failed miserably to build a framework able to ensure that the vital interests of their society can prevail. Will they succeed in making up for lost time and tackle the crisis that has long haunted Lebanon before it threatens the country's chance of having any future at all? We fear that when the economic and financial crisis breaks, the reaction will be one of communal recrimination. Gathered behind its president, each of the big communities will accuse the other two of having ruined national economy through egoistic opportunism. In keeping with what has become tradition, the three presidents (to whose company two or three other personalities must be added) will keep passing the buck, waving ostensible proof of all the other's responsibility for pushing the country over the edge. In this apocalyptic duel neither communities nor presidents will be entirely wrong. However, no one really wants to admit that evil has a long history, and is digging its claws deeper at each twist and turn of the system. The rejection of a common identification of evil is precisely what, until now, has made this evil incurable. The real evil is none other than this rejection.

The hardest conundrums, which the current Lebanese system is failing to address peacefully, are the normal and common changes that are unavoidable in any modern society. What is more inevitable than shifts in demographic composition (in particular in a multicommunal society), the spread of mass education and the ensuing ambitions, improvements in institutions, changes in the relative importance of different groups in the national economy, etc.? All are transformations that the confessionalist system has never taken into account because it has always failed to recognize them. It took 15 years of ravaging the country's body and soul for the system to become aware enough of these phenomena to register a lame reaction.

Against the Fifty-Fifty

However, these transformations continue. Consider the most notorious (and least mentioned) example. According to most estimates, the Lebanese population is roughly two thirds Muslim and one third Christian. Doing all they can to avoid reality, Christians – but also Muslims that benefit from the status quo – would rather not rock the fifty-fifty boat. They find useless words to conceal this inequity – undermining the law of numbers, upsetting the system, which is supposed to be a consociational democracy, a reminder of the necessity to leave to the Christians of the Middle East this little pied-à-terre, where, contrary to all Arab countries, they still have a real possibility of demonstrating their cultural presence, etc. Words! Words! Words! The law of numbers cannot be so casually avoided in a consociational or any other democracy. One can imagine some weighting rule that guarantees minorities the right to a voice in the matter or to avoid underrepresentation. That is completely different from the rule of 2 to 1! Already, Muslims, males and females, dare rebel, in the name of equality, against the Koranic law that grants "the male the share of two females" in matters of inheritance. We understand that the maxim "for one Christian, the share of two Muslims" is unsustainable in the long run. Mind you, the same maxim does not apply to divisions between Maronites and Greek Orthodox, for example, or between Druze and Shiites. If, however, to the passing stranger, Lebanon appears to be an Islamo-Christian society, to the insider, it appears (at least in times of peace!) to be a collection of 18 confessional communities rather than two religious communities. On the other hand, we cannot help but note that before their political contract can be dubbed a "consociational democracy" Lebanese communities would have to demonstrate their detachment from the mode of tribal organization and mobilization and their respect for citizens' rights and liberties, the essence of which is considerably reduced by compulsory communal affiliation. Finally, the argument drawn from the Christians' regional situation, even if it answers an undeniable reality, cannot convince Lebanese Muslims. Why should they have to pay for regional re-equilibrium, when those who call for it are the first to refuse to suffer the consequences of the plague that handicaps our region?

Not Even a War!

Why do we hesitate to look the defects sabotaging our future in the eye? By agreeing to do so, we certainly face great risks. But we are already caught in a predicament we cannot get out of! What are we waiting for then? A new war? Not even that! Because confessionalism or not, we no longer want a war, neither "for others" nor for ourselves.

Selected Bibliography

Âmil, Mahdî, *Madkhal ila Naqd al-Fikr al-tâ'ifî* (Introduction to the Refutation of Confessionalist Thought) (Beirut: Markaz al-Abhâth al-filistînî, 1980).
Beydoun, Ahmad, *Identité confessionnelle et temps social chez les historiens libanais contemporains* (Confessional Identity and Social Time for Lebanese Contemporary Historians) (Beirut: Publications of the Lebanese University, 1984).
Beydoun, Ahmad, *Al-Jumhûrîya al-mutaqatti³a* (The Occasional Republic) (Beirut: Dar Annahar, 1999).
Chahîn, Fuâd, *Al-Tâ'ifîya fî Lubnân* (Confessionalism in Lebanon) (Beirut: Dâr al-Hadâtha, 1980).
Charâra, Waddâh, *Fî Usûl Lubnân al-tâ'ifî* (At the Roots of Confessionalist Lebanon) (Beirut: Dâr al-Talî'a, 1975).
Chiha, Michel, *Politique intérieure* (Internal Policy) (Beirut: Éditions du Trident, 1964).
Corm, Georges, *Madkhal ila Lubnân wa al-Lubnânîyîn* (Introduction to Lebanon and the Lebanese) (Beirut: Dâr al-Jadîd, 1996).
Haddad, Grégoire, *Al-'Almânîya al-châmila* (Global Secularism) (Beirut: no ed., 1999).
Messarra, Antoine, *Le modèle politique libanais et sa survie* (The Political Lebanese Model and its Survival) (Beirut: Publications of the Lebanese University, 1983).
Messarra, Antoine, *Théorie générale du système politique libanais* (General Theory of the Lebanese Political System) (Paris: Cariscript, 1994).
Nassar, Nassif, *Nahwa Mujtama' Jadîd* (Towards a New Society) (Beirut: Dâr Annahâr, 1970).
Qazma Khûrî, Yûsuf (ed.), *Al-Tâ'ifîya fî Lubnân min khilâl Munâqachât Majlis al-Nuwwâb* (Confessionalism in Lebanon through Parliamentary Debates) (Beirut: Dâr al-Hamrâ', 1989).
Rabbath, Edmond, *La formation historique du Liban politique et constitutionnel* (The Historical Structure of Politics and Constitution in Lebanon) (Beirut: Publications of the Lebanese University, 1973).
Salam, Nawwaf, *Al-Islâh al-mumkin wa al-Islâh al-manchûd* (Possible Reform and Desired Reform) (Beirut: al-Mu'assasa al-Jâmiaaîya lil-Dirâsât, 1989).
Samad, Riyâdh, *Al-Tâ'ifîya wa Lu³bat al-Hukm fî Lubnân* (Confessionalism and the Power Game in Lebanon) (Beirut: no ed. 1977).
Sâyigh, Anîs, *Lubnân al-tâ'ifî* (The Confessionalist Lebanon) (Beirut: Dâr al-Sir'a al-fikrî, 1955).
Sâyigh, Dâwûd, *Al-Nizâm al-lubnânî fî Thawâbitih wa Tahawwulâtih* (The Lebanese System: Constants and Variables) (Beirut: Dar Annahar, 2000).
Taqi al-Dîn, Sulaymân, *Al-Mas'ala al-tâ'ifîya fî Lubnân* (The Issue of Confessionalism in Lebanon) (Beirut: Dâr Ibn Khaldûn, no date).

A Polity in an Uncertain Regional Environment

Samir Kassir

When a war has been as complex as the Lebanese war, the postwar era is unlikely to be any simpler. Indeed, the predominant feature of the Lebanese war – that it was not strictly Lebanese, but (at the risk of oversimplifying) a mix of domestic and regional conflicts – is also a feature of the postwar era. Thus, postwar Lebanon cannot be fully understood without considering it in its regional context, in particular the persistent uncertainty throughout the period and the overwhelming dominance of one regional power.

This essay deals with the external dimension of Lebanon's postwar politics, and in particular with three issues: first, Israel's continued occupation of South Lebanon long after the war had ended, and the intersecting regional strategies and local dynamics that fueled that conflict; second, the lingering question of the Palestinian refugees and its effect on Lebanon's society and polity; and third, and arguably the most important, what is commonly referred to as "the privileged relations" between Lebanon and Syria.

In all three issues, special attention will be given to the interplay between external actors and internal dynamics, and to the inputs of various Arab and foreign powers. This essay will focus primarily on the Syrian factor, a persistent influence in postwar Lebanon, whether from an external or internal perspective. The guidelines used here are those set by the Lebanese political agenda itself, which is dominated by Syrian-Lebanese relations, as reflected in the daily headlines. Owing to the so-called privileged relations, Syria plays a leading role in all spheres of Lebanese public life. Hence, the significance of that expression needs to be closely examined, particularly because the symmetry it assumes has yet to be realized. Instead of establishing an equitable relationship between two equal partners, "privileged relations" is code for control and domination: Syria is the center of power and decision-making in postwar Lebanon's society and polity. This has strongly influenced Lebanon's regional stance, particularly in respect of the peace process, as the coupling of Syrian-Israeli negotiations and Lebanese-Israeli negotiations – "*talazum al-masarayn*" – has gained tremendous credence. Indeed, this catchphrase has been a key factor in projecting the long-lasting stalemate in the regional peace process into the domestic arena, where it has constrained postwar politics and frozen the political game. One example of this is the extension of President Elias Hrawi's term of office in 1995, when an alleged "strategic interest" was put forward to justify the constitutional amendment necessary for that purpose.

The advent of peace in Lebanon after fifteen years of armed conflict and civil strife opened a new chapter in the history of the country. Nevertheless, the start of the peace process after the Gulf War clouded the significance of this new chapter and its importance for postwar Lebanon. Although the Middle East peace process initially nurtured great hopes of an end to the Arab-Israeli conflict, the slow pace of progress at the Madrid Peace Conference generated uncertainty. Given this atmosphere of uncertainty and the persistent ambiguities in Lebanon, the Lebanese political elite adopted a wait-and-see position, and acquiesced in Syria's extension of *de facto* control over the entire country through its security apparatus.

Peace from Abroad

In many respects, the manner in which internal peace was established in Lebanon explains the country's postwar hypersensitivity to the uncertainty of its regional environment. It is worth recalling that the Lebanese war was ended by two major events, both the result of decisions by foreign actors.

The first was the Taef Agreement of 1989, an agreement between the surviving members of the 1972 parliament. Although Lebanese participation was intensively prepared under the aegis of Speaker Hussein Husseini, the agreement itself was brokered by a special envoy from the Arab League, Lakhdar Ibrahimi, under the supervision of a tripartite Arab commission comprising Algeria, Morocco, and Saudi Arabia. The latter in particular, through its minister of foreign affairs, Prince Saud al-Faysal, and Rafiq Hariri, a Saudi-Lebanese billionaire and future prime minister of Lebanon, was instrumental in achieving the agreement. The Saudi influence was strongly felt by all Lebanese lawmakers gathered in Taef. While Syria did not formally take part in the talks, a special partnership between it and Saudi Arabia, combined with regional *realpolitik*, ensured that it would play a role in the implementation of the Agreement. In addition, the meeting in Taef was closely watched by France, the United States, and the Vatican. The Agreement was not put into effect immediately. The assassination of René Moawad, the newly elected Lebanese president, and choice of Elias Hrawi as his successor, undermined efforts to broker a compromise that would have enabled the reluctant General Michel Aoun to endorse the Agreement. It formally entered into force after the Syrian army ousted General Aoun in October 1990.

This Syrian military victory was the second of the two major events that ended the war. For the first time since Syrian intervention in Lebanon, its air force attacked its Lebanese foes, a sign that it had received the "green light" from the US, the broker of the Syrian-Israeli agreement of 1976.[1] America undoubtedly granted informal permission in the hope that Syrian troops would join Egyptian troops in the US-led coalition

---

1 On the 1976 agreement, cf. Yair Evron, *War and Intervention in Lebanon. The Israeli-Syrian Deterrence Dialogue* (London: Croom Helm, 1987): pp. 46-47, 52, and 59. See also Adeed Dawisha, *Syria and the Lebanese Crisis* (London: MacMillan, 1980): pp. 134 and 180.

against Iraq. The Gulf crisis also explains why Saudi Arabia was no longer in a position to supervise the implementation of the Taef Agreement, which allowed Syria to gain the upper hand in this process. Moreover, the signing of the Syrian-Lebanese Treaty of Brotherhood, Cooperation, and Coordination in May 1991 confirmed that the Syrian interpretation would prevail. In the following years, Saudi influence was limited to matters of finance, in spite of the close ties between the Saudi royal family and Prime Minister Rafiq Hariri, in office from 1992 to 1998 and again since 2000.

These local developments acquired increased importance because the first Bush administration was preparing a peace process in the Middle East. Syria and Lebanon attended the opening of the Madrid Peace Conference in October 1991 and subsequently several sessions of bilateral talks in Washington. Alas, it soon became clear that the peace process was a process of attrition, for all its protagonists. The occupation of the southern part of Lebanon by the Israeli army would continue for another nine years, as would armed resistance to it. On four occasions the Israeli army extended its operations well beyond the borders of the southern zone, in the form of massive bombardments from the air and the sea: in 1993 (the so-called air invasion code-named "Operation Accountability"), in 1996 (a massive campaign of Israeli air and sea bombardments code-named "Grapes of Wrath" and concluded by the April Understanding) and in 1999 and 2000 (the bombing of power stations near Beirut).

In the meantime, the Syrian interpretation of the Taef Agreement and its implementation gained strength and legitimacy. The withdrawal of Syrian troops from the capital and the central territory scheduled under the Agreement for September 1992 was not formally announced until the spring of 2002 – following a smaller redeployment in 2001. Even then, the withdrawal of army personnel, framed as the implementation of one of the clauses of the Agreement, failed to include the apparatus of the *mukhabarat*, the Syrian security forces. Throughout this time, Syrian officials were either unconcerned about delays in implementing Taef, or used delays in the regional peace process to justify its stalling. Their indifference was not only an expression of their complete hold over the Lebanese polity, but also of American blessing, or as former Speaker of Parliament Hussein Husseini put it, an informal American agreement to postpone withdrawal of their (i. e. Syrian) troops until the liberation of South Lebanon from Israeli military occupation.[2] It is worth noting, however, that both Lebanon and Syria refrained from any diplomatic maneuver that would have hastened the withdrawal of Israeli forces from occupied South Lebanon. No less interesting is the fact that after Israel finally withdrew in May 2000, the US did not insist on Syria pulling out its troops, as if pending uncertainty in the border area justified further postponement of the full implementation of the Taef Agreement.

---

2 Interview with the author.

Shifting Doctrines

Lebanese diplomacy was straightforward and consistent regarding the Israeli occupation of South Lebanon from the time it was established in March 1978 (when the United Nations Interim Force in Lebanon, or UNIFIL, was deployed) up to the early 90s: full implementation of UN Resolution 425. It was a logical policy that sought to separate the quest for a settlement of the Lebanese conflict in general and the Israeli occupation in particular from the Arab-Israeli conflict and any regional peace process.[3] However, this consistent Lebanese doctrine was incompatible with the proposed framework of the peace process launched at the Madrid Conference in 1991. Lebanese officials gradually embraced a perspective eventually known as "*talazum al-masarayn*", which coupled the Syrian-Israeli track with the Lebanese-Israeli track, subsequently upgraded to "*wihdat al-masar wa-l-masir*" or the "unity of the [negotiating] track and destiny". The alliteration of the last version is intended to reflect the (alleged) harmony between Lebanon and Syria on all issues, including the peace process. This implied that the basis for Syrian-Israeli negotiations would also apply to Lebanese-Israeli negotiations and, owing to its more general scope, UN Resolution 242 would supersede Resolution 425.

Before the specific nature of Resolution 425 was subsumed under Resolution 242, Lebanese officials had expressed reservations about the Madrid Conference. Salim Hoss, then prime minister, was inclined to turn down the invitation, but Lebanon could not afford to stay away from the Conference when all its Arab counterparts, particularly Syria, were present. In the end, after receiving a letter of assurances from the American administration,[4] Lebanon settled for the dubious position of attending with the explicit intention of *obtaining* the implementation of 425, and not of *negotiating* its implementation. As Foreign Minister Fares Boueiz put it in his speech to the Madrid Conference, Lebanon viewed Resolution 425 as independent of the whole negotiating process.[5]

As the stakes at the Conference were no less than a "just and lasting peace" (*salâm 'adil wa shâmil*), the Lebanese position was hardly defensible. Given the lack of coordination between the Arab parties concerned with the peace process, Lebanese diplomacy was able, however, to stand its ground by distancing itself from the entire process, except for matters pertaining to UN Resolution 425. Thus, Lebanon was not tempted to resist Syrian pressure to boycott the first session of multilateral negotiations in Moscow in early 1992 (in what effectively anticipated the *talazum*). In consenting to the boycott, Lebanon succeeded in pleasing Syria, but also in remaining true to its own inconsistent position, to be a party to the negotiations but to abstain from negotiating.

---

3 On Resolution 425 and Lebanese position on its implementation, see Ghassan Tuéni, *Une guerre pour les autres* (Paris: Lattès, 1984) and *Rasa'il ila Elias Sarkis* (Beirut: Dar an-Nahar, 1995).
4 The letter of invitation to the Madrid Conference and the letter of assurances were published in *The Beirut Review*, No. 3 (Spring 1992).
5 Speech published in *Revue d'études palestiniennes*, No. 42 (Winter 1992): p. 64.

How do we explain Lebanon's shift from obsessive pursuit of Resolution 425 as the only rationale for its presence in Madrid and Washington to its commitment to Resolution 242? Therein lies the crux of *talazum*: the consent, if only implicit, to the land for peace equation. Lebanese and Syrian land, that is.

The shift appears to have taken place in 1993, more precisely, after the ninth session of the Lebanese-Israeli negotiations, when news were leaked of an Israeli paper presented to the Lebanese negotiating team in Washington that called for guarantees of security in exchange for a gradual withdrawal – *as-Safir*, a Lebanese daily, was suspended for publishing the paper.[6] When Simon Karam, Lebanon's ambassador to Washington, resigned several weeks later, the crisis unraveling behind the scenes became public. Months earlier, President Elias Hrawi had personally entrusted Ambassador Karam with exploring the possibility of a gradual solution, the so-called "Jezzine first" option.[7] The crisis suggested that, prior to that point, Lebanese officials and their Syrian counterparts might have not been completely opposed to a gradual implementation of 425, possibly as a confidence-building measure between Syria and Israel. Needless to say, that pattern would have provided a more suitable framework for coordinating Lebanese and Syrian negotiating efforts, in contrast to the present situation in which Lebanon takes its cue from Syria at every step.

The implementation of Resolution 425 was not the only option for Syria. It has been widely said that the late President Hafez Assad was far more interested in the process of negotiation, any process of negotiation, than in the outcome of this process. This view must be moderated in retrospect, given the genuine Syrian concessions at Shepardstown in 1999 and early 2000, in contrast to Israel's inability to make concessions. However, Syria showed at an early stage it could afford to delay negotiations indefinitely, despite the competition that became palpable between the Syrian track and the Palestinian track in 1992 and 1993 – and which might explain the haste of Oslo. In the meantime, it began to strengthen its position at the negotiating table by using the Lebanese front and Hezbollah's increasingly efficient military resistance, to exert direct pressure on Israel.

Occupation and Resistance

Resistance to the Israeli occupation in Lebanon went through three major stages. From 1982 to 1985, a multilateral front was extremely successful in harassing the Israeli military presence, which led to the first major withdrawal of the occupiers. This was followed by years of low-intensity resistance, generally unnoticed by the Israeli public and the international media. In the third and final stage from 1993–1994, the resistance, now conducted solely by Hezbollah, gained in efficiency and legitimacy until it reached the intensity of a war of liberation, eventually resulting in the withdrawal of Israel and its surrogates from the remaining land they occupied in South Lebanon.

---

6 *Al-Safir*, May 11, 1993.
7 Karam's interview in *L'Orient-Express*, No. 6 (May 1996).

The first stage, in the aftermath of the 1982 invasion, was two-pronged: armed action and massive popular protests. The military resistance, which started during the occupation of Beirut in September 1982, was conducted as the Lebanese National Resistance Front which embraced left-wing and nationalist parties, including the Communist Party, the Organization for Communist Action in Lebanon (OCAL), the Syrian Social Nationalist Party (SSNP), and what remained of the PLO apparatus in the country. It kept up a high level of activity for about three years. Simultaneously, the Shi'i Amal movement was playing a key role in the growing popular resistance, along with Shi'a radical religious factions, which often originated in its ranks and later united to form Hezbollah in 1985. These religious factions, armed and trained by Iran's Pasdarans, also contributed to the armed resistance, resorting to suicide bombings as early as the fall of 1982. However spectacular these actions were, it was the continuous pressure on the Israeli Army by both the popular protests and the low-profile but efficient actions of the Lebanese National Resistance Front that earned Lebanon its reputation of a valley of tears in the eyes of the Israeli public. Indeed, Israeli casualties in this period were far heavier than at any later date. Indeed, the actions of this Resistance Front triggered the first Israeli withdrawal from the cities of Sidon, Tyre, Nabatiyyeh and most of South Lebanon in 1985.[8]

The subsequent decrease in pressure by the resistance was the result of a number of factors. Firstly, the Israeli army redeployed in the southern tip of Lebanon and started to use the surrogate South Lebanon Army (SLA) as a shield in the "security belt" it still occupied.[9] Secondly, the Amal movement moved against the left-wing parties and, with the Syrian blessing, neutralized the Palestinian component of the resistance during the "war of the camps" (1985–1988). The Resistance Front was still able to orchestrate spectacular acts, such as the assassination attempt on General Antoine Lahd, the head of the SLA, by a female Communist activist, and a number of bombings and suicide bombings organized by political parties with no religious affiliations. Not all such attempts were effective against the occupiers. In that period, resistance seemed residual, if existent at all, which allowed the national unity government in Israel to convince its constituency that its army was no longer occupying South Lebanon. For the Lebanese, the occupation was very real, spreading and stoking unease and unrest in South Lebanon, where Hezbollah, a formal movement since 1985, was gaining support amongst the population of the liberated territory. Owing to the special partnership between Iran, Hezbollah's ideological patron, and Syria, party members were allowed to ignore restrictions on movement and the carrying of arms imposed on left-wing parties.

After armed conflict ceased in central Lebanon, the occupation of the southern tip continued. Owing to the special partnership between Iran and Syria, and Syria's desire to empower the Amal movement, the *Muqawama* or "Resistance" was exempted from mi-

---

8 Samir Kassir, "La résistance nationale libanaise" and "Chronique de la lutte populaire", *Revue d'études palestiniennes*, No. 16 (Summer 1985). See also Mahmoud Soueid, Mahmoud Soueid, *Israël au Liban:La fin de trente ans d'occupation?* (Paris: Editions de la Revue d'études palestiniennes, 2000).

9 See Munzer Jaber, *Al-Sharit al-lubnani al-muhtall* (Beirut: Institute for Palestine Studies, 1999).

litia demobilization in 1991. As there were never any specific criteria for identifying the Resistance, there were no clear criteria for compliance and exemption. From empirical observation, it appears that those exempted included Hezbollah and Amal, while pro-Syrian Lebanese proxies like the SSNP had room to maneuver. Amal brandished the banner of the Resistance to maintain its hegemony over the South, only to be challenged by Hezbollah. The Communist Party, lacking external support since the collapse of the Soviet Union, had been dealt fatal blows by the Amal movement in the years preceding the end of the war. By then its relations with Syria were embittered, as were those of the Organization for Communist Action in Lebanon (OCAL). After 1991, the SSNP was closely associated to the circles of power and, willingly or unwillingly, refrained from acts of armed resistance in the South, while continuing to celebrate its past contribution to the Resistance. All in all, Hezbollah alone remained an active resistance movement.

Hezbollah chose to focus on the South, without neglecting its original stronghold in Baalbek and its environs. At the end of the war in central Lebanon, it appeared to be in firm control of the dynamics of resistance. By then, armed resistance was very different than in 1982–1985. One of the key differences was the launching of operations from outside the boundaries of the occupied zone. Consequently, enemy losses were lighter, and therefore not noticed by the Israeli public. But they inflicted enough harm and damage for the Israeli command to retaliate, most notably by abducting Shaykh Abdel-Karim Obeid, a Hezbollah leader, in 1989, and assassinating Shaykh Abbas Mussawi, general secretary of the party, in February 1992; he was replaced by *Sayyid* Hasan Nasrallah. Only after 1993 did the effectiveness of the Islamic Resistance (as it was referred to in official parlance) improve, a fact that some party officials admitted to in private.[10] Continuing resistance – and the rhetoric of resistance – enabled Hezbollah to enhance its stand in the national arena even before then. The arithmetic of parliamentary representation after the Syrian-engineered elections of 1992, for instance, reflected their clout. It is an open question whether the increasing efficacy of resistance operations was the incentive behind Syria's support, or vice versa. The Israeli air campaign, "Operation Accountability", in July 1993 provided an answer of sorts.[11]

This attack by the Israelis acknowledged Syria's gamble with the Resistance on the Lebanese front. The attack on the Resistance was an attempt to break Syrian leverage and alter its position. It is worth recalling here that Yitzhak Rabin, who had fueled competition between the Palestinian and Syrian negotiation tracks, changed his diplomacy decisively after the attacks of July 1993. Realizing that the Syrian track had failed to make any progress – the last attempt was that of US Secretary of State Warren Christopher – he reluctantly agreed to pursue the Oslo track, as advocated by Shimon Peres.[12]

---

10 Interviews with the author.
11 Mahmoud Soueid (ed.), *Harb al-ayyam al-sab'a 'ala Lubnan: 'Amaliyyat Tasfiyat al-hisabat* (Beirut: Institute for Palestine Studies, 1993).
12 Itamar Rabinovich, *Brink of Peace. The Israeli-Syrian Negotiations* (Princeton University Press, 1998).

Hezbollah still had to endure one last test before full integration into the power structure of postwar Lebanon. On September 13, 1993, the day that the Oslo Agreement was signed on the White House lawn, Hezbollah organized a protest in the suburbs of Beirut, which was bloodily suppressed. Several Hezbollah members were killed by Lebanese army fire. Contrary to widespread expectations, this incident marked the first and last instance of tension between Hezbollah, on the one hand, and the Lebanese army and/or the Syrian security apparatus on the other hand. The territorial hegemony of the party remained unchallenged: it was complete in the southern suburbs of Beirut, the area surrounding Baalbek in the Bekaa Valley, and the Iqlîm at-Tuffah area in the South near the boundaries of the occupied zone. Five years later, under General Emile Lahoud, and, as always, after Syrian prodding, toleration of Hezbollah was consolidated into close coordination between the party and the reshuffled Lebanese *mukhabarat*. In the meantime, *"talazum al-masarayn"*, which had gained in strength in conjunction with official backing of the Resistance, had become the core of the official policy of the Lebanese state.

In retrospect, it appears that the turning point of Lebanese diplomacy occurred in the summer of 1993. Between the Israeli attack in July and the White House ceremony in September the notion of *talazum* became a national mantra, a proposal deemed superior to all others on the table, and more advanced, with which every party concerned in the process was expected to engage. Be that as it may, the Lebanese-Israeli track became deadlocked in September 1993, after the eleventh and last session of negotiations.[13] As for Resolution 425, it became clear that the Lebanese position of "independence" from the negotiating process was purely rhetorical.[14]

By the time of "Grapes of Wrath", the second large-scale Israeli attack beyond the borders of the occupied zone, in April of 1996,[15] the credibility of *talazum* was caught in the front-page headline of the country's second-largest daily, as-Safir: "The blood of Lebanon summons the whole world to Damascus" – ironically intended to express support for Syria.[16] Cynicism aside, the Syrian regime had every reason to congratulate itself. The impact of the Israeli bombing of a UNIFIL shelter in Qana – which claimed more than a 100 civilian lives and was viewed as an unforgivable mistake by the American, European and Israeli public – accelerated efforts to end its short campaign of attrition; the solution underscored the full integration of *talazum*. The conflict was resolved with the April Understanding, monitored by a multilateral commission, a conflict management entity, composed of the USA, France, Israel, Lebanon, and Syria.[17]

---

13 On the negotiations process, see the series of articles by Georges Bkassini in *al-Mustaqbal* (Beirut, throughout May 2001).

14 Michael Young, "La 425 ou comment s'en sortir", in *L'Orient-Express*, No. 6 (May 1996), and "The different faces of Resolution 425", in *The Lebanon Report* (Spring 1998): pp. 43- 46.

15 Mahmoud Soueid (ed.), *Siyâsat al-ard al-mahruqa wa-l-hall al-mafrud: min Tasfiyat al-hisabat 1993 ila 'Anaqid al-ghadab 1996* (Beirut: Institute for Palestine Studies, 1996).

16 *Al-Safir*, April 20th 1996.

17 Eric Canal-Forgues, "La surveillance de l'application de l'arrangement du 26 avril 1996 (Israël-Liban)", in *Revue générale de droit public international* (July-September 1998)3: pp. 723-746.

The April Understanding gave Syria an official role for the first time in the lingering conflict over south Lebanon. In 1978, it had refused an official role in controlling the PLO.[18] The change in outlook was made possible by the legitimization of a resistance movement Syria was controlling, as the Understanding stipulated that parties to the conflict, i. e., the Resistance and the Israeli army, should refrain from attacks against civilians, which implied that attacks against non-civilians were allowed. It should be added that the unanimous outrage on the part of Lebanese society against the Israeli military campaign translated into support and increased popularity for the Resistance.

Yet, if the Israeli attack generated evidence that Lebanese society was – at last – able to mobilize itself to defend the South without second thoughts, the April Understanding was confirmation of the marginalization of the Lebanese state. Unable and unwilling to be an independent actor in the peace process, the Lebanese state did not have much to show for itself when the Israelis raised the option of withdrawal.

Undesirable Victory

To understand the reasons for Israel's withdrawal proposal, one needs to look at Israel's interests in Lebanon. There is little doubt that between 1978 and 1982 Israel was interested in establishing a zone of influence in Lebanon as a precursor to a peace treaty and a friendlier regime in Beirut. However, the consequences of the 1982 invasion (the Sabra and Shatila massacres, the intervention of the multilateral force and its departure, renewed civil war, the resignation of Prime Minister Menachem Begin, etc.) were a significant setback for Israel. With the failure of the May 17 Agreement, Israel could no longer pretend to exert significant influence on the Lebanese polity. By 1985, after withdrawing from most of South Lebanon – which was presented as a withdrawal from all Lebanon – Israel was strictly concerned with security, day-to-day security, not strategic security. The latter was no longer an option, as it was evident from a statement by Yitzhak Rabin in September 1994 in which he said that he would prefer to see two Syrian armored divisions in the Lebanese Bekaa than on the Golan Heights.

Given Israel's downgrading of Lebanon's strategic importance, the cost of military occupation was felt to be more burdensome, although lighter in absolute terms than during the period 1982–1985, or the current war in Palestine. Israel's further withdrawal from Lebanon in May 2000 was greeted with relief, even satisfaction.

In the meantime, Syria was able to resume its role as regional power. That its moves were purely tactical is attested by the countertactics Israel eventually adopted when it eventually abandoned what remained of its Lebanese ambitions. First, the Netanyahu government recognized Resolution 425 and then Ehud Barak, Netanyahu's successor, set a deadline for the withdrawal of the Israeli army. Had the retaliatory exchange not been the backdrop to Lebanese tragedies, the Syrian and Israeli maneuvers could easily be ar-

---

18 Samir Kassir, *La guerre du Liban. De la dissension nationale au conflit régional (1975-1982)* (Paris: Karthala, 1994): pp. 308-309.

chived amongst the best of their kind in the art of war – or more accurately: in the art of avoiding war as well as peace.

In the midst of the maneuvering and retaliation, there was real reason for rejoicing: the liberation of the South. Yet, joy was overcome by anxiety. The position of the Lebanese state was consistent with its inconsistency until the eve of that tremendous event. For months, Lebanese officials in the front row, and their Syrian counterparts in the second, had not been fully convinced of Israel's decision to withdraw. Worse still, they gave the impression that they did not want the Israelis to withdraw, thus harming Lebanon's credibility with the United Nations. When Israel withdrew on schedule in late May 2000, suspicions about Israeli intentions were extended to include UN efforts to establish a Blue Line in order to verify the end of the occupation – which the UN nonetheless succeeded in drawing.[19] Yet, in spite of the spirit of Resolution 425 and of a unique declaration by President Emile Lahoud,[20] Lebanon chose to ignore the framework of the 1949 Armistice Convention, once the cornerstone of Lebanese diplomacy. Indeed, the deployment of the Lebanese army in the border area, presented as a means of ensuring Israel's security, was now regarded as contrary to Lebanon's interests and rejected.

Lebanese officials gave several reasons for their caution. Some of them, such as the holding of Lebanese prisoners in Israel and the refusal of the Israeli military to hand over maps of mines,[21] were legitimate. The UN also made mistakes in drawing the Blue Line, which were corrected in the weeks following the withdrawal. Although genuine, those concerns also reflected suspicion and, moreover, overt intentions to keep the file on South Lebanon open. A policy ostensibly to avoid giving the enemy credit or comfort before a comprehensive Arab-Israeli peace agreement in general, and the liberation of the Golan in particular, it also ensured that Lebanon was the last field of fighting in the Arab-Israeli conflict, with the Resistance transformed into a full-time fighting force. With the rediscovery of the Shib'a farms this ploy was revealed in all its transparency. Once an object of dispute between Lebanon and Syria, this patch of territory at the foot of the Golan Heights had long been forgotten. Shortly before the Israeli withdrawal, and more insistently after its completion, Lebanon claimed that the area was part of Lebanon, and, against all odds, Syrian officials recognized this claim. However, the two governments failed to convince the UN of the claim, since the redrawing of the border would have required a treaty, which they were not inclined to sign.

The Shib'a farms, or the "shooting field" as one high-ranking Hezbollah official ironically put it,[22] served Lebanese and Syrian contention that the Lebanese-Israeli territorial dispute was not over, and therefore the Resistance should not disarm. The United States exerted pressure to prevent the issue from getting out of hand – especially with a

---

19 Frederic Hof, "Beyond the Boundary: Lebanon, Israel and the Challenge of Change", in *Middle East Insight* (2000).
20 Interview with CNN, May 26, 2000.
21 It was not before the fall of 2002 that Israel handed over the mining maps to the UNIFIL.
22 Interview with the author.

new Intifada in Palestine and the growing possibility of a regional war following the election of Ariel Sharon in Israel, and above all after the September 11 attacks. Lebanese and Syrian perceptions of this American interest lead to controlled escalation on several occasions, for instance on the eve of visits by US envoys to the Middle East.[23]

The interests of the Resistance were not limited to this territorial dispute over the Shib'a farms. Hezbollah saw in the new Palestinian uprising that started four months after the liberation of South Lebanon a way to broaden its scope from Lebanon to the Middle East as a whole and to sustain its own ideological agenda, if only through behind-the-scenes alliances with other radical Islamic organizations (Hamas, Jihad) and the rhetoric of al-Manar, its TV satellite channel. The Lebanese state also referred to the ongoing war in Palestine as a reason not to disarm the Resistance or to deploy the army in the South. Even prior to this, Lebanese officials used the Palestinian issue to justify their refusal to guarantee the security of the border area. In April 2000, on the eve of the Israeli withdrawal, President Lahoud went as far as to express the right of Palestinians to use Lebanon as a base to fight for their land, a reversal of the position Lebanon had held since the abrogation of the Cairo Agreement in 1985. This stance may have won Lahoud some support in the Palestinian camps, but it was clearly no more than a gesture. Not only was the blockade of the camps not eased, but Lebanese officials, including Lahoud, continue to play the *tawtîn* card, i. e., the threat posed by the permanent resettlement of Palestinian refugees, in everyday politics.

The Palestinian Pretext

Tawtîn refers to the resettlement of the Palestinian refugees in Lebanon, but the word from which derives, *watan* or homeland, endows it with a special resonance – a more accurate translation would be "impatriation". The word itself is not that old, although the question of settling Palestinian refugees in their host countries was raised in the 50s, with no success. Twenty years later, in the mid-70s, Lebanese Christian factions claimed they were fighting to prevent Palestinians taking over their country. A number of statements attributed to Henry Kissinger, a former US secretary of state, the idea of replacing the Christians with Palestinians. Among those that spread the rumor was former President Suleiman Frangieh, who reported that Ambassador Dean Brown, an envoy of US President Ford, presented him with a proposal to settle the Christians of Lebanon in Canada![24] The *tawtîn* referred to nowadays is slightly different. By virtue of its precise semantics (the reference to *watan*) and its practical vagueness (who would do it?), it has come to be used by nearly everybody, including Maronite Christians and Muslim Shi'a,

---

[23] On the situation in South Lebanon after the Israeli withdrawal, see Elizabeth Picard, "Autorité et souveraineté de l'état à l'épreuve du Liban sud", in *Maghreb-Machrek*, No. 169 (July-September 2000): pp. 32-42. See also *Old Game, New Rules* (Brussels: International Crisis Group (ed.), 2002).

[24] An allegation Dean Brown has refuted time and time again. Cf. Fadia Nassif, *Les rumeurs dans la guerre du Liban. Les mots de la violence* (Paris: CNRS éditions, 1999): pp. 195-199.

regardless of their ideology. These two groups seem to have a heightened sensitivity to *tawtîn*'s demographic and sectarian significance, as permanent settlement of the mostly Sunni Palestinians would change the sectarian balance to their respective disadvantage.

The first recorded use of the word *tawtîn* is in 1978, in the aftermath of Anwar Sadat's visit to Jerusalem and Menachem Begin's "peace plan" that stipulated that Palestinians from the diaspora would only be allowed to settle in autonomous areas in the occupied territories if they obtained the agreement of a trilateral commission, one of whose members would be Israel – which meant, in effect, that the Palestinians in the diaspora would stay where they were, in Jordan, Syria, and Lebanon. If the origin is fairly clear, its progress is less so. Curiously, the word underwent a paradigmatic shift owing to confusion between the PLO's de facto power in some areas of the South in the late 70s and the prospect of Palestinians becoming part of the Lebanese community. As a result, the idea of *tawtîn* was implicitly attributed to the Palestinians, who would be the victims of its implementation, rather than to Israel. Such calculations failed to take into account that any integration of Palestinians would put an end to the official ambitions of the PLO and its project by undermining its *raison d'être*. In that sense, integration was only feasible after conclusion of the Palestinian project. This confusion, or miscalculation, was embedded in the matrix of Lebanese-Palestinian relations and shaped by them. On the one hand, there was the antagonism with the Christian front and, on the other, the tension with Shi'a circles, fueled by the war in the South. The departure of the PLO from Beirut and the South following the 1982 Israeli invasion did little to allay such fears. When the war resumed after the failure of national entente under President Amin Gemayel, the Shi'a protagonists' obsession with *tawtîn* coincided with Syrian ambitions to eliminate independent Palestinian control of the camps and fueled an armed conflict known as "the war of the camps" that lasted from 1985 until 1988.

This obsession with *tawtîn*, with all its vague significance, persisted well into the postwar period. *Rafd al-tawtîn* (or rejection of resettlement) was formalized in the text of the Taef Agreement and later in the constitution. The collateral impact of this official formulation has prevented any debate on the future of Lebanese-Palestinian relations; worse, it has legitimized institutionalized discrimination against the refugees in the conduct of their daily lives.[25] It is difficult to gauge how seriously the populace takes *tawtîn*, but it is a very popular concept in the rhetoric of the political class, and most notoriously among some Christian politicians whose legitimacy is questioned because of their open compliance with Syrian positions and who need to remind their constituency that their real enemy is the Palestinians, not the Syrians. Aside from this extreme instrumentalization, various politicians, and government officials, use the fear of *tawtîn* in connection with of Syrian-Lebanese relations to justify reliance on the Syrian army.

---

25 Souheil al-Natour, "The Legal Status of Palestinians in Lebanon", paper presented to the conference on "Palestinians in Lebanon", organized by the Center for Lebanese Studies and the Refugee Studies Programme, Oxford, September 1996. Edited selection of this paper and others in the special issue of the *Journal of Refugee Studies*, Vol. 10, No. 3.

In the past few years, a minority group of intellectuals and politicians has spearheaded a change in the discussion. It started with the effort to re-examine and explain the meaning of *rafd al-tawtîn*, i. e., the refusal of a massive naturalization of Palestinians. Palestinians would be granted full civil rights, but they would be able to exercise their political rights only in the Palestinian national arena, or what would eventually become the Palestinian state.[26] This change in intellectuals understanding of *tawtîn* and *rafd al-tawtîn* has yet to inform official policy of the Lebanese state. Everyday life in the camps remains dire, restrictions on construction permits inside the camps are still in effect, and the army maintains a strict blockade around each camp to prevent people from bringing in, among other things, construction materials.

However irrational the matrix of Lebanese-Palestinian relations might seem, they cannot be understood without considering the wider framework. It may be useful here to speak of a Lebanese-Palestinian-Syrian triad, deeply scarred by the legacy of the war.[27] The structure of this framework explains why the official Lebanese position prefers to present the remaining camps as intolerable *juzur amniyya* or "islands of [self-policed] security", rather than acknowledge the authority of the PLO and its largest component, the Fatah movement, as stable representatives.[28] Accordingly, the return of the Fatah movement to most camps after a period of forced absence gave rise to new tensions, leading to legal action against senior Fatah officials, including Yasser Arafat's representative in Lebanon, who was sentenced to death *in absentia* in 1999.

To the outside observer, the situation in the camps has not changed since 1991. In North Lebanon, the camps are controlled by Syria through the *mukhabarat* and pro-Syrian Palestinian factions, such as the Popular Front for the Liberation of Palestine – General Command (PFLP-GC). In Beirut, the camps are also in the grip of the Syrian *mukhabarat* and pro-Syrian factions, though their hold is less solid. In the southernmost area, near Tyre, the camps are controlled by Fatah. The only contested terrain, so to speak, is the over-crowded Ayn el-Hilweh camp,[29] on the outskirts of Sidon, where Fatah is extremely active, but not allowed to stake an official claim to the camp, which gives newly emergent fundamentalist groups some room to maneuver. This framework explains why the staunchly pro-Syrian PFLP-GC is allowed to keep a base in the foothills of Na'ameh, at the southern tip of Beirut, and why fundamentalist groups have been allowed to build mosques and recruit members inside the camps, in spite of the prohibition on bringing in construction materials. The position of President Emile La-

---

26 Nawaf Salam, "Between Repatriation and Resettlement: Palestinian Refugees in Lebanon", in *Journal of Palestine Studies*, Vol. XXIV, No. 1 (Autumn 1994).
27 Rosemary Sayigh, *Too Many Enemies: The Palestinian Experience in Lebanon* (London: Zed Books 1994).
28 Bernard Rougier, "Le 'destin mêlé' des Palestiniens et des Libanais au Liban", in *Maghreb-Machrek*, No. 169 (July-September 2000): pp. 43-54.
29 On Ayn el-Hilweh, see Jaber Suleiman, "Report from Lebanon. The Current Political, Organizational and Security Situation in the Palestinian Refugee Camps of Lebanon", in *Journal of Palestine Studies*, XXIX, No. 1 (Autumn 1999): pp. 66-80.

houd is a glaring illustration of this paradox: although his army surrounds the camps, in April 2000 he proclaimed the Palestinians' right to armed struggle in order to justify official Lebanese reluctance to accept the withdrawal of Israeli forces.

A Syrian Protectorate

From all what been said about the South and the Palestinian refugees, it should be clear that Syria is the key actor in shaping Lebanon's foreign policy. But Syria's role is even more extensive and intensive: Syrian hegemony was and is the decisive factor in Lebanese *internal* politics. This is not to play down local factors endemic to the Lebanese polity, such as aggravated sectarianism,[30] the all-pervasive mercantilism, and the factionalism described by Michael Hudson[31] which still corrodes public life. However, Syrian hegemony is the dominant feature in postwar Lebanon.[32]

The first phase of the Lebanese war, from 1975 to 1982, ended with Israel's failure to turn Lebanon into a satellite state. The second phase, 1982–1990, marked the transformation of the country into a Syrian dominion. Yet, the two projects are by no means comparable. The relationship between Lebanese society and its eastern and northern neighbour is too close, whether from historical social, anthropoligical, religious or even familial perspectives, to permit an analogy with a hostile state and society that has always seen itself as an "outside" entity, at least until the vision of the Middle East that Shimon Peres presented during the Oslo negotiations. For the Syrian regime, this deep and complex connective meshwork was the backdrop against which it established its domination in Lebanon. This relationship enabled Syria to penetrate into the far reaches of Lebanese society in much the way as it did in its own society, using fear to control both at a distance. That was at the heart of Syrian deployment in the areas once deemed defiant that it "reconquered" in the 80s and early 90s: Tripoli in 1985, West Beirut in 1987, and the Christian enclaves in 1990.

Does this mean one could go further and speak of "Syrian occupation", as some Lebanese do? The legacy of the war, and specifically the bitter memory of clashes between the Syrian army and Christian forces from 1978 to the end of the "war of liberation" launched by General Aoun in 1989, has widely popularized this concept in – mainly but not exclusively – Christian Lebanese circles. This appears too simplistic a description of Syrian goals and practices in Lebanon, although one wonders if the Syrian decision-makers themselves are not indifferent to such nuances.

One of the arguments that discourages one from describing Syrian hegemony as occupation is the fact that beyond close "coordination" at all levels, the Lebanese army and

---

[30] Elizabeth Picard, "Les habits neufs du communautarisme libanais", in *Culture et conflits*, 15/16 (Autumn-Winter 1994.
[31] Michael Hudson, *The Precarious Republic. Political Modernization in Lebanon* (Boulder: Westview Encore Edition, 1985; first edition 1968): p. 214.
[32] Samir Kassir, "Dix ans après, comment ne pas réconcilier une société divisée?", in *Maghreb-Machrek*, No. 69 (July-September 2000): pp. 6-22.

other services are clearly and obviously responsible for security in the postwar era; the majority of soldiers at check points are Lebanese. The positions of Syrian soldiers around greater Beirut and in central Lebanon tend to be static before their withdrawal in 2002. The situation may differ a little in eastern and northern Lebanon, but even here the paradigm is not very useful, whether by virtue of common sense or comparison. This is not to say that the Syrian military presence is not resented by the Lebanese. On the contrary, this resèntment takes the form of growing xenophobia and racism against all Syrians – across all communities. However, close examination of Syrian control shows close similarities with the system in Syria. Lebanese should be aware they are confronted with more or less the same situation Syrians have experience for decades: a military hegemony policed principally by the *mukhabarat*. In the case of Lebanon, Syrian hegemony is also policed by the Lebanese *mukhabarat*.

Under the omnipresent shadow of this omnipresent actor, whose status as a regional power is combined with its mastery of the underworld, no single Lebanese entity has been able to successfully claim even the pretence of autonomy. Alliance parties are fundamentally undermined by their clientelist bonds with the Syrian hegemon, and the bridges of alliance are very vulnerable to Syria's capacity to fuel rivalry in their midst. As for overt opponents, they have been marginalized since the October 1990 "victory".[33]

The political class currently in power in Lebanon emerged in the 80s and 90s. Even for those who participated in the war prior to the Israeli invasion of 1982, the decisive turn in their career came after the "return" of Syria in 1983, and for many of them in the early postwar moments. Therein lies Syria's greatest asset in securing its dominion: the current Lebanese political class accepts the disequilibrium between the two states. There are various reasons for acquiescence, ranging from interest – those who would not occupy the positions they do without allegiance to Damascus –, lack of courage – those with bitter experiences of past confrontation –, and conviction – those who think that a withdrawal of Syrian troops would lead to chaos.

Therefore, instead of Syrian occupation, it would be more useful and accurate to speak of a Syrian protectorate. The intricate network of interests that webs Syrian officialdom and the Lebanese ruling elite is another argument against interpreting this hegemony as occupation. The fabric of this network is far too complex to be forced into an occupier/collaborator dyad, particularly because it is not a one-way track. Syria's Lebanese clients are able to influence Syrian policy in Lebanon via a myriad channels. Two of the most public instances were the presidential battles: the extension of President Hrawi's mandate in 1995[34] and the intense lobbying for General Emile Lahoud in 1998, presented as the rationalization of the country's relationship with Syria. But aside from internal competition, the Lebanese political class seems to have come to terms with its

---

33 Elizabeth Picard, *The demobilization of the Lebanese Militia* (Oxford: Centre for Lebanese Studies, 1994).
34 See Samir Kassir, "Coup de force institutionnel au Liban", in *Le Monde diplomatique*, November 1995.

own impotence. Lebanon is thus a rare example of a protectorate in which the "protected" elite does not seek to broaden its margins of autonomy, except in so far as it momentarily serves to resolve petty squabbles.[35]

This extended collusion points to another specificity of Syrian-Lebanese relationships, which lies in pervasive across-the-border clientelism, political as well as economical. Not only that the price of peace has been a transfer of sovereignty at the national scale, but furthermore in the sense that "protection" and promotion are rewards for daily compliance and have to be "bought" time and again, either by symbolic gestures of allegiance or by very mundane offerings, and often by both. As a result, the undergirding socio-economic structure of the Syrian protectorate became woven with a mafia-type pattern of racketeering. Hence Syria's interests in Lebanon involve not only geopolitical considerations; they also contribute to the survival of the regime.

Geopolitical and/or Domestic Explanations

Years ago, Fred Lawson proposed a "domestic conflict explanation" for Hafez Assad's decision to intervene in Lebanon in June 1976. Convincing in many respects, his argument failed to provide a complete background for the decision-making process in this matter.[36] Lawson's domestic explanation gains credibility by evaluating Syrian policy in Lebanon in the long run and answering the question of what Syria wants from Lebanon.

Geopolitics was of pivotal importance in Syria's 1976 military intervention. On the one hand, Syria wanted to avoid being weakened by an unstable neighbor, and on the other hand it sought to strengthen its bargaining power vis-à-vis the United States at the prospective Geneva conference. In spite of the departure of the PLO from Lebanon in 1982–83, this consideration remained. It was reinforced in the 1990s after the end of the internal wars in Lebanon and the simultaneous launch of the Madrid peace process. Open Syrian support for the armed resistance in South Lebanon was understood as a means to increase its leverage in the rounds of negotiation with Israel. This explains why Syrian officials and their Lebanese clients were so uneasy with the Israeli decision to evacuate South Lebanon, because it eliminated Syria's most valuable bargaining card.

However, it would be naïve to think that nearly a quarter of a century of military domination and political hegemony have not changed the way Syria looks at Lebanon. Two changes are of the utmost importance for Syria's own destiny. The first is the realization among Syria's elite that its present status as a regional brokering power has been molded by its intervention in Lebanon, and the understanding that maintaining this regional status hinges on sustaining its hold over Lebanon. The second transformation is

---

35 For some examples, see Samir Kassir, "Au Liban un pouvoir sans responsabilité, des querelles sans enjeux", in *Le Monde diplomatique*, October 1994.
36 Fred Lawson, "Syria's Intervention in the Lebanese Civil War. A Domestic Conflict Explanation", in *International Organization*, Vol. 38, No. 3 (1984). For a discussion, see Kassir, *La guerre du Liban*, op. cit., p. 210.

the result of Lebanon's pivotal role in shaping the distribution of power and wealth in the highest circles of the Syrian regime, and the perception that any weakening of Syria's hold over Lebanon would entail severe setbacks in this respect. Such a role goes beyond the usual bribery and illegal border-traffic of the early years of Syrian intervention. Since the mid-1980s, Lebanon has become the realm where Syria can manage its informal economic sector, allowing the regime to buy time and stall on introducing urgent measures that would entail a radical shift in economic policy towards openness and modernization. In the 1990s, this economic role was enhanced by reconstruction projects in Lebanon, which, under the aegis of hegemony, significantly expanded economic opportunities for Syrians. High-ranking Syrian officers claimed a large stake in large deals, and were provided with opportunities to white-wash the capital accumulation of themselves and their kin in the shadow of the prevailing official socialist rhetoric.

In nearly a quarter of a century of hegemony, the Syrian regime was and is not ready to risk lessening its grip on its dominion, particularly in the transitional period of Hafez Assad's last years and the succession of his son Bashar. A peaceful settlement with Israel, even if delayed, will involve drastic changes for a state apparatus overwhelming shaped by the military and the *mukhabarat*. In addition, the internal succession itself was risky, and provided a critical occasion to reshape the distribution of power and wealth. This background was apparently the main factor behind choosing General Emile Lahoud and his military team to manage Lebanese affairs, for Syria had long kept the Lebanese military at arm's length, even after it had been successfully "rehabilitated" following the ousting of General Michel Aoun.

The most striking evidence of Lebanon's role in Syrian internal politics was yet to come, namely the promotion in the fall of 2002 of General Ghazi Kanaan, for almost two decades head of Syrian intelligence in Lebanon and ostensibly the informal governor of Lebanon since the implementation of the Taef Agreement, to head of Political Security in Syria. Although his actual role is not really understood, it is clear that his appointment to a central position in Syria is a tribute to his tremendous success in "normalizing" Lebanon.[37]

Lebanon as *trompe-l'œil*

Lebanon's "normalization", though a result of brilliant maneuvering by Syrian officials, owes its success to a rare absence of challenge. At the domestic level, the compliance of the political class with Syrian desires is a permanent guarantee against any meaningful change in the protectorate's operating system. The surrounding context was no less unchallenged.

On the contrary, Syria's domination was encouraged from the outset by the behavior of regional and foreign powers. This was especially true of the United States, or at least

---

37 Samir Kassir, "La lutte pour la démocratie en Syrie et l'indépendance libanaise", in *Confluences-Méditerranée*, n° 44 (Paris, Winter 2002-2003), pp. 83-95.

perceived as such after the Syrian troops bombed the Baabda Palace to oust General Michel Aoun, a move inconceivable without the tacit approval of Israel and, hence, the green light from the US. But, as Syrian domination evolved into a lasting protectorate, none of the foreign powers who had an interest in Lebanon could regain any independent influence, even had they wanted to do so. Any relationship between Lebanon and another country is constrained by the Syrian agenda, or explicitly channeled through Damascus.

Since the end of the war, Lebanon has arguably reclaimed admission to the international arena, maintaining a semblance of diplomatic life, such as hosting foreign officials and exchanging visits. However the country has not been able to effectively develop an autonomous foreign policy, despite the extended network of international friendships of which Prime Minister Rafiq Hariri boasts. The backing from Saudi Arabia and the Gulf States, by virtue of Hariri's personal connections in the region, has not led to independent diplomacy, either. On a number of occasions, Hariri himself has paraded as a public relations officer for the Syrian regime.

The constraints reflect the general pressure that Syrian domination exerts on Lebanon, as well as from the reshuffling of the administration, in which the key positions are offered only to trusted appointees. The distribution of power amongst Syria's Lebanese clients guarantees that no initiative will be considered unless it is consistent with the credo of "privileged relations" and *talazum al-masarayn*. Ironically, this is particularly manifest in inter-Arab relations, as Syrian officials and their Lebanese cronies jealously guarded Lebanese external relations against any interference by fellow Arab countries. If the long lasting dispute over Lebanon's "Arabness" is now resolved,[38] the very idea of Arabness has been distorted to the exclusive benefit of the Syrian regime: Lebanon's Arabness means exclusively "privileged relations" with Syria, and in particular- with "Assad's Syria" (Sûriyya al-Assad) – according to the propaganda. Lebanon can have economic relations with other Arab countries, but not political ties.

The paradox in this vision of Arabism is that it isolates Lebanon from the larger reality of the Arab world. The equilibrium of forces in the Middle East is now seen through Syrian eyes. Palestinian influence, once vibrant in various sectors of Lebanese society, has been severely repressed, and Palestine as such no longer stands as the gateway to the Arab realm. Furthermore, in the aftermath of the Oslo agreement, respect for Palestinians declined. Lebanese with open ties to Palestinians became suspect, were characterized as "capitulationists" and even worse as "Israeli agents" – at least till the outbreak of the Intifada. At a practical level, it was difficult for non-resident Palestinians, especially those coming from the autonomous territories, to get entry visas for the country.

Other Arab countries that have traditionally had ties with Lebanon have not been able to improve them. Iraq, once an influential protagonist with ties through the Ba'ath Party and a host of Arab nationalist and leftists parties in the 60s and 70s, which were re-

---

38 Ahmad Beydoun, "Sur l'arabité du Liban", in *Maghreb-Machrek*, No. 169 (July-September 2000): pp. 23-31.

newed in the 80s though its backing of the Lebanese Forces and General Aoun, has been marginalized. In the last years of Hafez Assad's rule, Syria managed to renew relations with Baghdad, in the process subsuming relations between Lebanon and Iraq. While Iraq the food-for-oil program has enabled Iraq to resume trade with Lebanon, Syrian priorities set the terms of trade. Lebanese industrialists are barred from broadening their range of exports, and informal trade is controlled by Syrian and pro-Syrian intermediaries. Without any intention of interfering with Syrian interests, the Iraqi regime inaugurated a new practice of "friendship" from 1998 onwards by bestowing gifts to various Lebanese in the form of oil coupons at below market prices. Libya, another protagonist with influence in the Lebanese war, lost its leverage after the war, partly because of its own isolation – and isolationism – and partly because of lingering hard feelings in the Shi'i establishment caused by the disappearance of Imam Moussa Sadr on a visit to Tripoli in 1978.

Saudi Arabia, less visible during the war, but no less active, was expected to carry serious clout in the postwar because of its sponsorship of the Taef Agreement and the links between the royal family and Lebanese Prime Minister Rafiq Hariri. On the one hand, as a consequence of the Gulf War, inter-Arab diplomacy came to a halt, and the Saudi kingdom was no longer able to translate its weight into an active policy. On the other hand, Saudi Arabia and various Gulf states have failed time and time again to keep their financial promises to Lebanon, which has marginalized their influence.

Egypt also suffered from the general freeze on inter-Arab diplomacy in the 90s. Hariri managed to restore relations with Egyptian officials and has hosted the Egyptian premier on numerous occasions. However, in the overall scheme of things, Egypt has maintained a low profile in Lebanon. The one exception came after a massive Israeli strike against Lebanon's infrastructure in February 2000, on the eve of the Israeli withdrawal, when President Mubarak took the initiative and paid a visit to Lebanon. Furthermore, Egypt encouraged an extraordinary meeting of the Arab League Council in Beirut. Officially, the venue was chosen to express Arab solidarity with Lebanon; but unofficially it was said that Arab exposure would help Lebanon to loosen Syria's grip. Some Egyptian officials went so far as to announce – in private – that Egypt had decided to "get back to Lebanon". However, nothing more happened, and two years later President Mubarak did not attend the Arab summit in Beirut. In the meantime, the Syrian-Lebanese management of the Israeli withdrawal clearly discouraged Egyptian involvement.

Whatever Arab countries may feel about establishing relationships with Lebanon, the subservience of Lebanese officials to Syria's domination is definitely a deterrent. Furthermore, Syrian hegemony as a guarantee against the resumption of internal feuding has also influenced the behavior of European countries, including France. While inclined to preserve the international autonomy of the Lebanese state, since the Taef Agreement France has been cautious about endorsing Syrian control, in order to avoid criticism of neo-colonialism. At a more practical level, Lebanon was able to sign a partnership agreement with the EU in 2002 because, as one European official put it, Syria wanted its own agreement with Brussels.[39]

The constraints of Syrian domination on Lebanese diplomacy were obvious in the preparations and choice of venue of the Arab summit in Beirut in March 2002. This summit arguably meant that Beirut was back as a capital of some importance, and that Lebanon was regaining some Arab and international prestige. Indeed, the protocol was Lebanese, the security also, and everything was done to convince the guests that Lebanon was a sovereign state. Everything, that is, except the contents and the proceedings of the conference, as was demonstrated during the opening ceremony, when President Lahoud, complying with Syria's disapproval of the Palestinian authority, prevented Yasser Arafat from speaking to the conference from Ramallah where he was besieged. The policy Lebanon defended during the drafting of the Arab peace plan also reflected Syria's views. The francophone summit, six months later, could have had a more specific Lebanese agenda, since Syria, not a member of the Francophone organization, did not attend. But Lebanese officials strictly avoided any display of autonomy. At both meetings, Lebanon's role as host was a fiction or, more accurately, a kind of political *trompe-l'œil*.

While pointing out the fictitious autonomy of Lebanese policy, such a situation, heralded by Lebanese officials and applauded by most of the Lebanese political class, indicates how the postwar era has been used to confirm orientations set at the beginning. For the Lebanese leadership, it is no longer an era of waiting. Some Lebanese officials may be waiting for a change in the regional environment to reassert some autonomy. But the behavior of the majority, especially as the movement towards war in Iraq escalates, demonstrates that the Syrian-oriented Lebanese state is primarily interested in creating and perpetuating *faits accomplis*, regardless of what might happen in the region.

---

39 Interview with the author.

On Roots and Routes:
The Reassertion of Primordial Loyalties

SAMIR KHALAF

> "Most societies seem allergic to internal anonymity, homogeneity and amnesia."
> *Ernest Gellner* (1988)

Almost 35 years ago I preambled an essay I wrote, on the interplay between primordial ties and politics in Lebanon, with the following salient characterization:
> *By the admission of many dispassionate observers – indigenous and foreign alike – the political system in Lebanon stands as a curious but happy phenomenon. A pluralistic confessional society, it enjoys a parliamentary system of government with a freely elected Chamber of Deputies. Outwardly the country appears to be bolstered by liberal and democratic traditions, yet Lebanon hardly possesses any of the political instruments of a civil polity. A National Pact, a sort of Christian-Moslem entente, sustains its so-called national entity – al-kayan, yet this sense of identity is neither national nor civic. Its politicians, masterminds at the art of flexibility and compromise, are local za'ims not national heroes.*
>
> *The few parties that do exist are so closely identified with sectarian groups and so unconcerned with a larger national identity that they can easily engender political disintegration. Likewise, its political blocs and fronts are so absorbed with parochial and personal rivalries that they fail to serve the larger national purpose of mobilizing the population for the broader aims of society. Politicians and pressure groups alike have not been able to transcend their petty personal feuds to grapple effectively with the public issues of the country.*

I went on to argue that precarious as the political system was at the time, it had nonetheless managed to maintain a balance of power among its heterogeneous, confessional, kinship and communal groups. Except for the crisis of 1958, for nearly a century the country's pluralistic allegiances and loyalties had been relatively stable and viable. It also demonstrated a noted resilience in resisting the ideological and political turmoil that had overwhelmed its adjacent Arab states. Writing at a time when perspectives of developmentalism and comparative modernization were still in vogue, it was argued that political modernization in Lebanon need not involve a transfer of sovereignty from primordial allegiances to secular, liberal and ideological commitments. Given the persistence of primordial sentiments, the metamorphosis of political life in the country may never involve such a sharp transformation. Adopting a dialectical rather than a dichotomous relationship between the forces of tradition and modernity, the paper (contrary to the neo-evolutionary models rampant at the time) cast doubt as to whether Lebanese society can ever be a duplicate of a purely rational, secular and egalitarian society based exclusively on achievement-oriented and universalistic criteria. Nor can it be a reactionary throwback on an ossified, unbending and incompliant social order where traditional norms and practices are mindlessly adhered to. Instead the problem boils down to a question of fusion and assimilation: how to assimilate certain selective features of traditional culture into the culture of a rational and secular society without undermining both.

Prefiguring much of the subsequent concerns with issues associated with the so-called "crisis of identity", the paper advanced another caveat: given the survival, indeed retrenchment of traditional ties and loyalties, it is not surprising that the average Lebanese citizen should continue to elicit greater satisfaction and security from his primordial attachments than from his involvement or participation in purely rational and ideological associations. Within such a setting, and contrary to what is often proposed, this perpetual crisis of identity cannot be resolved by fiat. Legislation cannot turn a confessional, kinship and personalistic society into a nation-state overnight. Nor can a wilful sense of government legitimacy be created by constitutional arrangements and a representative electoral system alone. These constitutional prerequisites have long been guaranteed in Lebanon but primordial loyalties have lost little of their verve or resilience.

Such realities, I maintained in 1968, cannot or should not be wished away, bypassed or dismissed as futile nostalgic gestures to seek shelter in the relics of a dead, disinherited or imagined past. These hybrid entities, often a viable fusion of seemingly disparate ties and networks, have proved to be – particularly when their inhibitive and intransigent elements were contained or neutralized – effective mediating agencies.

By documenting the resilience of primordialism, I was not proposing that the system was a paragon of political virtues. The country's shortcomings and pitfalls were readily recognized. Yet throughout its checkered political history, Lebanon I argued, was fairly successful in integrating its pluralistic factions, guarantee a modicum of freedom of expression and civil liberties, evolve a coherent foreign policy, protect and encourage a liberal economy and most of all safeguard a free, independent, prosperous and peaceful society. In subsequent research (Khalaf, 1991, 2002). I advanced five further inferences regarding the primacy and survival of primordialism:

1. The sweeping changes Lebanon has been subjected to, from internal insurrections to centralized and direct rule by foreign powers or the more gradual and spontaneous changes associated with rapid urbanization, spread of market economy, and the exposure of a growing portion of the population to secular, liberal, and radical ideologies, etc., did little to weaken or erode the intensity of primordial loyalties. Indeed, in times

of social unrest and political turmoil such loyalties are inclined to become sharper and often supersede other ties and allegiances. Hence, it is not uncommon that protest movements and other forms of collective mobilization of social unrest, sparked by genuine grievances and unresolved public issues, should be, as was frequently the case in such episodes, deflected into confessional rivalries.

2. Primordial loyalties have not only survived and retained their primacy; they continue to serve as viable sources of communal solidarity. They inspire local and personal initiative and account for much of the resourcefulness and cultural diversity and vitality of the Lebanese. But they also undermine civic consciousness and commitment to Lebanon as a nation-state. Expressed more poignantly, the forces which motivate and sustain harmony, balance, and prosperity are also the very forces which on occasion pull the society apart and contribute to conflict, tension and civil disorder. The ties that bind, in other words, also unbind.

3. From the aborted accord of Shakib Effendi (the partition scheme of 1843) to the current discourse over the "Ta'if Accord", Lebanon grappled with successive strategies, pacts, covenants, concordats, and other political and territorial rearrangements to identify and safeguard the country's sovereignty and autonomy as a plural society. To a large degree, the most viable of these efforts were more the byproduct of volition, collective acts of will, consent, habits of discussion, and compromise – even courtesy – rather than coercion, force or cruelty. Cruelty only begot further cruelty.

4. Clearly, not all the persisting internal disparities which have plagued Lebanon for so long, should be attributed to foreign intervention. Nor were they exclusively generated by unplanned and fortuitous circumstances. Foreign powers, by virtue of their preferential and shifting patronage of different communities, must have also contributed to the accentuation of such gaps and dislocations. This is most visible in their direct involvement, often as principal architects of covenants and pacts or in negotiating terms of settlements on behalf of their client groups or protégés. Such wilful and deliberate involvement carries their intervention to its ultimate degree. Without exception all pacts in Lebanon, particularly those coming in the wake of armed struggle, were brokered by foreign governments either unilaterally or through their trusted local or regional allies.

Despite sharp differences in their visions, all the foreign powers involved in the various settlement schemes ended up, wilfully or otherwise, by consolidating the confessional foundation of the political order. I wish to argue that the schemes which were fairly successfully (particularly the *Règlement Organique* of 1861 and the *Mithaq* of 1943), had recognized the realities of confessional affiliation but sought to secularize sectarianism in such a manner as to encourage harmonious coexistence between the various confessional groups. In short, they made efforts to transform some of its divisive and pathological features into a more enabling and constructive system.

5. When external sources of instability are contained and neutralized various Lebanese communities were able to evolve fairly adaptive and accommodating strategies for peaceful coexistence. The last and, perhaps most successful of these was the 'National Pact' of 1943 which survived for over 30 years. The ideology or philosophy which in-

spired the Pact perceives Lebanon neither as a society "closed against the outside world, nor a unitary society in which smaller communities were dissolved, but something between the two: a plural society in which communities, still different on the level of inherited religious loyalties and intimate family ties, co-existed within a common framework" (Hourani 1976:38).

Two decades of displaced and protracted collective violence along with the unsettling consequences of globalization, consumerism and popular and mass culture have reawakened interest in the character and role communal and primordial groupings are playing today. Of all such ties, confessionalism appear to elicit the most acute and contentious polemics. Most observers have been predisposed to document its disruptive and abusive features. Hence, the literature abounds with references to the evils of confessionalism, such as the bankruptcy of ideological parties and pressure groups, deficient civility, the paralysis of the Parliament, excessive meddling of religious leaders in the political life of the community, and the sacrifice of competence and efficiency on the altar of sectarian balance. Most damaging perhaps, recurrent cycles of political violence are often perceived as byproducts of crazed fanatics, or a reawakening of the deeply-rooted confessional bigotism lodged in the collective unconscious of warring communities, locked in and driven by little else other than the imagined or real hostility and intolerance they harbour towards others.

Eager to highlight the abuses of such tendencies – and they certainly cannot be minimized or dismissed – observers have nonetheless often misread their sources and consequences. Confessionalism in Lebanon is often made an expedient scapegoat for abuses whose roots lie elsewhere. For example, in my view, the abuses of *marja'yah* or *taba'iyah* (i. e. clientelism) are far more egregious in their character and pervasive implications. Indeed, the seemingly sanctimonious and self-righteous communal predispositions underlying sectarian loyalties become expedient disguises for the more aggrandizing and self-seeking interests which sustain patron-client ties.

Have the abusive features and manifestations of primordialism (particularly confessionalism) become so subversive that they are beginning to undermine whatever supportive or rehabilitative functions they might have once served? *Roots*, to invoke the metaphor of the essay's title, have been thus far effective *routes* for socio-cultural and psychological mobilization. At least during certain interludes, when stripped of their bigoted and intolerant features, they became the bases for equitable and judicious forms of power sharing and the articulation of new cultural identities germane for co-existence and multi-culturalism.

Couldn't this be done again? This is why Lebanon seems, today, gripped by all the tensions of this unfolding dialectics. Once again, in other words, the country seems delicately poised at a critical juncture: we are witnessing the erosion or substitution of one viable form of pluralism for a more regressive and pathological kind. We are destroying a system, imperfect as it has been, which permitted groups with a multiplicity of voices, divergent backgrounds, allegiances and expectations to live side by side.

What is emerging is a monolithic archetype that is hostile, or at least not receptive, to any form of co-existence and hybrid cultural encounters.

The paper is a reconsideration of both the enabling and disabling features of primordialism to reassess their impact on Lebanon's political culture in the context of the unsettling internal, regional and global transformations the country has been subjected to during the past three decades. It explores three related dimensions. First, and by way of framing the discussion within a comparative conceptual context, an attempt is made to identify the circumstances which have reinforced communal and sectarian cleavages. Second, this is followed by a more concrete and substantive documentation of how the three salient forms of primordialism (kinship, communal and confessional solidarities) have responded to the forces which undermine their cohesion and collective identities. Finally, I explore the prospects of how this longing to reconnect with one's abiding but threatened *roots* may again become *routes* for the articulation of new cultural identities more germane for civil and peaceful forms of pluralism and guarded co-existence.

The Resilience of Primordialism

For some time mainstream theoretical paradigms – i. e., those associated with modernization, Marxism and their offshoots – were quite tenacious in upholding their views regarding the erosion of primordial ties and loyalties. Despite the striking ideological differences underlying the two meta theories, they shared the conviction that ties of fealty, religion and community – which cemented societies together and accounted for social and political distinctions – were beginning to lose their grip and would, ultimately, become irrelevant. Indeed, to proponents of modernization theory, notions like familism, tribalism, confessionalism were not only pejoratively dismissed and trivialized, they were seen as obstacles to modernity. So-called "traditional" societies, in other words, were expected to break away and disengage themselves from such relics of pre-modern times if they are to enjoy the presumed fruits of modernity or to become full-fledged nation states. Given the resilience of traditional loyalties, some proponents made allowances for interim periods where so-called "transitional" societies might linger for a while. Eventually, however, all such precarious hybrids will have to pass. They cannot, and will not, it was argued by a generation of social scientists in the sixties and seventies, be able to resist the overpowering forces of industrialization, urbanization and secularization.

Likewise to Marxists, communist and socialist regimes were perceived as "giant brooms" expected to sweep away pre-existing loyalties. If non-class attachments and interests survive or resurface, they are treated as forms of "false consciousness" to mask or veil fundamental economic and social contradictions. In short, ethnic and primordial loyalties were treated, as Theodore Hanf (1995) put it, as transitory phenomenon by modernization theorists and as epiphenomenon by Marxists. Both agreed, however, that primordialism was destined to disappear. Both, of course, have been wrong. It is a blatant misreading, if not distortion, of history in both advanced and developing societies.

It is a marvel in fact that such misrepresentations could have persisted given persuasive evidence to the contrary.

Ernest Gellner (1988) provides such evidence while exploring the nature of nationalism and cohesion in complex societies. He finds it conceptually fitting to re-examine the role of shared amnesia, collective forgetfulness and anonymity in the emergence of nation-states. Among other things, he argues that the presumed erosion of primordial allegiances is not a prerequisite to the formation of cohesive nation-states. Likewise, the formation of strong ruthless centralizing regimes is not the monopoly of any particular state or culture. Seemingly cohesive and integrated old states are not as culturally unified and homogeneous. More recently, David Lowenthal has also advanced a compelling plea for what he calls "artfully selective oblivion" which, in his view, is necessary to all societies. "Collective well being", he argues, "requires sanitizing what time renders unspeakable, unpalatable, even just inconveniently outdated" (Lowenthal, 1999:xii).

Of course here Ottoman Turkey became the prototype of the "mosaic" where ethnic and religious groups not only retained much of the so-called primordial and archaic identities, but they were positively instructed – through edicts, centralization, fiat, etc. – never to forget. As such, the Ottomans were tolerant of other religions but they were strictly segregated from the Muslims. The various "millets," in other words, mixed but were never truly combined in a homogeneous and unified society. Today such a dread of collective amnesia is amply visible in the dramatic events surrounding the collapse of the USSR and the unfolding disintegration of Eastern Europe.

Nor are the nascent new nations today bereft of the loyalties and institutions often attributed exclusively to civil and secular nation-states. Perhaps conditions of anonymity are true in time of swift or revolutionary social changes and turmoil. But after the upheavals, when the deluge subsides, when social order is restored, internal cleavages and continuities resurface. New memories are invented when the old ones are destroyed. Indeed, "most societies," Gellner reiterates, "seem allergic to internal anonymity, homogeneity and amnesia." (Gellner, 1988:9).

Lebanon's political history, both in good and bad times, reinforces this self-evident but often overlooked or misconstrued reality. Throughout its epochal transformations – the emergence of the "principality" in the seventeenth and eighteenth centuries, the upheavals of the mid-nineteenth century and the consequent creation of the Mutesarrifate of Mount Lebanon (1860-1920), down to the creation of Greater Lebanon in 1920, the National Pact of 1943, the restoration of unity and stability after the civil war of 1958, and the aftermath of almost two decades of protracted violence – some salient realities about the ubiquity of recurring "retribalisation" are reconfirmed. One might argue that Lebanon has not been detribalized sufficiently to be experiencing retribalisation. The term, nonetheless, is being employed here rather loosely as a catchall phrase to refer to the resurgence of communal loyalties, particularly the convergence of confessional and territorial identities. As has been demonstrated by a score of socio-economic and political historians, the sweeping changes Lebanon has been subjected to, from internal insurrections to centralized and direct rule by foreign powers or the more gradual and spontaneous changes associated with rapid urbanization, spread of market economy and the exposure of a growing portion of the population to secular, liberal and radical ideologies, etc...did little to weaken or erode the intensity of confessional or sectarian loyalties. Indeed, in times of social unrest and political turmoil such loyalties became sharper and often superseded other ties and allegiances. (For supportive evidence see, among others, Chevallier, 1971; Harik 1968; Khalaf 1979; Picard 1996; Salibi 1969).

As the cruelties of protracted violence became more menacing, it is understandable why traumatized and threatened groups should seek shelter in their communal solidarities and cloistered spaces. Confessional sentiments and their supportive loyalties, even in times of relative peace and stability, have always been effective sources of social support and political mobilization. But these are not, as Lebanon's fractious history amply demonstrates, unmixed blessings. While they cushion individuals and groups against the anomie and alienation of public life, they also heighten the density of communal hostility and enmity. Such processes have been particularly acute largely because class, ideological and other secular forms of group affiliation have been comparatively more distant and abstract and, consequently, of less relevance to the psychic and social needs of the uprooted and traumatized. Hence, more and more Lebanese are today brandishing their confessionalism, if we may invoke a dual metaphor, as both emblem and armour. Emblem, because confessional identity has become the most viable medium for asserting presence and securing vital needs and benefits. It is only when an individual is placed within a confessional context that his ideas and assertions are rendered meaningful or worthwhile. Confessionalism is also being used as armour, because it has become a shield against real or imagined threats. The more vulnerable the emblem, the thicker the armour. Conversely, the thicker the armour, the more vulnerable and paranoid other communities become. It is precisely this dialectic between threatened communities and the urge to seek shelter in cloistered worlds which has plagued Lebanon for so long.

Massive population shifts, particularly since they are accompanied by the reintegration of displaced groups into more homogeneous, self-contained and exclusive communities, have also reinforced communal solidarity. Consequently, territorial and confessional identities, more so perhaps than at any other time in Lebanon's history, are beginning to converge. It is in this sense that "retribalisation" is becoming sharper and more assertive. Some of its subtle, implicit and nuanced earlier manifestations have become much more explicit. Political leaders, spokesmen of various communities, opinion makers and ordinary citizens are not as reticent in recognizing and incorporating such features in their daily behaviour or in bargaining for rights and privileges and validating their identities. Even normally less self-conscious and more open communities such as Greek Orthodox, Catholics and Sunni Muslims, are beginning to experiment with measures for enhancing and reinventing their special heritage and particular identity.

Recently such symptoms of "retribalisation" have become more pronounced. Ironically, during the pre-war and pre-Ta'if periods when confessionalism was recognized, its manifestations and outward expression were often subtle and attenuated. Groups seemed shy, as it were, to be identified by such labels. More so during the decades of the 50s and 60s when nationalism and often secular and so-called progressive and ideological venues for group affiliation had special appeal. (See Melikian, L and L. Diab, 1974). Today, as the sectarian or confessional logic is consecrated by Ta'if and, to the same extent, by public opinion, the overt expression of communal and sectarian identities have become much more assertive. Political leaders and spokesmen of various communities, of all persuasions, are not at all reticent or shy in invoking such parochial claims. Indeed, dormant and quiescent communal identities are being reawakened, often reinvented, to validate claims for special privileges.

Universities, colleges, research foundations, voluntary associations, special advocacy groups, radio and TV stations are all being established with explicit and well-defined communal identities. So are cultural and popular recreational events and awards to recognize excellence and encourage creative and intellectual output. Even competitive sports, normally a transcending and neutral human encounter, have been factionalized by sectarian rivalries.

These and other such efforts can no longer be wished away or mystified. They must be recognized for what they are: strategies for the empowerment of threatened groups and their incorporation into the torrent of public life. The coalition of confessional and territorial entities, since it draws upon a potentially much larger base of support, is doubtless a more viable vector for political mobilization than kinship, fealty or sectarian loyalties. Hence, as has been demonstrated elsewhere, it was not uncommon that protest movements and other forms of collective mobilization of social unrest, sparked by genuine grievances and unresolved public issues, were often deflected into confessional or communal rivalries (Khalaf, 2002).

Theodor Hanf (1995) coins the term "ethnurgy" to highlight such conscious invention and politicization of ethnic identity. Circumstances associated with the emergence and mobilization of such identities are instrumental in accounting for the pattern and intensity of intra - and interstate conflict. Since all societies are, to varying degrees, horizontally stratified with vertical cultural cleavages, conflict is bound to reflect both the horizontal socio-economic disparities and the deep cultural divisions. By themselves, however, the strata and cleavages will not become sources of political mobilization unless groups are also made conscious of their distinctive identities. Differences in themselves, horizontal or vertical, become politicized only when those who share common distinctive attributes also share awareness of their distinctiveness. Analogically Hanf translates Marx's "class-by-itself" and "class-for-itself" into ethnic group loyalties. Hence, only an ethnic group "for itself" can become a source of political mobilization.

Within this context it is neither uncommon nor surprising that one should come across recurrent circumstances in Lebanon's socio-political and cultural history which heighten and mobilize the political and radical consciousness of communal and confessional identities. Of course technically speaking, communal and confessional attachments are not strictly "ethnic" in character, if by that is meant that the assignment of special or distinct status, within a culture or social system is arrived at on the basis of purely racial or physical characteristics. But if "ethnicity" is broadened to incorporate variable traits associated with religion, communal, ancestral affiliations, dialect and other behavioral and sub-cultural distinctions, then confessional and sectarian identities may well assume some ethnic attributes (Horowitz, 1985:xi). It is also then that these identities become sharper and more militant. They acquire a density of their own and coalesce around sentiments of solidarity and collective self-consciousness.

Popular accounts, particularly during the early rounds of fighting, were keen on depicting, often with noted amazement, the eagerness with which impressionable teenagers flocked to the barricades, just as their older brothers only a few years back had taken to frivolous pastimes, such as night-clubbing, fast cars, pinball machines and sleazy entertainments. (Randal, 1984:112-3). This is all the more remarkable since we are dealing with a fairly quiescent political culture, one without much background or tradition in military service, conscription or prior experience in para-military organizations.

In short, what these and other manifestations imply is that religion is not resorted to as a spiritual or ecclesiastical force. It is not a matter of communing with the divine as a redemptive longing to restore one's sense of well-being. Rather, it is sought largely as a form of ideological and communal mobilization. Indeed, it is often people's only means of asserting their threatened identities. Without it, groups are literally rootless, nameless and voiceless.

Such realities, incidentally, are certainly not unique to Lebanon. In an insightful and thoroughly documented study of Hindu-Muslim rioting and violence in India, Sudhir Kakar (1996) reaches essentially the same conclusion. The author also draws on other historical encounters- – such as the anti-Semitic pogroms in Spain in the fourteenth century, or sixteenth century Catholic-Protestant violence in France, and anti-Catholic riots in eighteenth century London – to validate the inference that all such instances of collective mobilization were more a byproduct of cultural identities and communalism rather than a reflection of religiosity or revitalization of religious zeal as such:

> ...*if we look closely at individual cases around the world, we will find that the much-touted revival is less of religiosity than of cultural identities based on religious affiliation. In other words, there may not be any great ferment taking place in the world of religious ideas, beliefs, rituals, or any marked increase in the sum of human spirituality. Where the resurgence is most visible is in the organization of collective identities around religion, in the formation and strengthening of communities of believers. What we are witnessing today is less the resurgence of religion than (in the felicitous Indian usage) of communalism where a community of believers not only has religious affiliation but also social, economic, and political interests in common which may conflict with the corresponding interests of another community of believers sharing the same geographical space.* (Kakar, 1996:166-7)

To Kakar, communalism then is a state of mind elicited by the individual's assertion of being part of a religious community, preceded by the awareness of belonging to such a community. He goes further to maintain that only when, what he terms, the *"We-ness of the community"* is transformed into the *"We are of communalism"* can we better understand the circumstances which translate or deflect the potential or predispositions for intolerance, enmity and hostility and how these are ultimately released into outward violence (Kakar, 1996:192). Enmity after all can remain at a latent level. As Lebanon's checkered history with protracted collective strife amply demonstrates, hostility between the various communities did not always erupt in bloody confrontations. Rather, it managed, and for comparatively long stretches, to express itself in a wide gamut of non-violent outlets and arrangements ranging from mild contempt, indifference, guarded contacts, distancing to consociational political strategies and territorial bonding in exclusive spaces.

This is why it is instructive to identify those interludes – the critical watersheds so-to-speak – during which feelings of communal identity are undermined and when the vague, undefined threats and fears become sharper and more focused. It is also during such moments that communities sought efforts to reconnect and revive communal solidarity and mobilization. Identifying with and glorifying the threatened virtues of one's own group is heightened and rendered more righteous – as the psychology of in-group/out-group conflict reveals – if it is reinforced by enmity towards the out-group. (For further elaboration, see Kelman, 1987; Group for the Advancement of Psychiatry, 1987). If uncontained, especially when amplified by rumours and stoked by religious demagogues, the hostility could easily erupt into open violence. By then only the slightest of sparks is needed for a violent explosion.

A drop of blood here and there, in moments of aroused communal passions, always begets a carnage. If I were to express this prosaically or more crudely, there is a relationship after all between hot-headedness and cold-blooded violence. The more impassioned and impetuous groups are, the more likely they are to be merciless and guilt-free in their brutality. Hotheadedness should not here be mistaken for mindlessness. Hardcore fighters, both by virtue of their youthfulness and effective resocialisation, are normally impelled by an ardent, often sacrificial, commitment to the cause and strategies of combat. Hostility is thus made more legitimate by dehumanizing, depersonalizing and reducing the enemy into a mere category; a target to be acted upon or eliminated. The "other" becomes no more than an object whose body is worthy of being dispensed with (see Volkan, 1979 and 1985; Keen, 1986; Zur, 1987). Assailants can now commit their cruelties with abandon and without shame or guilt. It is also then that collective violence degenerates into barbarism and incivility.

The Three Salient Modes of Primordialism

As the scares and the scars of war became more savaging and cruel, it is understandable that traumatized groups should seek refuge in their most trusted and deeply embedded primordial ties and loyalties, particularly those which coalesce around the family, sect, and community. Even in times of relative harmony and stability, kinship and communal groupings were always effective as mediating agencies. They have served as accessible and often innovative venues or routes for sociopsychological support, political mobilization and cultural change.

Among other things the cruelties of protracted and diffused hostility had drastically rearranged the country's social geography. Massive population shifts, particularly since they involved the reintegration of displaced groups into homogeneous and exclusive communities, rendered territorial identities sharper and more spatially anchored. It is in this sense that "retribalisation" became more pervasive. The term is employed here loosely to refer to the reinforcement of kinship, confessional and communal loyalties - especially since they also converged on tightly-knit spatial enclosures. Lebanon, in other words, is being retribalised precisely because in each of the three basic groupings (i. e. family, community, and sect) loyalties and obligations and the density of social interaction which binds groups together are increasingly becoming sources of intense solidarity. A word about each is in order, by way of elucidating some of the salient manifestations and consequences of such resurgent primordialism.

Familism

The Lebanese family has always been a resilient institution. Despite the inevitable decline in the sense of kinship the family experienced in the prewar years – generated by increasing urbanization, mobility, and secularization – it continued to have a social and psychological reality that pervaded virtually all aspects of society. As repeated studies have demonstrated, there was hardly a dimension of one's life which was untouched by the survival of family loyalty and its associated norms and agencies. To considerable extent, a person's status, occupation, politics, personal values, living conditions and life style were largely defined by kinship affiliation. So intense and encompassing were these attachments that the average Lebanese continued to seek and find refuge and identity within close family circles. This was most apparent in the emergence and survival of family associations-perhaps unique to Lebanon. Even when other secular and civic voluntary associations were available, the family was always sought as a mediating agency to offer people access to a variety of welfare and socioeconomic services (Khalaf 1971).

The war years have shored up the family's prominence. A significantly larger number of people found themselves, willingly or otherwise, enfolded within the family. By their own testimonies, they were drawn closer to members of their immediate and extended family than they had been before the war. They were also expending more effort, resources, and sentiments on family obligations and interests. As a result, the traditional boundaries of the family expanded even further to assume added economic, social, and recreational functions.

For example the concept of kin, *ahl* or *'ayleh*, became more encompassing and extended beyond the limited confines of a nuclear family. The results of an empirical survey conducted in 1983, in the wake of the Israeli invasion of 1982, reconfirms the manifestations of such resurgent familism. For example only 12 percent of the respondents perceived the boundaries of their family to be limited to spouses and children. Almost 40 percent extended their definition to include both parents. Another 22 percent stretched if further to include paternal and maternal uncles. The remaining 27 percent extended the boundaries even further to encompass all relatives. The family was not only becoming more encompassing. It was also becoming more intimate and affectionate, reinforced by repeated visits and mutual help. Close to 60 percent evaluated their family relations in such highly positive terms. The remaining 38 percent considered them as moderately so. Only 2 percent admitted that their family relations were distant, cold and had no sign of any mutual help or support.

As shown in Table 1, more than 58 percent of the respondents referred that their ties and relationships with their immediate families had been strengthened by the war. The incidence fell to about 23 percent for relatives and dropped to as low as 18.8 percent for colleagues. The respondents were also asked to indicate, on the conventional 5-point scale, the degree of their involvement in domestic and family affairs. More concretely an effort was made to assess the extent to which such family concerns were becoming more, remaining the same or becoming less important since the outbreak of civil hostilities. Here as well, and for understandable reasons, more than 60 percent of the respondents indicated that they had become more preoccupied with domestic and family affairs. Thirty-eight percent felt that there was no change in such relations during the war, and only 2 percent reported that domestic and family-centred interests became less important for them.

Given the large-scale devastation of state and other secular agencies and institutions, the family was one of the few remaining social edifices in which people could seek and find refuge in its reassuring domesticity and privacy. It became, to borrow Christopher Lasch's apt title, a "haven in a heartless world" (Lasch 1979). Whether the family will be able to withstand such mounting pressure remains to be seen. What is clear though is that during the war it had to reinvent and extend itself to assume added functions. For example, beyond absorbing a larger share of the leisure, recreational, welfare, and benevolent needs of its members, it also served as an economic and commercial base. Many, particularly lawyers, craftsmen, retailers, and agents, were forced to convert their homes into offices for business operations. Housewives, too, were known to have used their homes to conduct a variety of transactions and to sell clothing, accessories, and other such items.

Table 1: Impact of the War on the Nature and Identity of social Relations

	Immediate family	Relatives	Friends	Colleagues
Strengthened	58.2%	22.9%	27.6%	18.8%
About the same	39.4%	65.4%	57.5%	68.6%
Weakened	2.4%	11.7%	14.9%	12.6%
Total	100.0%	100.0%	100.0%	100.0%

Here as well, in other words, the enclosure within family circles and networks, has not meant that family members, particularly women, are doomed to a constricted life of idleness, servitude and bondage. Many were able to transform such seemingly parochial and non-rational ties into venues for economic, commercial and cultural participation in the public sphere.

Their longing to take shelter in the security and emotional sustenance of family ties and ancestral roots, in times of uncertainty and ambivalence, is understandable. But so is their need to step out into the public world. The one does not preclude or pre-empt the other. While women are eligible, they continue to be disproportionately represented in the political life of the country. Their access, however, to employment opportunities in both the private and public sectors has increased considerably over the past few decades. Indeed in some ventures, particularly the informal economy and leadership in voluntary associations, women continue to predominate (see *al-Raida*, 1998; CAWTAR, 2001 for supportive evidence).

Persisting uncertainties of the post-war interlude along with the unsettling transformations generated by the forces of globalism, consumerism, popular culture and mass entertainment have had added strains on the family. Demographic pressures, associated with the disproportionate outmigration of young professionals, skewed sex ratios, postponement of marriage, are generating acute tensions and sharper dissonance between parental authority and the liberalization of sexual norms and conduct youthful groups are prone to be receptive to.

Coping with this dissonance has not been effortless or unproblematic. The seeming abandon with which some of the young appear to display symptoms of permissiveness and relaxation of sexual standards should not, however, be taken to mean that such liberal life styles and licentious behaviour, have been uniformly accepted without resistance or conflict. Therapists and counsellors speak of enhanced manifestations of anxiety, depression and demoralization. These, if anything, are naturally symptomatic of unresolved tensions and the failure to reconcile the contradictions inherent in these inconsistent normative expectations. Given the relative scarcity of eligible bachelors, young women are expected to be, indeed encouraged and condoned, when they are sexually attractive. Hence, considerable resources and emotions are invested on eroticizing their bodies and outward appearance. An aggressive and scintillating cosmetic, fashion and popular entertainment industries have reinforced such proclivities to embrace these amatory self-images and the allures of the public gaze and being longed for as sexual objects.

While young women are condoned for rendering themselves more sexually attractive, they are however condemned if they become sexually active. Shuttling between these two inconsistent normative expectations has been fraught with ambivalence and social hypocricy. It has also been a boon for the thriving cosmetic industry and rehabilitative plastic surgery.

Another inveterate feature of the resilience of kinship solidarities is the manner with which family ties and personalistic loyalties continue to shape the political process. In more than one respect, I argued in 1968, that the whole political history of Lebanon can be described in terms of a handful of prominent families competing to reaffirm their name, power and privilege in their respective regions or political constituencies. Competition for political succession, particularly as it manifests itself in contentious electoral companies, remain the broadest arenas where such factional rivalries vent themselves. Nothing has transpired over the past three decades to dilute or undermine such elements.

As in other personalistic and kinship societies, local and national elections in Lebanon are not merely a process of electing representatives or a device through which the ruling elite seeks to perpetuate itself. It is not an ideological contest between political systems or figures. Rarely, if ever, have elections been sought and fought on programmatic and impersonal basis. In more cases than not it is a bitter and long-standing conflict between extended families and communal factions. It is a chance to vindicate some of the old feuds which have traditionally mobilized and divided electoral districts. Irrespective of the positions of the contestants, the contest is almost always a source of friction and hostility. Since elections are fought in a personal and vindictive manner, the results bring glory to the victors and shame to the losers. The former take their victory with indulgence; the later accept their defeat with bitterness and humiliation. Needless to say, a personal and familial rivalry needs few ideological platforms. It leaves no room for organized debates where contestants can challenge the ideas of their rivals. Gaining access to voters is still largely accomplished through traditional contacts; visits, social calls, and through the services of 'Election Keys' who act as self-appointed intermediaries between candidates and voters. They organize meetings, arrange for contacts, and sometimes go as far as to guarantee a certain number of votes and returns.

Virtually all the prominent political families manage to find the circumstances to perpetuate their re-election into the parliament. I have elsewhere provided evidence to substantiate the magnitude and survival of such a reality (Khalaf 1980). Indeed, over the entire span of fifty years of parliamentary life (1920-72), 425 deputies belonging to 245 families have occupied a total of 965 seats in 16 assemblies. It must be borne in mind that deputies are considered to belong to the same family if they are characterized by close kinship ties and carry the same name. For example, Deputies with a surname of al-Khuri – one of the most numerous families in the Parliament – are not all descendants of the same lineage. Khalil of Aley, Ilyas of Babda, Shahid of Jbeil, and Rashid of Zahrani are all unrelated Khuris who occupied seats in the 1964 Chamber. The same is true of the Beydoun, Al-Husayni, and Shihab families, to mention a few. Care was taken to keep such distinctions in mind in identifying family units. If distant relatives and those related through intermarriage were to be included then the estimate would certainly not exceed two hundred families.

It is revealing that only 129 Deputies (28 percent) of all parliamentary representatives are unrelated to other parliamentarians. The remainder, with the exception of approximately 10 percent of the earlier pre-Independence cases whose family ties could not be ascertained, bear some close or distant relation to other deputies. As shown in Table 2, 45 percent of all parliamentarians can be considered closely related, through direct kinship descent or marriage, to other colleagues in the Chamber. Another 17 percent might be considered distant relatives. Altogether, in other words, 62 percent of the entire universe of Deputies have some kinship attachments to other parliamentary families.

Table 2: Kinship Ties among 425 Parliamentarians

Kinship Ties	Number	Percentage
Fathers[a]	36	9
Sons[b]	41	10
Brothers	33	7
Cousins	37	8
Nephews	12	3
Uncles	19	4
Brothers-in-Law	16	4
Distant relatives	76	17
Unrelated	129	28
Not determined	44	10
Total	443	100

[a]Includes two grandparents; Qabalan, Frangieh and Ahmad al-Khatib.
[b]Includes two grandchildren; Antoine Frangieh and Zahir al-Khatib.
Source: Messarra 1974:201

That there are oligarchic or "dynastic" tendencies is also apparent in the disproportionate share of parliamentary seats a few of the prominent families have enjoyed. Table 3 identifies the year each of those families were initiated into politics, the number of assemblies they served in and the parliamentary seats they occupied. Altogether, not more than twenty six families have monopolized 35 percent of all parliamentary seats since 1920. What this means in more concrete terms is that 10 percent of the parliamentary families have produced nearly one-fourth of the deputies and occupied more than one-third of all available seats.

Table 3: Prominent Parliamentary Families (1920-1972)

Family	Year of Initiation	No. of Deputies	No. of Seats	No. of Chambers
Arslan	1922	4	19	15
Zayn	1920	5	18	13
Fadl	1922	4	17	10
Husayni	1922	4	17	14
Khazin	1920	6	16	15
As'ad	1925	4	16	12
'Usayran	1922	3	15	13
Haydar	1920	3	15	13
Edde	1922	3	15	13
Hamadeh	1925	1	14	14
Junblat	1920	3	14	13
Al-Solh	1943	5	14	7
Al-Khuri	1925	5	13	12
Skaff	1925	4	13	11
Frangieh	1929	4	13	12
Ghusn	1920	2	12	12
Salem	1925	3	11	10
Qaz'oun	1922	3	11	11
Lahhoud	1943	5	11	8
Al-Khatib	1937	5	10	8
Beydoun	1937	7	10	7
Zuwayn	1925	2	9	9
Karami	1937	3	9	9
Gemayel	1960	3	9	4
Harawi	1943	5	9	8
Chamoun	1934	2	9	
Total		98		339

A few other striking features of family succession are worth noting. Once initiated into political life, almost all the families have virtually had uninterrupted tenure in all successive Chambers. With the exception of one family (Gemayel), which entered the Parliament in 1960, the majority had initiated their political career in the 1920s. this is quite telling, considering the prominent and decisive role the Gemayels, Pierre and his two sons Amin and Bashir, came to play in the political life of the country during the past three decades.

In some instances, it is one man (Sabri Hamadeh), or fathers and sons (Arslan, Edde, Karameh, Ghusn, Khazin, As'ad, Skafff, Khuri, Zayn, Zuwaym, Gemayel), brothers (Zayn, Edde, Shahin, Skaff), cousins (the five Solhs, four Khazins, two Gemayels, two

Sihnawis, and two Kayruzes), or brothers-in-law (Hamadeh-As'ad, Salam-Karami, Arslan-Junblat, Safiuddin-Arab) who perpetuate family succesion. In two particular instances – Frangieh and Khatib – three successive generations of grand fathers, fathers, and sons have already ensured the continuity of their family mandate in Parliament. This is rather remarkable given the comparative recency of Lebanon's experience with parliamentary life.

The staying power of the family is particularly demonstrated during by-elections. In several instances when a parliamentary seats is vacated in mid term, the deputy is succeeded by a son, if he has an apparent successor, or relative. Magid Arslan, Kamel al-As'ad, Antoine and Suleiman Frangieh, Zahir al-Khatib, Bahij al-Fadl, Maurice Zuwayn, Myrna Bustani, Abdallatif al Zayn, Amin Gemayel, Philip Taqla, Ma'rouf and Mustapha Saad – to mention a few – have all inherited their seats from a father, brother, or uncle.

Because no general parliamentary elections were held for twenty years (1972-92), such familial succession often takes place outside the official or constitutional political process. In typical patrimonial and feudal fashion, sons – their qualifications notwithstanding – are bequeathed their fathers' political "estates". Given the resigned and unchallenged attitudes that sustain the survival of this tradition, the succession often assumes all the attributes of an endowed estate in the very strict meaning of the term.

Elite circulation, as measured by incidence of general deputy turnover and new entrants into the ten successive Chambers since independence, is considerably high. Though the incidence witnessed periodic variations, it stabilized to about 40 percent in 1972. This, incidentally is considerably higher than comparable rates observed in some Western democracies (see Froman, 1967:170; Ross, 1949:107; Mathews 1960:240). By 1992 the rate of new entrants doubled to about 80 percent (al-Khazin, 1993:71-2). Such deceptively high rates of elite circulation doubtlessly reflect changes in size of the Chamber. For example, the Chambers of 1951, 1957 and 1960 marked an increase of 22 deputies each. From 1960-1972 it stabilized at 99 and then leaped, as stipulated in the Ta'if Accord, to 128 in 1992. But if one probes into the background of the new entrants, particularly their kinship ties and process by which they are normally co-opted or recruited by other political veterans, the manifest rates might well disguise other latent considerations. Indeed, 48 percent of all presumably new entrants are descendants of families with a history of parliamentary representation. The incidence of such family succession became even higher (56 percent) during the three successive Chambers of 1964, 1968 and 1972 (see Khalaf 1980:133 for further details).

Nearly all other *aqtab*, with an eye on their imminent retirement, have made manifest and unhesitant efforts to bequeath their political capital and influence to their children. Camille Chamoun, Saeb Salam, Suleiman Frangieh, Pierre Gemayel, Kamal and Walid Junblat, Ma'rouf and Mustafa Saad, among others, encouraged their sons to assume more visible public roles and relegated to them some of their official and unofficial responsibilities.

The above evidence is hopefully sufficient to confirm the continuity of kinship ties in political succession. In terms of both the number of seats they occupied and the successive assemblies they served in, it is clear that a disproportionately small number of families have been able to retain and extend their power positions. Expressed differently, at least a significantly larger number of families have demonstrated staying power in comparison to those whose political fortunes have suffered sudden set-backs. The political casualty rate among prominent families, in other words, is remarkably low. Only nine such families – Daouk, Beyhum, Sa'd, Thabet, Trad, Munthir, Nammur, Istfan, Abdel-Razzaq – who were prominent politically in the pre-Independence era have since lost or disinherited their positions.

Table 4: Family Succession in Nine Lebanese Parliaments: Sons of Deputies

	1943	1947	1951	1953	1957	1960	1964	1968	1972
Sons of Deputies	6	4	13	11	12	12	23	21	13
Percentage of Membership	10.9	7.3	16.9	25.0	18.2	12.1	23.2	21.2	13.1
Number of Seats	55	55	77	44	66	99	99	99	99

What is even more striking is that this trend in kinship succession does not at all, contrary to what Harik (1975:210-11) suggests, evince any decline. If the ten successive Parliaments since Independence are any measure, both the incidence of sons of Deputies and descendants of parliamentary families have definitely persisted. In fact, in all prewar parliaments, the proportion of sons who have "inherited" their seats from their fathers is close to 20 percent compared to 10.9 percent in 1943. Nearly the same magnitude of change occurred among the deputies who are descendants of families with a history of parliamentary representation. The incidence of such family succession increased from 41-8 percent in 1943 to 44.4 percent by 1972. By 1992, despite all the assumed secularizing changes, it declined to about 39% (see El-Khazin 1993:74-5).

Table 5: Family Succession in Ten Lebanese Parliaments: Descendants of Parliamentary Families

	1943	1947	1951	1953	1957	1960	1964	1968	1972	1992
Deputies from Parliamentary Families	23	27	40	26	33	35	50	48	44	49
Percentage of Membership	41.8	49.1	51.9	59.1	50.0	35.3	50.5	48.5	44.4	38.3
Numbers of Seats	55	55	77	44	66	99	99	99	99	128

Source for 1992, el-Khazin, 1993:74

The indelible weakness of party affiliation and their failure to serve as an alternate source of socio-cultural and ideological mobilization account, no doubt, for the persisting saliency of family attachments. In the pre-war period, many of the leading political parties, precarious as they were, had failed to gain any recognizable inroads or undermine the hegemony of the prominent family oligarchies. This was most notable in South Lebanon, Beqa' and the North. Zahle, in particular, was popularly labelled as the "grave yard of political parties" (see Chawool, 1993:178). By 1992 party representation in North Lebanon, particularly because of the boycott of elections by Christian parties, dropped sharply from 46 percent in 1972 to 25 percent in 1992. South Lebanon is the only region where party representation increased to 30 percent. Indeed, political parties like Hisballah, PPS, Amal, Al-Jama'a al-Islamiyya, al-Wa'ad managed to enter the seemingly exclusive sanctuary of the Parliament for the first time (for further details see Beydoun, 1993).

Table 6: Changes in Party Representation in the Lebanese Parliament

	1972 N	1972 %	1992 N	1992 %
National Liberal	7	10.9	---	---
Al-Kata'ib	3	6.9	---	---
National Bloc	3	2.9	---	---
Hizballah	---	---	8	10.0
PPS	---	---	6	7.6
Socialists	5	5.0	5	6.0
Al-Wa'ad	---	---	2	2.5
Al-Ahbash	---	---	1	1.0
Al-Ba'ath	1	1.0	2	2.5

Source: Messarra 1972, El-Khazin 1993

More damaging perhaps are the opportunities those in power have under their disposal, particularly in a postwar setting pregnant with massive reconstruction projects, to tilt such privileging ventures in favour of their direct kin and political clients. The recent public outcry over the magnitude of corruption and the egregious squandering of public funds are symptomatic of such rampant clientelism. The stakes involved in such disputes are normally so high (e.g. the "cellular deadlock" over selling off two competing cellular licenses) that prospects for the privatization of public ventures such as water, electricity, public transport, television, have all precipitated debilitating government crises.

The persistence of such kinship rivalry and the political dominance of prominent families, has among other things, given the political process a rather personalistic, opportunistic and non-ideological character. Hence today's political alliances, parliamentary blocs and oppositional fronts and coalitions, much like their predecessors, continue to be initiated and sustained by personal, segmental and non-ideological considerations.

A caveat is in order. Opportunistic and unprogrammatic as most personal relationships are, it is erroneous to assume that the whole structure of the body politic is sustained by personal and kinship alliances. The radicalization of the Shi'ites in the South, Beirut's suburbs, the Beqa'a or elsewhere, clearly speak otherwise. So does the divisive rift between those who differ regarding the presence and implications of Syria's intractable hegemony over Lebanon. What these and other such instances suggest is that the continuing dominance of personalistic loyalties does not preclude the existence of ideological rivalries. The political history of Lebanon – both remote and more recent – is replete with instances where purely personal and kinship rivalries are transformed into doctrinal conflicts and , conversely, where doctrinal and political issues have been reinforced by kinship loyalty. Despite the avowed and celebrated expressions and tokens of family solidarity, instances of political divisions and discord within families are legion. Virtually all prominent political families, particularly those with perpetual seats in the Chamber of Deputies, cannot claim that they are the uncontested political spokesmen of their respective families. For example, the political standing of families such as Franjieh, al-Khazin, Murr, Lahhoud, Hrawi, Asaad, Zein, Salam, Karameh, Khalil - to mention a few – have all been splintered by inveterate schisms.

Communalism

Manifestations of resurgent primordialism have also been resurfacing at the communal level with, perhaps, greater intensity. Since the boundaries and horizons within which groups have been circulating are becoming more constricted, it is natural that these tightly knit localities should become breeding grounds for heightening communal and territorial identities. Inevitably, such bonding in exclusive spaces was bound to generate deeper commitments towards one's community and corresponding distance from others. In-group/out-group sentiments are consequently becoming sharper. Segmental and parochial loyalties are also more pronounced. So have the sociocultural, psychological, and ideological cleavages. In this sense the community, locality, neighbourhood, or quarter are no longer simply a space to occupy or a place to live in and identify with. They have become akin to an ideology – an orientation or a frame of reference through which groups interact and perceive others. It is then, that the community is transferred into a form of communalism.

Two unsettling, often pathological, features of such "retribalisation" are worth highlighting again. More and more communities, in the wake of protracted hostilities, started to assume some of the egregious attributes of "closed" and "total" entities. The two are naturally related. Comparatively mixed, hybrid, and open communities were becoming more homogeneous and closed to outsiders. Such polarization was bound to engender and sustain the growth of almost totally self-sufficient communities and neighbourhoods.

Since early in the initial stages of the war the traditional city centre and its adjoining residential quarters witnessed some of the fiercest rounds of fighting and destruction, the episodes were accompanied by a quickening succession of massive population shifts and decentralization. In no time business establishments and virtually all the major public and private institutions – including universities, schools, banks, embassies, travel agencies, and the like – took measures to establish headquarters or branch offices in more than one district. This clearly facilitated the proliferation of self-sufficient urban enclaves. Before the war, people by necessity were compelled to traverse communal boundaries to attend to some of their public services and amenities. Gradually the urge to cross over became superfluous and undesirable. As a result, a rather substantial number of Lebanese are now living, working, shopping, and meeting their recreational, cultural, medical and educational needs within constricted communal circles. More compelling, generations of children and adolescents have grown up thinking that their social world could not extend beyond the confines of the ever smaller communities within which they have been entrapped.

Some of the sociopsychological and political implications of such reversion to "enclosed" communities are grievous. The psychological barriers and accompanying sociocultural differences are becoming deeper and more in-grown. More and more Lebanese have been forced over the past two decades to restructure and redefine their lives into smaller circles. What is rather unsettling in all this is that they don't seem to particularly resent such restrictions.

A few results of the empirical survey we conducted in 1983, particularly those which reinforce the proclivity of groups to seek shelter in cloistered spatial enclosures and their corresponding inclination to maintain distance from other communities, are worth nothing. Around 70 percent of the respondents indicated that their daily movements are restricted to the area or neighbourhood they live in. Surprisingly, a slightly larger number desire to live, work and confine their movements to such restricted areas. Only 22 percent were moving at the time, albeit furtively, between different sectors of the city.

The religious composition of the three broad communities from which the samples were drawn (Ras-Beirut, Basta, and Achrafieh), must have, no doubt, enhanced their receptivity to sustain and encourage feelings of communal solidarity and to entertain unfriendly and hostile feelings toward other groups. The sectarian composition of our respondents corresponds to the religious profile we generally associate with those urban districts. As shown in Table 7, Ras Beirut is the only fairly mixed district. The majority (40%) are Orthodox, followed by Sunnis and Protestants. The rest are almost equally distributed among Maronites, Catholics, Shi'ites, and Druze, with a few Armenians and other Christian minorities. On the whole, however, Ras Beirut is more than two-thirds Christian and around 27 percent Muslim. On the other hand, Basta is almost exclusively Muslim in composition, just as Achrafieh is also exclusively Christian. The proportion of Maronites, Catholics, and Protestants is as negligible in Basta as is the proportion of Sunnis, Shi'ites, and Druze in Achrafieh. The only exception is perhaps the Orthodox. It is the only sect which is represented in the three communities, although to a much lesser degree in Basta.

Table 7: Religious Composition of the Three Communities (in percent)

	Ras Beirut	Basta	Achrafieh	Total
Maronites	9.1	2	40	17.2
Catholics	7.3	2	13.5	7.6
Orthodox	40.0	7.8	30.8	26.2
Protestants	15.4	0	1.9	5.8
Armenians	1.8	2	5.7	3.2
Sunnis	17.3	60.8	3.8	27.3
Shi'ites	5.5	15.5	3.8	8.3
Druze	3.6	9.8	0	4.4
Percent	100.0	100.0	100.0	100.0
N	110	51	52	213

It is natural that residents of such closely knit and homogenous communities should begin to display particular attitudes towards other sectarian groups. The war, judging by some of our preliminary results, has apparently sharpened such sentiments. The respondents were asked: "How do you evaluate your present feelings and opinions towards the groups listed below? Do you feel closer to them now than before the war, or do you have unchanged feelings, or do you feel more distant?"

The results, as summarized in Table 8, reveal some obvious and expected tendencies that reflect the roles the various communities played during the war at the time of the survey and the consequent social distance between them. If we take the sample as a whole, 39 and 38 percent have grown more distant from the Kurds and Druze respectively and harbour hostility toward them. Next come Maronites (29%), Shi'ites (26%) and Sunnites (23%), followed by Syriacs (18%) and Armenians (17%). The rest, namely Catholics, Christian minorities, Orthodox, and Protestants evoke little or no hostility or negative feelings. Conversely, the respondents feel closer to Maronites (22%), Orthodox (19%) and Sunnites and Shi'ites (15%). Groups that elicit least sympathy are Druze (8%), Armenians (5%) and Kurds (1.6%).

Table 8: Enmity and Social Distance (in percent)

	Closer	Unchanged	More Distant
Maronites	22.0	40.0	29.0
Orthodox	19.0	62.0	8.0
Catholics	10.0	71.0	7.0
Protestants	7.0	73.0	8.0
Xian Minorities	8.0	72.0	7.0
Sunnites	15.0	50.0	23.0
Shi'ites	15.0	47.0	26.0
Druze	8.0	44.0	38.0
Kurds	1.6	45.0	39.0
Armenians	5.0	64.0	17.0
Syriacs	8.0	60.0	18.0

Distant from		Closer to	
Kurds	39	Maronites	22
Druze	38	Orthodox	19
Maronites	29	Shi'ites/Sunnites	15
Shi'ites	26		
Sunnites	23		

It is interesting to note that, with the exception of the Druze, attitudes toward belligerent sects (Maronites, Sunnis, Shi'ites) invite both extremes. Nearly the same proportion who indicate that they have grown closer to a particular sect also display enmity and distance toward them. They are equally admired and admonished. It is also interesting in this regard, to observe that attitudes toward nonbelligerent groups or those who were not directly involved in the fighting, (i. e. Protestants, Christian minorities, Catholics, and Greek Orthodox) remained largely unchanged.

A few other, albeit self-evident, variations are also worth nothing. Ras Beiruties on the whole feel far closer toward Maronites (32%) and Orthodox (23%) than they do toward Sunnis (16%) and Shi'ites (15%). The Druze received the lowest score (5%). They have grown distant from the Druze (56%) and then almost equally from Shi'ites (30%), Sunnis (26%), and Maronites (24%). The Basta residents feel closer toward Shi'ites (27%) and to a slightly lesser degree, Sunnis, Druze and Orthodox (23%). The bulk of their resentment is directed toward the Maronites. The Achrafieh residents are naturally closest to Maronites (51%), followed by Orthodox (35%) and Catholics (27%). Their resentment is directed toward the Druze (57%) and to a much lesser degree, Shi'ites (30%) and Sunnis (22%).

Communities in Lebanon have been becoming more "closed" in still another and perhaps, more vital and disturbing sense. A few of these communities are beginning to evince features akin to a total, even "totalitarian" character in several significant respects. I borrow the term here employed by Erving Goffamn (1961) in his analysis of total institutions such as prisons, hospitals, monasteries, mental asylums and the like.

1. Because of the massive population shifts and decentralization, accompanied by the fear and terror of intercommunal hostilities, communities became increasingly self-sufficient. A full range of human activities has developed within each of those communities.

2. As a result, even where entry and exit into and from these communities remained largely voluntary, an increasing number of people were reluctant to cross over. The boundaries, incidentally, are not merely spatial. Sometimes an imaginary "green line", a bridge, a road network, might well serve as the delimiting borders. More important, the barriers are becoming psychological, cultural, and ideological. Hence, there emerges within each of those communities a distinct atmosphere of a cultural, social and intellectual world closed to "outsiders". It is for this reason that the social distance and the barriers between the various communities are also becoming sharper. The barriers are often dramatized by deliberately exaggerating differences. Such dramatization serves to rationalize and justify the maintenance of distance. It also mitigates part of the associated feelings of guilt for indulging in avoidance.

The same kinds of barriers which had polarized Beirut during the war into "East" and "West" started to appear elsewhere. For example Residents of "East" Beirut were inclined to depict the Western suburbs as an insecure, chaotic, disorderly mass of alien, unattached, and unanchored groups aroused by borrowed ideologies and an insatiable appetite for lawlessness and boorish decadence. In turn, residents of Western Beirut depicted the Eastern suburbs as a self-enclosed "ghetto" dominated by overpowering control and hegemony of a one-party system where strangers are suspect and treated with contempt. In short, both communities were cordoned off and viewed with considerable fear and foreboding. Each vowed to rid or liberate society from the despicable evil inherent in the other!

3. A total institution, often in subtle and unobtrusive ways, involves and effort to remake or resocialise individuals and groups within it. This, by necessity, requires that prior values, ideas and patterns of behaviour be dislodged and then be replaced by new ones. To varying degrees such manifestations of resocialisation became visible at the early stages of the war. The various communities and warring factions, supported by an extremely well developed and sophisticated media – with their own broadcasting stations, newspapers, periodicals, pamphlets, slogans, symbols and motifs – competed in gaining access to potential recruits, clients, and converts. Each developed its own ethnocentric interpretation of the war, its own version of the social and political history of Lebanon, and proposed diametrically opposed views and programs for the socioeconomic and political reconstruction of the country. The differences do not stop here. They have pervaded virtually every dimension of everyday life: the national figures and popular heroes they identify with, their life style, public and private concerns, and their perceptions of the basic issues in society are being drastically reshaped and redefined.

As a result, there are very few national symbols or fundamental issues with which all the Lebanese can identify. It is facts of this sort that prompt me to argue that Lebanon's pluralism, particularly if those same parochial loyalties and sentiments are maintained, remains more of a divisive force than a viable source of organic solidarity and national unity.

4. Finally, one can also discern signs of total control. Individuals and groups, particularly in areas where private militias and political groups enjoy a large measure of hegemony, are subjected to increasing forms of social controls – ranging from direct measures of conscription, taxation, impositions, censure to the more subtle forms of intervention in individual freedom and modes of expression and mobility. Some of these measures became so pervasive at different interludes of the war that at times nothing was held to be morally or legally exempt from the scope and unlimited extension of the group in power.

Confessionalism

Symptoms of primordialism are, doubtlessly, most visible in the reassertion of religious and confessional consciousness. What makes this particularly interesting is that religious and confessional loyalties manifest a few paradoxical and seemingly inconsistent features that reveal the sharp distinctions between them. Clearly religiosity and confessionalism are not and need not be conterminous. Indeed results of the 1982-83 empirical survey revealed some sharp distinctions between the two.

Curiously, as respondents indicated, their religiosity – as measured by the degree of changes in the intensity of their spiritual beliefs, religious commitments, and observation of rituals, practices, and duties of their faith – was declining. Their confessional and sectarian identities however were becoming sharper. When the respondents were asked whether the war has had an impact on the religious practices and activities, the majority (85%) admitted that they had not changed in this regard.

One could infer from such findings that the Lebanese are not taking recourse in religion in an effort to find some spiritual comfort or solace to allay their rampant fear and anxiety. To a large extent this kind of refuge is better sought and served in the family and community. Religion is therefore clearly serving some other secular – indeed socio-economic and ideological – function. Some of the results clearly support such an inference. It is, in a way, revealing that when it comes to matters that reflect their religious tolerance and their willingness to associate and live with other sectarian or religious groups – such as the schooling of their children, their attitudes toward interconfessional marriages and their residential preferences – confessional considerations begin to assume prominence.

When asked, for example, whether they would agree to send their children to a school affiliated with a sect other than their own, close to 30 percent of the respondents answered in the negative – i. e. a preference to educate their children in schools with similar sectarian background. Their attitudes toward mixed sectarian or religious marriages – for both males and females – reveal much of the same sentiments. Close to 28 percent disapprove of such religiously mixed marriages for males and 32 percent for females. Similar predispositions were expressed regarding their preferences to live in a locality that has a majority of people from their own sect. Around 21 percent were sympathetic with such a prospect.

Altogether, a surprisingly large proportion of what presumably is a literate, cosmopolitan, and sophisticated sample of professionals, university and college teachers, intellectuals, journalists, and the like, displayed strong confessional biases, and a distance from and intolerance toward other groups. This was apparent, in their disapproval of interconfessional marriages, their preference for parochial schooling for their children, and their reluctance to associate and live with other sectarian and religious groups. More poignant, perhaps, it was also becoming increasingly visible in this rather narcissistic preoccupation with one's community, with its corresponding exclusionary sentiments and phobic proclivities towards others. This heightened confessional consciousness, understandable in times of sectarian hostility and fear, started to assume fanatic and militant expressions of devotion to and glorification of one's group. The relative ease with which the various communities were politically resocialised into militancy was largely an expression of such aroused sectarian consciousness.

Pre-war confessional sentiments were on the whole subtle and nuanced, even if at times a bit wilily and insidious. They rarely assumed, however, explicit or overt manifestations. At worst, they were recognized as necessary aberrations to be tamed and reformed. They were rarely flaunted, with so much abandon and guilt-free aplomb, as boastful collective emblems and privileging identities or as gambits to distance oneself from or defile the other. Virtually the entire fabric of the body politic of the country is now suffused, wilfully or otherwise, with sectarian considerations. On both the weighty issues of national sovereignty or the mundane politics of everyday life, it is extremely difficult to keep such avowed expressions in check.

It is understandable, given the depth of such sentiments and their inherent association with feelings of collective security, solidarity and well-being of various groups, that they could be readily aroused in times of public discourse over the contested issues of power-sharing, electoral reforms, national identity, foreign policy, civil marriage and the like. But virtually all other debates, with no direct or visible link to sectarian interests or loyalties, become embroiled nonetheless in such overriding consciousness. In earlier epochs the expressions of confessional sentiments were nuanced, subtle and furtive. If and when invoked, it was always perceived as a pathology to be wished away or contained. Today the dissonance between its rhetorical expressions and explicit behaviour manifestations are more acute and poignant. It has also become much more invasive. It intrudes virtually every national discourse or public issue, substantive or prosaic. Hence, not only debates over electoral reforms, civil marriage, foreign policy, school curricula but even common-place and quotidian parliamentary debates on the budget, economic rehabilitation, monopolies etc… become suffused with confessional undertones. Willy-nilly, they begin to spark off confessional hostility and paranoia. For example, the government efforts to remove import monopolies has been quite contentious, given the underlying confessional tone which imperil the controversy. Since a disproportionate number of Christian entrepreneurs enjoy such protection, the measures are seen as another pernicious design to undermine further the socio-economic standing of the Christian community.

Incidentally, the whole, *sine-qua-non* of the Ta'if Accord was supposed to allay such visceral tears. Its legacy thus far has not been very felicitous in this regard. Ta'if, it must be recalled, was predicated on the effort not only to put an end to 15 years of protracted and displaced hostility, but to bring about a more balanced and equitable formula for power sharing among the belligerent communities. Accordingly, while Tai'f preserved the custom of the Maronite presidency, the Shi'a speakership and the Sunni premiership, it greatly undermined the powers of the Maronite president while enhancing those of the prime minister, the council of ministers and the speaker. More unsettling are the explicit transformations which engendered the further marginalization of the Christian community. At least three circumstances stand out in this regard: the electoral laws of 1992 and 1996, the naturalization decree of 1994 and the rehabilitation of the displaced. A word about each is in order.

The size of the electoral district, a hotly contested issue, has naturally direct bearing on the hegemony and scope of political influence the various communities can yield. The electoral laws of 1992 and 1996, by rearranging the size of electoral constituencies, contributed in no small measure to curtailing the impact of Christian voters on the election of Christian deputies. The post-Ta'if electoral laws were such that they assigned large districts in predominantly Muslim regions where Christian deputies were elected by Muslim votes than Muslim deputies elected by Christian votes. In his methodical analysis of the conduct and outcome of the two post-Ta'if elections (1992 and 1996), Farid el-Khazin substantiates such anomalies. In both elections, for example, Greek Orthodox and Greek Catholic voters had little or no impact on choosing any of their deputies in their respective constituencies. This was not true, however, of Muslim representatives who were brought to parliament by the votes of their co-religionists (el-Khazen 1998:27)

Such manifestations of political dispossession and disinheritance, particularly among the Maronites, have been spilling over to other dimensions of the political system, which serve to heighten further the feelings of marginalization and disenchantment (*ihbat*). Christian representatives on the Executive, in successive cabinets, have also been of lesser stature and credibility in comparison to those of Muslims. On the whole, the three leading Muslim communities continue to be represented by their most established and credible political leaders. Rafic Hariri for the Sunnis, Nabih Berri for the Shi'a, and Walid Jumblatt for the Druze all enjoy a wellspring of popular support and almost uncontested power-base which wields considerable bargaining strength on behalf of their constituencies. In stark contrast, Christian communities, with rare exceptions, are bereft of such consequential public spokesmen. Those who command such standing are either excluded from public office or are in voluntary or, more likely, involuntary exile.

The collective fears and anxieties of Christians are exacerbated by two other momentous problems with dire consequences for intercommunal balance and harmony: The return of the displaced and the spectre of naturalization. Ta'if makes a passing and declarative reference to the former: "the problem of the Lebanese evacuees shall be solved fundamentally, and the right of every Lebanese evicted since 1975 to return to the place from which he has been evicted shall be established. Legislation to guarantee this right and to ensure the means of reconstruction shall be issued."

The problem of the displaced and the prospects for their return is a complex issue fraught with an interrelated set of economic, sociocultural and psychological implications. In sheer magnitude it is immense. Close to 827,000 (about one-third of the country's resident population) were displaced between 1975 and 1989. Christians, however, bore a disproportionate burden of its misfortunes. The same source (Labaki and Abu Rjeily 1998) reveals that of those, 670,000 are Christians and only 157,500 are Muslims, roughly a ratio of 7 to 1. Also 70 percent of those who have not as yet reclaimed their homes and property are Christians. This is notably true of areas like Aley and Chouf where displaced Christian families continue to harbour misgivings about their return.

The measures of the government have taken thus far are not only fickle. They have also been mired in charges and counter-charges of corruption, favouritism, and mismanagement of resources. The special fund established in 1993, attached to the Prime Minister's Office and administered by the Ministry of the Displaced, has drained more than $ 600,000 million. I say drained, because close to 80 percent of the fund's budget has been squandered on indemnifying squatters to reclaim houses and premises they have illegally occupied in Beirut and elsewhere.

The problem of naturalization, though not attributed to Ta'if, has also aroused the apprehensions of Christians since this, too, carries with it the dread of their demographic marginalization. The naturalization decree (ratified by the parliament on June 20, 1994) has reawakened their fears, particularly since the religious breakdown of those who were recently naturalized is skewed heavily in favor of Muslims: about 80 percent compared to only 20 percent Christians (el-Khazin 1999:7-8). The problem is compounded by two further unsettling considerations: A large proportion of those granted citizenship (about 40,000) were UNRWA–registered Palestinian refugees. More disruptive, efforts were made to register the new citizens in selected mixed villages and town to tilt the demographic profile of these electoral constituencies in favor of known pro-government candidates (for further details, see Atallah 1997).

Given such reawakened fears, more so since these are being exacerbated by the unsettling regional and global transformations, it is understandable that marginalized communities should seek shelter in their tested cloistered, communal and territorial solidarities. Indeed, this compulsion to huddle in compact, homogeneous enclosures has been reinforcing Lebanon's "balkanized" social geography. There is a curious and painful irony here. Despite the many differences which divide the Lebanese, they are all in sense homogenized by fear, grief and trauma. Fear, at it were, is the tie that binds and holds them together – three primal fears, in fact: the fear of being marginalized, assimilated, or exiled. But it is also those fears which keep the Lebanese apart. This "geography of fear" is not sustained by walls or artificial barriers as one observes in other comparable instances of ghettoisation of minorities and ethnic groups. Rather, it is sustained by the psychology of dread, hostile bonding and ideologies of enmity. Massive population shifts, particularly since they are accompanied by the reintegration of displaced groups into more homogeneous, self-contained and exclusive spaces, have also reinforced communal solidarity. Consequently, territorial and confessional identities, more so perhaps than at any other time, are beginning to converge. For example, 44 percent of all villages and towns before the outbreaks of hostilities included inhabitants of more than one sect. The sharp sectarian redistribution, as Salim Nasr (1993) has shown, has reshuffled this mixed composition. While the proportion of Christians living in the southern regions of Mount Lebanon (i. e. Shouf, Aley, Upper Metn) was 55 percent in 1975, it shrunk to about 5 percent by the late 1980s. The same is true of West Beirut and its suburbs. Likewise, the proportion of Muslims living in the eastern suburbs of Beirut has also been reduced from 40 percent to about 5 percent over the same period (Nasr, 1993).

Within urban areas, such territorial solidarities assume all the trappings and mythology of aggressive and defensive "urban *'asabiyyas*" which exist, Seurat (1985) tells us, only through its opposition to other quarters. In this sense, the stronger the identification with one's quarter, the deeper the enmity and rejection of the other. Seurat's study also suggests that, once such a process is under way, a mythology of the quarter can develop. In it, the quarter is seen not only as the location where a beleaguered community fights for its survival, but also as a territorial base from which the community may set out to create a utopia, a world where one may live a "pure" and "authentic" life, in conformity with the community's traditions and values. The neighbourhood community may even be invested with a redemptive role and mission (such as the defence of Sunni Islam in the case of Bab Tebbane in Tripoli which Seurat was studying). Hence, the dialectics between identity and politics may be better appreciated. Politics implies negotiation, compromise, and living side by side with 'the other'. Heightened feelings of identity, however, may lead one to a refusal to compromise, if negotiation comes to be perceived as containing the seeds of treachery that may undermine the traditions, values and 'honour' of one's community. In such a context, violence and polarization become inevitable: precisely the phenomena that have plagued Lebanon for so long.

Beyond Ta'if

To assert that sectarian affiliations have been reinforced by the war is, in many respects, documenting the obvious. It is, nonetheless, an affirmation worth belabouring, given some of the curious and pervasive features and consequences of Lebanese confessionalism. Lebanon's political history is replete with instances where sectarian loyalties evolved a dynamic of their own and became the most compelling forces underlying some of the major socio-cultural and political transformations in society. Even during periods of relative stability and normality, confessional allegiances have almost always operated, touching virtually all dimensions of everyday life. All the momentous events in a person's life cycle continue to be shaped by sectarian affiliation. It is a reality one cannot renounce. Early socialization, access to education, employment, welfare, hospital care, as well as many other vital services and personal benefits, are mediated through or controlled by sectarian foundations or agencies. Even a person's civil rights and duties as a citizen are largely, an expression of one's sectarian identity. The *sine qua non* of the state is, after all, an embodiment of a pact – transfigured at times into a sacred covenant – between the various sects to preserve this delicate balance.

Although the two decades of rapid socio-economic change which preceded the outbreak of the war had ushered in some of the inevitable manifestations of secularization, the residues of seventeen years of civil unrest and random violence have eroded many of them. At least, the burgeoning class identities depicted, and at times heralded, by many observers prior to the outbreak of the civil war, have been grossly undermined. Indeed, sectarian sentiments and their associated clientelistic loyalties appear to have reaffirmed themselves more powerfully than ever before. Military and economic reasons have doubtless played a crucial role in this process, as affiliations with militias rapidly became the most effective means for ensuring one's physical security, as well as providing access to vital goods and services.

More pressing perhaps, is the role of sectarian organizations in dispensing relief and shelter and attending to much of the war-stricken needs of the homeless and traumatized. In this context, it is scarcely surprising the sectarian mobilization and the accompanying exacerbation of religious tensions and passions should become more pronounced. Indeed, confessional loyalties have become to intense that they now account for much of the bigotry and paranoia permeating the entire social fabric. More surprising, they bear an inverse relationship to the degree of religiosity. As we have seen while religiosity, measured by the extent of changes in beliefs and the practices of religious duties has been declining, confessional and religious biases and prejudices are becoming more pronounced. This implies, among other things, that religion is not resorted to as a spiritual force to restore one's sense of well-being, but as a means of communal and ideological mobilization.

Equally enlightening is the way Ta'if enshrined intercommunal consensus to sustain its solemn pact of communal coexistence (*al aysh al-mushtarak*) and safeguard the strained features of power-sharing and distributive justice as the defining elements of its political culture. This is at least a tacit recognition on the part of the architects of the Accord that nearly two decades of civil strife had done little by way of undermining the intensity of communal and sectarian loyalties in society. Ta'if, in other words, has judiciously opted to embrace, as Joseph Maila has argued, the "consensual, sectarian logic and accepted its dictates." This, once again, renders Lebanon "more of a contractual, consociative country than one based on a constitution. According to this tradition, the formal, legal framework is always subordinate to pragmatic, consensual approach to mitigating conflict within the country, and to managing national and communal strains" (Maila 1994:31).

Such auspicious features notwithstanding, Ta'ifs record for nearly a decade now does not provide an encouraging outlook regarding it future prospects either as a peacemaking venture or as a covenant for achieving a more balanced and harmonious intercommunal coexistence. Since its inception, in fact, the Accord has been a source of heated controversy. Some observers continue to maintain that its flaws are congenital. Others suggest that these inborn defects were compounded by the setting and the history surrounding the three-week diplomatic bonanza at Ta'if. It was clear that some of the conferees were acting under duress. Although they were freely elected participants, the charged atmosphere imposed constraints on how far they could have ranged beyond some of the pre-prepared texts and agendas. They were left with a very limited margin to maneuver or to work out alternative schemes and proposals.

Even these who found no fault with the text still had misgivings about its lofty overtones, rendering it altogether more "declarative than definitive" (Maila:1994:37). Hence, at the operational level virtually all the concrete proposals for reform have either been "violated or derailed" (el-Khazen 1999:2). Political deconfessionalisation, let alone the aspired hope of transforming Lebanon into a truly secular society, has yet to be achieved. Most grievous perhaps is the pronounced and uneven shift in the relative political standing of the various communities. Ta'if's political reforms, particularly in laying the foundation for a more balanced system of power-sharing or sectarian representation, were expected to redress some of the internal gaps and disparities. For example the transfer of executive powers of the President to the Chamber of Deputies and the Cabinet rendered the position of a Maronite president more ceremonial and symbolic in character. The political standing of the Maronites has been unevenly undermined in other more disparaging respects.

It is ironical that at a time when other repressed groups throughout the world are liberating themselves from the repressive yokes of their servility, Lebanon is now being engulfed by all the disheartening manifestations of mounting disempowerment and subjugation. The guns might have been muted but deep-seated hostility and paranoia are far from being quelled. This is most visible in the redrawing of the country's social geography and other symptoms of retribalization. Unappeased hostility and fear predispose threatened and marginalized groups to find refuge in cloistered spatial localities and, hence become distant from or indifferent to other communities. Coexistence, let alone the professed goals of national reconciliation, become all the more elusive.

Naturally one cannot but lament the erosion of these and other enabling features of Lebanon's political culture, particularly the virtues of compromise, pluralism and a penchant for adaptive change and volunteerism. Off and on these have managed to reinforce its consociational character and jealous regard for civil liberties. In stark contrast to other authoritarian regimes in the region, Lebanon continues to enjoy more than just a modicum of civil liberties, tolerance and openness. For more than a century, and a century is a long interlude in the life of a young republic, Lebanon sustained a rather vibrant civil society which manifested itself in a lively press and multi-cultural communication networks, an inventive system of private education, a virile, often impetuous and risk-prone entrepreneurship and informal economy, and a spirited voluntary sector. Though momentarily at risk, one must single out an auspicious feature which remains a source of expectant hope: marginalized groups are not as yet bereft of collective voice to mobilize their sense of outrage and grievances. This polyphony of voices of a variety of dissenting coalitions, advocacy groups and recalcitrant assemblies (e.g. "Qornet Shehwan", "The Democratic Platform", "Renewal Movement", "Panel of National Action", "Consultative Gathering".)are far from muffled. They remain visibly vocal in issuing platforms and manifestos for political reform. They might not amount to much by way of restoring the frayed symptoms of state sovereignty and autonomy. They do though serve as vectors for inciting other furtive and silenced groups to partake in the collective discourse. By doing so they assist in the much-needed cultivation of free public opinion and the education of citizens into the ways of civil virtues. Here again, *roots* could well become the *routes* or venues through which seemingly cloistered communities could retain their local and parochial attachments while being receptive to new cultural encounters.

The politics of civil society, as John Keane (2001), John Friedman (1998), Iris Young (1990) among others insist on reminding us, is emancipatory in at least two vital senses. First, they enlarge the sphere of autonomy, particularly by providing public spaces based on trust, reciprocity and dialogue. Second, they provide venues for the mobilization of multiple voices and, hence, political empowerment. Incidentally, Young here makes a useful distinction between *autonomy* which is largely the sphere of the private, where groups can make decisions that affect primarily their own welfare without interference by others, and *political empowerment* which calls for effective participation in all decisions that affect the public welfare (Young, 1990:250-52).

Both are particularly relevant strategies at this critical watershed in Lebanon's history, caught between the throes of postwar rehabilitation and the disquieting manifestations of global and postmodern transformations. The promise of autonomy is inherent after all in its ability to encourage the active engagement and self management of the myriad of local voluntary associations which have mushroomed during the past decade. Among other things this calls for a dissenting and oppositional politics and the provision of venues for cultural resistance. Political empowerment, on the other hand, implies a shift from the essentially private and parochial concerns of civil society to the sphere of political community. Here politics become a struggle for inclusion, an opportunity for self actualization and a form of social justice that acknowledges the needs and priorities of different groups.

There is also another sense through which the concern for autonomy and empowerment can be particularly redemptive in Lebanon. Given the regional and global constraints, it is understandable why Lebanon might not be able to safeguard its national sovereignty or contain some of the global forces which undermine its political independence and economic well-being. At the socio-cultural and psychic level, however, the opportunities to participate in such voluntary outlets can do much to nurture some of the civil virtues which will reinforce prospects for greater measures of autonomy and empowerment.

Postwar interludes, particularly those coming in the wake of prolonged periods of civil disorder, anarchy and reckless bloodletting normally generate moods of restraints, disengagement and moderation, War-weary people are inclined to curb their ordinary impulses and become more self-controlled in the interest or reassessing the legacy of their belligerent past and redefining their future options. Somehow, postwar Lebanon has begotten the adverse reactions. Rather than releasing the Lebanese from their pre-war excesses, it has unleashed appetites and inflamed people with insatiable desires for extravagant consumerism, acquisitiveness and longing for immoderate forms of leisure and sterile recreative outlets. Some of the dismaying byproducts of such mindless excesses, particularly those which continue to defile the country's habitat and living spaces have become more egregious. Here as well, the active engagement in the burgeoning voluntary sector can be effective in resisting the forces of excessive commodification, government dysfunction, drain in public resources and corruption.

Concerted efforts must be made in this regard to shift or redirect the obsessive and effete interest of the Lebanese in the hedonistic and ephemeral pleasures of consumerism to more productive and resourceful outlets. Consumption is essentially a passive preoccupation when compared to the more productive and creative pursuits of doing things for oneself in association with others. This distinction is not as benign or self-evident as it may seem. Nor should it be belittled as a source of collective healing and rejuvenation. All productive activities, as John Friedman (1998:33-5) reminds us, are inherently cooperative. Hence any active engagement in a medley of activities – be in sports, music, neighborhood improvement, social welfar, human rights, programs for continuing special education or participation in advocacy groups on behalf of the excluded and marginalized – are all destined to become transformative and transcending experiences.

By transforming the private concerns of autonomy into sites of political empowerment, where issues of public concern are debated and addressed, such venues will also become the ultimate and most redemptive settings for the cultivation of civil virtues. It is in such hybrid and open spaces that this cultivation in civility will allow groups to appreciate their differences without being indifferent to others. Is this not, after all, what the virtues of tolerance are all about?

References Cited

Atallah, Tony George, "Al-Mujannasun Fi Lubnan Ma Ba'dal Harb: Haqa'iq wa Arqam" (The Naturalized in Lebanon: Facts and Figures), in *Al-Abhath* 45 (1997): pp. 97-111.

Baydoun, Ahmad, "Al-Janoub: al-Masrah wa al-Rawaya", in F. El-Khazen and P. Salem (eds.) *First Postwar Elections in Lebanon* (Lebanese Policy Studies, 1993).

Center of Arab Women for Training and Research (CAWTAR), "Arab Women in the Informal Sector: Changing Trends", in *Globalization and Gender* (Tunis: CAWTAR, 2001): pp. 91-104.

Chawool, M. "Al-Beqa'a: Al-'Ailat al Murhaqah" (Beqa' Enfeebled Families), in F. El-Khazen and P. Salem (eds.) *First Postwar Elections in Lebanon* (Lebanese Policy Studies, 1993).

Chevallier, Dominique, "Western Development and Eastern Crisis in the Mid-Nineteenth Century: Syria Confronted with the European Economy", in William R. Polk and Richard L. Chambers (eds.) *The Beginning of Modernization in the Middle East* (Chicago: University of Chicago Press, 1968).

Froman, L., *The Congressional Process: Strategies, Roles and Procedures* (Boston: Little, Brown, 1967).

Gellner, Ernest, *Culture, Identity and Politics* (London: Cambridge University Press, 1988).

Goffman, Erving, *Asylums* (New York: Anchor Books, 1961).

Hanf, Theodor, *Coexistence in Wartime Lebanon. Decline of a State and Rise of a Nation* (Oxford and London: Centre for Lebanese Studies and I. B. Tauris, 1993).

Hanf, Theodor, "Ethnurgy: On the Analytical Use of Normative Abuse of the Concept of 'Ethnic Identity'", in Keebet von Benda-Bechman and M. Verhuyfen (eds.) *Nationalism, Ethnicity and Cultural Identity in Europe* (Utrecht: European Research Centre on Migration and Ethnic Relations, 1995): pp. 40-51.

Harik, Iliya, "Political Elites in Lebanon", in G. Levezowski (ed.) *Political Elites in the Middle East* (Washington: American Enterprise Institute for Public Policy Research, 1975)

Hourani, Albert, "Ideologies of the Mountain and the City", in Roger Owen (ed.) *Essays on the Crisis in Lebanon* (London: Ithaca Press, 1976): pp. 33-41

Kakar, Sudhir, *The Colors of Violence* (Chicago: University of Chicago Press, 1996).

Keen, Sam, *Faces of the Enemy: Reflections on the Hostile Imagination.* (New York: Harper and Row, 1986).

Kelman, H., "On the Sources of Attachment to the Nation", paper presented at the meeting of the International Society of Political Psychology. San Francisco 1987, July 6.

Khalaf, Samir, "Family Association in Lebanon", in *Journal of Comparative Family Studies* (Autumn 1971): pp. 235-250.

Khalaf, Samir, *Persistence and Change in 19th-Century* (Beirut: American University of Beirut, 1979).

Khalaf, Samir, "The Parliamentary Elite in Lebanon", in Jacob Landau and Ergun Osbudun (eds.) *Electoral Politics in The Middle East* (London: Croom Helm & Hoover Institution, 1980): pp. 243-71.

Khalaf, Samir, "Ties that Bind: Sectarian Loyalties and the Revival of Pluralism in Lebanon", in *The Beirut Review* 1 (1) (Spring 1991): pp. 12-61.

Khalaf, Samir, *Civil and Uncivil Violence in Lebanon* (Columbia University Press, 2002).

Khazen, Farid El, "Intikhabat Maqable al-Ta'if wa ma Ba'dahu", in F. El-Khazen and P. Salem (eds.) *Al-Intihabat al-Ulah fi Lubnan ma ba'd Al-Harb* (First Postwar Elections in Lebanon) (Lebanese Policy Studies, 1993).

Khazen, Farid El, 1999, "Shrinking Margins: The Christians in Postwar Lebanon", in Barbara Roberson (ed.) (in press).

Lasch, Christopher, *Haven in a Heartless World: The Family Besieged* (New York: Norton, 1979).

Lowenthal, David, "Preface", in Adrian Forty and Susanne Küchler (eds.) *The Art of Forgetting* (Oxford: Berg, 1999): pp. xi-xiii.

Maila, Joseph, "The Ta'if Accord: An Evaluation", in Deirdre Collings (ed.) *Peace for Lebanon: From War to Reconstruction* (Boulder: Lynne Rienner, 1994): pp. 31-44.

Matthew, D., *US Senators and Their World* (Chapel Hill: University of North Carolina Press, 1960).

Melikian, L. H. and L. N. Diab, "Stability and Change in Group Affiliations of University Students in the Middle East", in *The Journal of Social Psychology* 93 (1974): pp. 13-21.

Messarra, A., *La structure social du Parlement Libanais*. Thesis (Université de Strasbourg, 1974).

Nasr, Salim, "New Social Realities and Post-War Reconstruction", in Samir Khalaf and Philip S. Khoury (eds.) *Recovering Beirut* (Leiden: E. J. Brill, 1993): pp. 63-80.

Picard, Elizabeth, *Lebanon: A Shattered Country* (New York: Holmes and Meier, 1996).

Raida, Al, "Female Labor Force in Lebanon", in *al-Raida*, Vol. XV, No. 82 (1998): pp. 11-23.

Randal, Jonathan, C., *Going all the Way* (New York: Vintage, 1984).

Ross, J., *Parliamentary Representation* (New Haven: Yale University Press, 1949).

Salibi, Kamal, *The Modern History of Lebanon* (London: Weidenfeld and Nicolson, 1965).

Seurat, Michel, "Le Quartier de Bab Tabane à Tripoli (Liban): Etude d'une Asabiyya Urbain", in C.E.R.M.O.C. (ed.) *Mouvements Communautaires et Espaces Urbaines au Machreq* (Beirut: C.E.R.M.O.C, 1985): pp. 45-86.

Volkan, V. D., *Cyprus-War and Adaptation: A Psychoanalytic History of two Ethnic Groups in Conflict* (Charlottesville: University Press of Virginia, 1979).

Volkan, V. D., "The Need to Have Enemies and Allies: A Developmental Approach", in *Political Psychology* 6 (2) (1985): pp. 219-247.

Young, Iris, *Justice and Politics of Difference* (Princeton, N. J.: Princeton University Press, 1990).

Zur, O., "The Psychohistory of Warfare: The Co-Evolution of Culture-Psyche and Enemy", in *Journal of Peace Research* 24 (2) (1987): pp. 125-34.

The New Social Map

SALIM NASR

In the quarter of century that followed the eruption of the conflict in Lebanon, in 1975, the Lebanese society underwent a radical transformation of its demographic, territorial and societal base. Fifteen years of protracted "civil strife" and a decade of "reconstruction politics" produced a society much different from the pre-war Lebanon, in terms of demographic dynamics, population movements, social stratification, balance of communities, role of the state, or political economy.

A complex combination of factors, internal political and social implosions, penetration of the Palestinian Israeli and other regional conflicts, impact of the oil economy boom and bust, and differential influence of the various diasporas, all these and other factors led to a profound alteration in the composition and trends of the Lebanese society.

Lebanon enters the new century with thirty billion dollars of public debts; an oversized and unsustainable public sector; a mostly fragmented and uncompetitive private sector; a rentier economy heavily dependent on transfers, remittances, interests, real estate speculations and hot money; no cohesive national class but divided, dependent and costly post-war political elites; an increasing sectarian polarization in most walks of life; a partly repressed, partly depressed youth, often dreaming of emigration; an increased duality between two societies: A wealthy, extrovert, spending and ostentatious minority, living and moving at par with the globalised world elite to which it aspires to belong; and a pauperized, expanding majority, stuck with a receding economy, limited horizons and declining opportunities.

Relying on the limited available statistical data and social research conducted in the nineties, and some of the author's previously published work on social stratification in Lebanon, this brief suggestive essay will try to highlight some of the features of the social map of post war Lebanon. By doing so, it will lay no claims to be systematic or comprehensive, but will try to underlines what seems to be major trends that have affected and continue to affect the emerging post war Lebanese society.

The New Socio-Demographic Profile

One significant result of fifteen years of protracted hostility, with onerous ramifications for socio-economic reconstruction, was the fact that Lebanon had, for all practical purposes, a population that was stagnant. Indeed, in relative terms, the population has been declining. This, among other things, implied that the economic and political reconstruction of Lebanon had to be carried out in the context of demographic regression.

In 1975, the Lebanese resident population was estimated at 2.6 million, a figure that according to demographers' projections before the war was to reach the level of 3.6 million by 1990. In fact Lebanon's actual resident population in 1990, according to the UN estimates, was no more than 2.7 million, which means an almost zero population growth over sixteen years. The expected growth of one million between 1975 and 1990 has been drained and/or absorbed by three major factors, directly related to the effects of protected conflict in such a small country.

First, and most obviously, are the war-related casualties whose estimates vary considerably. A relatively conservative figure puts the number of dead at 120.000 and of wounded at 300.000. This means that 4.5 percent of the 1975 resident population was killed and 11.5 percent wounded. To understand the comparative magnitude of the impact of such figures one might mention for instance, that the total number of Arabs killed in all four Arab-Israeli wars since 1948 did not exceed 110.000 (as opposed to 20.000 Israelis).

A second factor accounting for this zero population growth is the phenomenal acceleration in the exodus of Lebanese from their country. Estimates of this emigration during the war vary, but can be reasonably put at somewhere between 800.000 and 900.000. Emigration, of course, is not new in Lebanon. For the last 150 years it has been a persistent safety valve, response to Lebanon's socio-political crises and scarce natural resources. The war, however, has dramatically escalated the average yearly outflow, particularly towards Canada, Australia, certain Arab and African states, Western Europe (mainly France) and the United States. From a yearly average of about 5.000 in the 1950s and 1960s, it rose to 10.000 in the early 1970s, to an average of 40.000 for the years between 1975 and 1988, and finally exceeded 70.000 in 1989 and 10.000 in 1990. The significance of this out-migration, as we shall see, does not merely reflect its unrelenting magnitude. Perhaps more grievous is the composition and qualifications of the migrant group.

A third factor accounting for the lack of population growth is a reduction in the natural growth rate owing to a substantial drop in fertility observed in many case studies and monographs on various local communities. An example from the Shiite community, which had grown very rapidly in the 1950s and 1960s, shows the extent of this demographic decline. There surveys conducted within segments of the Shiite community in 1970, 1978, and 1987 show that the proportion of the population under 15 years old dropped from 49 percent in 1970 to 41 percent in 1978 to 39 percent in 1987. Even more telling are the surveys concerning the number of children born to women by the time they had reached the end of their childbearing cycle. In 1971, the average number of children born to women aged 44 to 49 years old was 8.5, while surveys conducted among the same age group during the late 1970s to the late 1980s showed an average of 4.8 per woman; a drop of over 40 percent. Another interesting indicator, from a 1985 survey on the average size of household, showed both a general decline in the overall rate of fertility and a reduction in the gap between the fertility rates of the different communities. For the predominantly Shiite *cazas* (districts) of Baalbeck, Hermel, and South Lebanon, the average size of household was 6.5, while the average size of household for the three largely Christian cazas of Zghorta, Batroun, and Zahleh was 505. Compared to these mainly rural areas, urban centres not only showed smaller family size but also a further narrowing of the gap between communities. For example, the average household size in East and West Beirut is almost identical: 4.3 in the former and 4.9 in the latter.

In sum, Lebanon's population base had shrunk in real terms, being less than three million when normally it should have been over four million. Nonetheless, the fact that demographic trends have decelerated was not necessarily a negative feature. These and related trends could have very well alleviated some of the demographic pressures, particularly in meeting mounting demands for education, housing, child care, and health services. The narrowing of the differential growth rate between the communities can also be seen in positive terms. The fact that this gap, which led in the 1950s and 1960s to demographic shifts in the population distribution among the communities and to political pressures on the system, had reached a point of stabilization that should contribute to alleviating fears and anxieties in most Lebanese communities.

In the nineties, two surveys, respectively conducted by the Ministry of Social Affairs and the Administration of Central Statistics led to two significantly diverging estimates of the resident population, 3.1 million (for 1996) in the first case, and 4.0 million (for 1997) in the second case. Without getting into the methodological debate, it is safe to estimate the resident population in 2000 at 3.5 million. This figure is still below the projected population that should have been reached in 1990. The slowing population growth of the nineties is explained both by a continuously declining growth rate (now around 1,6 percent per year) and by renewed waves of out migration provoked by the chosen mode of economic reconstruction and the economic recession of the later part of the nineties.

New Trends of International Migrations

A land of old migration and emigration, a major receiver and sender, contemporary Lebanon has been both at the heart of one of the first global Diaspora and the objective of many in the region who aspired to and moved to become part of it.

For the past one hundred and fifty years, emigration waves that followed civil strife, economic crisis, world wars, and family and village networks, produced a global Diaspora of almost 14 million persons of Lebanese descent scattered around the world. This rough estimate includes 6 million in Brazil, 3 million in the rest of Latin America, 3 million in North America, and half a million in each of Africa, Europe, Australia and the Arab World. This Diaspora is about four times the current resident population of Lebanon, probably the highest ratio in the world. Although no systematic account or extensive research has been conducted on the considerable effects of the Diaspora on families, villages and towns of origin, the economy and institutions, there is evidence throughout the past century of the impact of Lebanese emigration. Through remittances, donations, investments, scholarships, religious endowments, and building of schools and local infrastructure, emigrants have contributed to the survival of resident Lebanese in times of duress, and to the upgrading of the assets and capacities of Lebanon in times of peace.

Although it is difficult to quantify their impact, it is well known that wealthy Lebanese emigrants who returned to Lebanon have contributed significantly to the development of sectors such as the textile and building material industries in the 1930s, banks in the 50s and 60s, and contracting and public works since the 70s.

In contrast with the considerable and continuing outflow of Lebanese, contemporary Lebanon has been a centre of attraction for successive waves of regional immigration, due to social pluralism, a liberal tradition, a market economy, and perceived opportunities. Merchant houses, industrial families, ambitious financiers and entrepreneurs as well as artists, writers, intellectuals and political activists, from the rest of the Middle East and more particularly from Egypt, Syria, Iraq, and Palestine immigrated to Lebanon from the thirties to the seventies. They were pushed out by the many regional conflicts, authoritarian regimes, nationalization, and increasing restrictions on dissent, innovation, and enterprise, contributing considerably to the development of the Lebanese bourgeoisie and professional classes and the consolidation of Beirut in the mid-70s as a regional centre of trade and finance, transit and international communications, artistic and cultural innovation, printing and publishing, and political and social change. Although this role was considerably diminished by the conflict of 1975-90, no other regional metropolis succeeded in replacing Beirut in the combination of functions and the social and cultural climate created in the preceding half century.

Contemporary Lebanon has, in parallel, attracted also groups of refugees, artisans, workers and labourers, including Armenians in the 1920s, Kurds since the 30s, Palestinians in 1948, and Syrians throughout the century, but more particularly since the 50s. These replaced departing unskilled and skilled Lebanese workers and contributed to the expansion and relative efficiency of segments of the industrial, construction, and agricultural sectors. Industries such as jewellery, wood products, shoes and ready-made cloth (Armenians), the citrus sector (Palestinians), and construction and public works (Palestinians, Syrians, and Kurds), have largely depended on this compensatory immigration. Since the 80s and more particularly in the 90s, Egyptians and East Asians have joined the replacement immigration, each group currently reaching an estimated hundred thousand workers, playing a key role in sectors such as gas stations and bakeries, hotels and restaurants, gardening and specialized agriculture, some manufacturing industries, domestic service, and others.

After the end of the conflict, in the early nineties tens of thousands of Lebanese entrepreneurs, professionals, and skilled workers returned, either attracted by the emerging opportunities of the reconstruction program and/or pushed out by the declining opportunities in West Africa, Canada, France, and the Arab Gulf countries. A new community of thousands of dual citizens emerged, living in Lebanon, some returning, some commuting, some departing according to economic and market opportunities in Lebanon, in their country of naturalization and elsewhere. Over 40,000 Lebanese-Canadian, 30,000 Lebanese-French and maybe 20,000 Lebanese-American resided in Lebanon in 2000. Lately, and in the context of the economic recession of 2000, this group seems to have shrunk, as many of the investment projects of the returnees ran into difficulties.

The recession has also affected all other categories of immigrants, including the largest, Syrian workers, very sensitive to the state of the economy, whose numbers may have fallen from an all time high of 600,000-700,000 in the mid-90s, at the peak of the reconstruction activities, to as low as about 250,000 in 2000. The slow but continuing departure of Palestinians residents, whenever they could find opportunities to emigrate, led to further shrinking of the Palestinian community, from an estimated number of 350,000 or 13,5% of the resident population in 1975 at the eve of the conflict, to an all time high of 470,000 and 18% in 1982 at the eve of the Israeli invasion, to an estimated 280,000 and less than 8% of the residents in 2000.

Some could read the balance of exchanges between Lebanon and the globalizing world as relatively negative. Lebanon lost over the last century and a half hundreds of thousands of its people. Since independence in 1943, it has been deprived, through the brain drain of its best minds, attracted by international centres and regional opportunities. This historical openness, say the critics, mainly operated as a safety valve to deflate internal social and economic crises and to reduce pressure for internal reforms and structural change within the contemporary polity and economy. Opting out has been a possibility in the minds of most Lebanese whenever confronted with rigidities, inequities, or threats. This phenomenon increased dramatically in the last quarter of the past century. Around 900,000 Lebanese permanently left the country during the 1975-1990 conflicts, almost a third of the 1975 resident population (1998 National Human Development Report).

Paradoxically and dramatically, hundreds of thousands of Lebanese left in the post-war decade (1991-2000). It is estimated that a yearly average of 50,000 people left in the early post-war period and the take-off of the reconstruction project (1991-1994). In the second half of the past decade, as the economy in general and reconstruction activity slowed and finally gave way to recession, tens of thousands of mainly young and highly qualified Lebanese continued to emigrate each year. A recent national survey of Lebanese households, conducted by Université Saint Joseph, found that young people aged from 18 to 35 form half the active population but represent 71 percent of the total unemployed. 37 percent of the young people declared wanting to leave the country mainly to find work, but additionally to escape the "general situation", or to join family abroad, or to obtain dual nationality. The number of young men wishing to emigrate is almost double that of young women.

The phenomenon of continuing migration poses the problematic nature of Lebanon's model of development. It also raises the issue of the weak capacity of that model to take advantage of historical capital accumulated by Lebanon, on national territory and for resident Lebanese.

A Changed Social Geography

Beyond the situation of demographic stagnation and changing trends of emigration and immigration, Lebanon has been the scene of massive internal population displacements that have totally redrawn the social geography of the country, thereby reducing the traditional heterogeneity that has long characterized the various communities. The successive waves of population movement, in the wake of inter-factional fighting, are doubtless one of the more dramatic and grievous consequences of Lebanon's internal war. It is bound to have an important impact on the political and economic reconstruction of the country. It is estimated that by 1989 more than 1.2 million Lebanese had been displaced from their previous places of residence (villages, neighbourhoods, etc.) on a long-term basis. This figure represents 45 percent of the Lebanese population in 1975, which means that half the population has been forcibly displaced. Furthermore, this estimate includes only those who moved from one area to another and who have not returned to their initial place of residence. If one were to add those who moved within the same politico-military zone or those who moved at least once but then returned to their original residence, the proportion of those who had experienced the hazards of involuntary displacement becomes considerably greater.

To appreciate the impact of this level of displacement in Lebanon's communal structure, one must go to the pre-war social setting. Of the traditional 24 districts or cazas of post-Independent Lebanon, five (the Shouf, Aley, Akkar, Zahleh, and West Beqaa) had populations that were relatively balanced between Christians and Muslims. Six districts (Zahrani, Jezzin, Marjayun, Jbeil, South Metn, and Baalbeck) had majorities of one group with substantial minorities of another. More than two thirds of the Lebanese population lived in homogenous regions. Another indicator of the magnitude of communal heterogeneity is the fact that 44 percent of the 1,330 villages and townships of Lebanon included inhabitants of more than one sect.

This mixed communal character was not only an attribute of rural regions. It was present, even to a higher degree, in urban areas, given the tremendous rural-urban migration Lebanon had witnessed for several decades before the outbreak of hostilities in 1975. As a result, Lebanon's urban population had leaped sharply from 25 percent of the overall population in 1950 to 65 percent in 1975. An important effect of this rural migration was to transform all the major cities into plural societies, at least at the market places and in many of the burgeoning quarters and neighbourhoods. More significant, this led to the growth of mixed urban centres and agglomerations in and around Beirut, Tripoli, Sidon, Zahleh, and other towns.

Altogether, sixteen years of protracted strife have profoundly altered the social geography of the country. The multi-secular trend toward pluralism and greater communal territorial admixture was reversed. Instead, two related patterns were becoming more distinct: a growing homogeneity among the various districts and a corresponding segregation of the population along sectarian lines. This change has profoundly undermined the social basis of the Lebanese consociation.

From the early stages of the conflict, inter-communal disputes were reflected territorially, resulting in a progressive division of the country into increasingly homogeneous enclaves. Two parallel trends were at work here: the gradual destruction of the country's "common space", and the increasing concentration of the various communities in separate areas. The centre of Beirut which represented the heart of the country and held the seat of Parliament, the main business district, the banking headquarter, the transportation hub and the thriving marketplace was largely looted and destroyed by various armed factions in 1975. Meanwhile, many of the communities that had developed between the traditional, communally based neighbourhoods were also being dismantled and depopulated, as they became battlegrounds for the warring factions. This was the case along both sides of the Beirut-Damascus road, from Minat al-Hosn, near the Beirut port, to Ras al-Nabaa in the middle of the town, and in large sections of Shiyyah and Ayn al-Rummaneh near the suburbs. The same phenomena occurred in several of the mixed neighbourhoods in the periphery of Tripoli and Zahleh.

Each armed faction strove to create its own homogeneous sectarian territory through intimidation, threats, and violence against political opponents within its community and against members of other communities living within the borders of its sectarian territory. The result, once again, was an acute segregation of the Lebanese communities.

Table: Sectarian Redistribution of Lebanese Communities

	1975	1989
Christians:		
Southern Mt. Lebanon (Shouf, Aley, Upper Metn)	55	5
West Beirut and Suburbs	35	5
Beqaa	40	15
South Lebanon	26	10
Muslims:		
Eastern Suburbs (Beirut)	40	5
South Lebanon (Security Belt)	50	10
Koura, Batroun	10	2
East Beirut	8	1

Figures in %

As shown in the table, the southern regions of Mt. Lebanon, historically a confessionally-mixed area, have experienced perhaps the most intensive degree of redrawing of its sectarian composition. The proportion of Christians residing in those
Districts have dropped sharply from fifty percent to five percent. West Beirut and its suburbs have also been drastically rearranged. The proportion of Christian groups has plummeted to not more than five percent. Conversely, the number of Muslims living, at the end of the conflict, in areas like the eastern suburbs of Beirut and the security zone in the South has also experienced a corresponding decline.
Over twelve years after the end of the conflict and in spite of hundred of millions of dollars spent on compensation and rehabilitation programs, some of them notoriously misappropriated, the most optimistic estimates claim that, on average, no more than 30% of the displaced have returned to their homes. Partial emigration, new lives reconstructed in other parts of the countries, remaining fears, continuing decline of livelihood means in the localities of origin, and other factors explain the limitation of the rate of the return and the more segregated social geography of post war Lebanon.

A Drastic Recomposition of Society

In considering the process of political and socioeconomic reconstruction of Lebanon in the nineties, it is important to keep in mind that the society has been profoundly altered by the war. The changes should not be dismissed as merely a reflection of geographic redistribution or temporary relocations of vital services and functions. Lebanon has undergone nothing short of profound social recomposition. We can no longer assume that it is essentially the same society as in 1975. The forced social mobility has resulted in the decline or even quasi-demise of some classes and the attrition of others. In some instances new strata have emerged. It is thus a profoundly transformed society that formed the basis of this political and economic reconstruction.

One element in this transformation is a major reshuffling of the entrepreneurial class. The pre-war bourgeoisie, or economic upper class – contractors, bankers, international financiers, international traders – has largely left the country. The assets of this potentially powerful group of self-exiled Lebanese – largely transnationalized and redeployed in Western Europe (Paris, London, Athens, Zurich) and in North America – are estimated at somewhere between $10 and $20 billion. Hence, one of the crucial questions of any reconstruction effort has been how, when, and to what extent this pre-war bourgeoisie could be re-attracted to Lebanon either as investors or to relocate at least some of their activities there. While one could not rely largely on or anticipate such likelihood, certainly a fraction of the group's assets would make a significant difference, provided they are channelled through a balanced, rational economic reconstruction plan and not scattered in an unbridled or random fashion. Needless to say, if Lebanon's relocated and transnationalized bourgeoisie would have been induced, for economic or national reasons, to participate in their country's reconstruction, Lebanon's task could have been considerably facilitated. Such prospects would, at the least, mitigate the magnitude of dependence on foreign aid or reliance on international agencies, banks, or Arab countries.

What is certain, however, is that the old entrepreneurial class has been largely replaced by a number of emergent groups inside Lebanon. Most notable among these is what has been called the "Gulf entrepreneurs": a growing nucleus of dynamic contractors returning to Lebanon after amassing quick and large fortunes in the Gulf. The most prominent, of course, is Prime Minister Rafik Hariri. There are, however, others, mostly Shiite émigrés returning from West Africa (Ali Jamal, Jamil Ibrahim, etc.). Added to these are strata of war profiteers and new riches that were associated with the militias.

The rise of new groups has led to a re-equilibration of the sectarian composition of the bourgeoisie, a phenomenon of considerable importance. In 1960, for example, 75 percent of the economic upper class of Lebanon had been Christian and only 25 percent Muslim. By 1975 the gap had already narrowed through various social transformations to reach some 65 percent Christian and 35 percent Muslim. By 1988-89, however, it had become roughly evenly divided between the two major groups.

Thus, while these transformations were underway prior to 1975, they were accelerated by the war. The result was a quasi-complete equilibration of the upper bourgeoisie in its Christian and Muslim components, which is very significant for the overall balance of the country, given the perceived or real disequilibrium between classes and communities in pre-war Lebanon. There was then an overrepresentation of Christians and under-representation of Muslims in the upper classes, while a reverse situation characterized much of the lower classes. The fact that today a very significant segment of the entrepreneurial class is Muslim, with a vested interest in the stabilization of the system and in the development of its economy, may thus be taken in a more positive light.

Another promising byproduct of this burgeoning Christian-Muslim re-equilibration in the upper economic strata is the increased number of associations between Christian and Muslim capital. In a study of the fourteen new banks established between 1975 and 1987, eleven were found to be characterized by religiously-mixed capital. This is a fairly new phenomenon, since most businesses before the war, being largely family enterprises, tended to reflect a single community. Consequently, this may be a reflection of a lesser will to national unity than an appreciation of the need for connections with various groups under the militia system as a prerequisite for operating in the eastern and western sectors. Be that as it may, these new associations became a new tradition, and many new enterprises are now joint sectarian ventures.

Another dimension of this social recomposition – with more grievous implications for the future – has been the attrition of the professional middle class and skilled workforce. Initially, the decline was gradual and hardly visible. As the war system, however, became more widespread and deeply entrenched in society, the attrition assumed a much greater magnitude. According to various estimates, this strategic group represents a very significant proportion of those who have been leaving the country since 1975. Of the estimated 900,000 émigrés – a figure that includes all age groups-about 250,000 –

300,000 would have been active in the workforce. Some 120,000 members of this economically active population are estimated to have been from the professional middle class and highly skilled or technical workforce, including over 30,000 professionals.

This out migration had already seriously endangered the functioning of many major institutions in Lebanon, including universities, where many of the senior faculty has left. Hospitals have lost some of their more competent physicians. The haemorrhage in utilities and large firms has been equally debilitating. If this outflow continues at the same rate, it could lead to the quasi-collapse of the cultural and techno-professional heritage of more than 150 years, a legacy that made Lebanon what it was.

This depletion in the country's most vital resource base, its economic backbone so-to-speak, is bound to have dire consequences. It is, to begin with, largely irreplaceable, or at best replaceable with considerable time and investment. The continuing haemorrhage of this higher stratum of the professional and skilled labour force will also affect what remains of the workforce. The less-qualified technicians, teachers, health workers, etc. are prone to lose much of their own efficiency when left on their own. The results are thus detrimental at two levels: Lebanon is first deprived of two strategic professional sectors and, consequently, suffers a loss in the overall productivity and efficiency of the remaining workforce.

Within this context, one of the major challenges facing post war Lebanon has been to re-attract a significant portion of those professionals and highly skilled workers before they get too settled in the lives and careers they were establishing in the Diaspora. Such re-absorption was essential for expediting the reconstruction and rehabilitation of the country's weakened institutions and infrastructure facilities. These returns were also supposed to restore or infuse the spirit of national consciousness and renew faith in the dynamic role Lebanese can play in the collective effort of rebuilding their own society and national economy. The initial return of several thousands professionals and entrepreneurs was slowed down if not halted, by the mid-nineties, by the combined effects of political clientelism, widespread corruption, limited investment opportunities and economic recession. On the contrary, a new and dangerous wave of brain drain was well underway in the late nineties.

The Inflated State and Unequal Development

For most of the period extending from independence to civil strife (1943-1975), the Lebanese state was mostly an ultraliberal state. It benefited from conflicts and instability in the Middle East and from the advantage Lebanon had relative to the region in educational and cultural terms. But the Lebanese state, except in the reformist period of President Fouad Chehab (1958-1964), did not capitalize sufficiently on this historical opportunity to consolidate its institutional and societal basis, through policies of national integration, social redistribution, and opening up more equal opportunities of education, employment and social mobility.

In the post-conflict decade, the Lebanese state increased dramatically its intervention in the economic and social spheres. Although some state expansion was certainly justified by the requirements of post-war reconstruction, the size and the modalities of state intervention resulted in considerable waste and an unsustainable public sector: the number of state employees rose from 75,000 in 1974 to 175,000 in 2000 or from 9 percent to 14 percent of the total manpower. At the same time, the weight of the state sector, including the servicing of the increasing public debt, reached an all time high of over 42 percent of GDP in 2000, compared to less than 20 percent in 1974 and 23 percent in 1993. As the state grew in size, it was declining in efficiency, because of the aging of the civil servant corps, a considerable vacancy rate in established posts, the practice of hiring a plethora of temporary staff and the war and post war legacy of hiring thousand of persons outside the formal procedure, on the basis of political clientelism and spoil sharing.

There is a clear and urgent need to revert this process and make the necessary adjustments in order to allow country's government and public services to function more efficiently, as without a streamlined and reformed state sector, the country's development and integration into the global economy will be further hampered.

In addition to the need to adjust the role of the state, Lebanon also needs to redress, in a systematic and sustainable manner, the uneven development between regions, social strata, sectors and communities.

Contemporary Lebanon has been and continues to be a land of high social contrasts between levels of resources, modes of consumption and ways of life that are similar to those of privileged strata in advanced societies, and levels of deprivation and lack of opportunities that are similar to those of underprivileged strata in the poorer societies.

Some recent national studies reveal the persistence of serious differences between Beirut and some of the peripheral districts in terms of socio-economic levels and satisfaction of basic needs. A 1998 UNDP study (Mapping of Living Conditions), which ranked geographic regions according to the degree of satisfaction of basic needs, found that over a third of the households were living below the basic needs satisfaction threshold. But in rural and peripheral areas such as Bint Jbeil, Hermel, Akkar, and Marjeyoun this percentage increased to between 60 and 67 percent of households. Social observation, family budget studies, and computation of the Gini coefficient underscore an even wider social gap of one-to-five in terms of income and resource distribution between the higher and lower social strata of the Lebanese society.

The territorial mode of development of contemporary Lebanon has been a macrocephalic, unipolar model with a concentration, in 1975, of more than fifty percent of the population, over two-thirds of the economic activities, two-thirds of the overall employment, the entire state administration, all of the country's higher education, and ninety-five percent of banking activity in the capital, Beirut.

Lebanon's 1975 primacy ratio – comparing the size of the largest city to the combined populations of the three next largest cities – was 2.8, a very high rate. In concrete terms, this means that Beirut (1,200,000) was almost three times larger than the combined population of Tripoli (250,000), Saida (75,000) and Zahleh (65,000). As a result of the vicissitudes of the war, this rate went down to 1.5 in 1990, or half of its 1975 level. The decline of Beirut (1,100,000) and the war related growth of regional poles – not only primary poles such as Tripoli (400,000), Saida (225,000) and Zahleh (100,000), but also secondary poles such as Zouk, Jounieh, Baalbeck, Nabatieh, Zghorta, Tyre, and Baakline, were the result of a number of factors: forced population movements, segmentation of the economic space, and the fact that most of the major phases of armed conflict took place in Beirut, which caused physical damage there far more extensive than elsewhere.

Another indicator of the trend towards de-concentration, linked to the shift away from Beirut, was the relocation of vital functions and services. Local branches of public utilities, universities, and private banks and firms have been established in various regions of the country. Local agricultural production has been revitalized in some areas, and some industries have relocated to different regions. There has also been the emergence of regional commercial networks and services not necessarily passing through Beirut.

These phenomena of forced de-concentration had mixed results: manpower imbalances among regions; redundant, unproductive, and uncompetitive activities and jobs; and the inability to sustain economies of scale in many cases. However, these developments could have been construed as positive and functional in a reconstruction project aiming at correcting the regional and territorial imbalances of pre-war period.

Instead reconstruction activities and the majority of public spending in the nineties have tended to re-concentrate activities and resources around the capital and some areas of central Lebanon and the cost. Based on the priority of rehabilitating or reconstructing existing pre-war public utilities and networks, and in the absence of a territorially based national planning, reconstruction expenditures neglected regions that were poorly equipped before the war. This pattern of regional imbalance is reflected in the following table of distribution of the Council of Reconstruction and Development expenditures in the first half of the post war period:

Table: Committed Reconstruction Expenditures (1992-1998)

	Distribution	Implemented	Under preparation	Not implemented
Beirut and Mount Lebanon	27.0	40.0	32.0	28.0
North Lebanon	8.0	3.2	25.5	71.2
Beqaa	5.5	3.3	12.0	84.7
South and Nabatiye	5.5	3.0	15.0	82.0
National Projects	54.0	50.4	14.8	34.8

Figures in %

Thus, at the end of the reconstruction decade, not only the greater Beirut area was the location of most of the nation wide projects, but it also attracted the majority of the region based projects and had a rate of project implementation ten times higher then that of the other provinces.

This trend translated into a new rise in the urban primacy ratio: Beirut's resident population can be estimated at 1,200,000 in 2000 (which represent the same population level as in 1975), while the resident population of Tripoli was now estimated at 275,000, Saida at 160,000 and Jounieh (now the fourth city before Zahleh) at 65,000. Thus Lebanon's privacy ratio went from 2.08 in 1975, down to 1.5 in 1990 and up again to 2.4. The partial return of some of the forced immigrants, the continuing departure of thousands of Palestinians mainly from the suburbs of Saida and Tripoli, the modalities of the reconstruction process as well as the new waves of out-migration from the poorer regions of the country, all have contributed to the restoration of the pre-1975 territorial macro cephalic mode of development, centred around Beirut.

In the hierarchy of regions, a very significant change was brought about by the social dynamics of the war and post war periods. The provinces of South Lebanon and the Beqaa used to be at the bottom end of the development hierarchy, in terms of income and education status, extent of poverty or access to basic services. Studies of the late nineties revealed that the province of North Lebanon has now fallen to the bottom end. This comparative improvement or deterioration, over the last two decades, could be partly explained by the increased political weight and representation of the Shiia community, translating in increased attention and influx of public aid, in addition to a growing volume of remittances and local investments by the Shiia Diaspora in Africa and the Gulf in their regions of origin in the South and the Beqaa. No equivalent trend benefited North Lebanon, which also suffered from state neglect because of the marginalization of the Northern Sunni political leadership by the increasing preeminence of the Beirut and Saida based Prime Minister Hariri.

The post war trend towards social polarization is very clearly reflected in the comparison between several estimates of the relative distribution between the three lower, middle and higher income groups in Lebanon, before and after the war.

Table: Distribution of Income Groups

	Lower Income	Middle Income	Higher Income
1973	22.0	68.0	10.0
1992	49.5	40.2	10.3
1999	61.9	29.3	8.8

Figures in %

Thus, in the aftermath of the conflict, in 1992, the weight of the middle and higher income groups diminished significantly in comparison with an enlarged lower income group that included now half the population against only one fifth in 1973. This was a clear indication of the degree of pauperization of the Lebanese population brought about by the protracted war. As significant, at the end of a decade of "reconstruction policies", the weight of the lower income group was still increasing to reach 62%, at the expense of a declining middle class, practically halved from 60% to 30% in the last quarter of a century. Several studies in the middle and end of the nineties gave various indications about this increasing pauperization: They found for example that more than 35% of the Lebanese households fall under the poverty line; that the average spending on food in family budgets rose from 26.6% in 1966 to 33.9% in 1997; that the average real wage declined by a cumulative 30% during the nineties; that only 28.3% of the Lebanese had a secure and regular medical insurance; that 46% of the Lebanese live in overcrowded housing, with an average of 4,8 individuals per bedroom, one of the highest in the world; that thousands of families were moving their children out of private schools and universities they could no longer afford into public schools and universities, in spite of their declining levels and quality; that unemployment and hidden unemployment were estimated to have reached over 30% of the labour force at the end of the nineties.

Table: Distribution of Students between School Systems

	Public Sector	Private Sector (Free)	Private Sector (Paying)
1995 - 1996	30.5	13.5	56.0
2000 - 2001	39.0	12.5	48.5

Figures in %

At the macro-economic level, the increased social polarization was manifested also in the decline of the share of wages and the parallel increase of the share of interest in the Lebanese Gross Domestic Product. The share of interests has been estimated at 9% of the GDP in 1990 and 23% in 1998, one of the highest in the world. This reflected the fact that the financing of the reconstruction expenditures was done mainly through high interest treasury bills subscribed predominantly by local banks and Lebanese and Arab financial oligarchs inside and outside Lebanon. Over the last decade, more than 13 billion dollars of interests have been already paid, a costly price for often oversized and unconnected public utilities and equipment projects. The enlarged wealth concentration can also be partially measured by the degree of concentration of deposits in the Lebanese banks: At the end of the nineties, 2% of bank accounts control more than 70% of total bank deposits.

In spite of significant (although costly) investments in the physical infrastructure and public and private construction activities (most spectacularly in the Beirut Central District), the Lebanese society seems to have failed until now to recover its pre-war productive base, to reach an internationally oriented level of competitiveness and productivity, to create a sustained and diversified entrepreneurial dynamism or to achieve an adequate level of social justice and integration. An apparently thriving leisure, food, entertainment and luxury-shopping sector, living of a minority of wealthy Lebanese or vacationers and shoppers from the Gulf cannot hide the fundamental crisis in the real economy, the steady decline in the quality of education, the limited amount of job creation, the high cost of the local factors of production, the continuing deterioration of the environment, the scarcity of investment opportunities or the burden of the public debt.

As long as through sound analysis, sustained dialogue and political commitment, a national consensus on the framework and priorities of a new paradigm for the development of Lebanon would not emerge, the social map will continue to reflect the distorted realities of the post war political economy. Only substantial political and social reforms could help the emergence of a comprehensive and integrated approach to the challenges facing the Lebanese economy and society into the next decades.

They would open the way to a joint project of reinventing Lebanon as a convivial, viable and creative community of the twenty first century.

Bibliography

Administration Centrale de La Statistique, *Conditions de vie des menages au Liban 1997* (Beirut: ACS, 1998).

Council for Development and Reconstruction (ed.), *Progress Reports 1998-2002* (Beirut, no date).

Courbage, Y. and Ph. Fargue, *La situation démographique au Liban* (Beirut: Publications de l'Université Libanaise, 1984).

Dubar, Claude and Salim Nasr, *Les classes sociales au Liban* (Paris: Presses de la Fondation Nationale des Sciences Politiques, 1976).

Faour, Ali, "The Displacement Crisis and Forced Migration in Beirut", in S. Nasr and Th. Hanf (eds.), *Urban Crisis and Social Movement: Arab and European Perspectives* (Beirut: The Euro-Arab Research Group, 1984): pp. 165-173.

Faour, Ali, *Beirut: 1975-1990, Demographic, Social and Economic Transformations* (Arabic) (Beirut: Geographic Institute, 1990).

Fawaz, Leila Tarazi, *Merchants and Migrants in Nineteenth-Century Beirut* (Cambridge, MA: Harvard University Press, 1983).

Feghali, Kamal, "Les déplacés au Liban. Stratégie du retour et développement", in *Lettre d'Information 11, Observatoire de Recherches sur Beyrouth et la Reconstruction*: (Beirut, 1999): pp. 11-18.

Harb el-Kak, Mona, "Toward a Regionally Balanced Development", in *UNDP Conference on Linking Economic Growth and Social Development in Lebanon* (Beirut: United Nations Development Programme, 2000): pp. 117-133.

Hatab, Zouhair, "The Effect of the War on the Structure of the Lebanese Family", in Muntada al-Fikr al-'Arabi, *The Lebanese Crisis: Social and Economic Aspects* (Amman: Conference Proceeding, 1988).

Khalaf, Chemali, Mona, *Youth Unemployment in Lebanon* (Beirut: International Labour Organization, 1998).

Khalidi, Mohammed Ali (ed), *Palestinian Refugees in Lebanon 2002*, (Beirut: Institute for Palestine Studies, 2002).

Labaki, Boutros, "Le Développement Equilibré au Liban", in *Lettre d'Information 11, Observatoire de Recherches sur Beyrouth et la* Reconstruction (1999): pp. 23-26.

Maroun, Ibrahim, "La question des classes moyennes au Liban", in *UNDP Conference on Linking Economic Growth and Social Development in Lebanon* (Beirut: United Nations Development Programme, 2000): pp. 167-183.

Ministry of Social Affairs – United Nations Development Programme, *Mapping of Living Conditions in Lebanon* (Beirut: MOSA-UNDP, 1998).

Ministry of Social Affairs – United Nations Population Fund, *Analytical Studies of Population and Housing Survey*, 6 volumes (Beirut: MOSA-UNFPA, 2000).

Nasr, Salim, "Morphologie sociale de la banlieue-est de Beyrouth", in *Maghreb-Machrek*, no. 73 (Juillet-Septembre 1976): pp. 78-88.

Nasr, Salim, "The Crisis of Lebanese Capitalism", in *MERIP Reports*, No. 73 (1978): 3-13.

Nasr, Salim, "Les formes de regroupement traditionnel (familles, confessions, communautés regionales) dans la société de Beyrouth", in D. Chevalier (ed.), *L'Espace social de la ville arabe* (Paris: Maisonneuve et Larose,1979): pp. 145-99.

Nasr, Salim, "Beyrouth et le conflit libanais. Restructuration de l'espace urbain", in F. Metral (ed.) *Politiques urbaines dans le Monde Arabe* (Paris: Maison de l'Orient, Etudes Sur le Monde Arabe, 1, 1983).

Nasr, Salim, "Guerre, migrations vers le Golfe et nouveaux investissements immobiliers dans le Grand Beyrouth", in CERMOC (ed.) *Migrations et changements sociaux dans l'Orient Arabe*" (Beirut, 1985): pp. 309-330.

Nasr, Salim, "Lebanon's War: Is the End in Sight?", in *MERIP Reports*, No. 162 (1990): pp. 5-8.

Nasr, Salim, *Anatomy of the Lebanese Conflict* (Washington: Conference on Lebanon, American Task Force for Lebanon, 1991).

Nasr, Salim, "New Social Realities and Post-War Lebanon: Issues for Reconstruction", in S. Khalaf and P. Khoury (eds.) *Recovering Beirut. Urban Design and Post-War Reconstruction* (Leiden: E. J. Brill, 1993): pp. 63-80.

National Human Development Report – Lebanon 2001-2002, *Globalization: Towards A Lebanese Agenda* (Beirut: UNDP, 2002).

Safa, Elie, *L'Emigration Libanaise* (Beirut: Université St. Joseph, 1960).

The Deepening Cleavage in the Educational System

Munir Bashshur

Introduction

In his speech a few days ago, on Army's Day, August 1, 2002, the President of the Lebanese republic General Lahhoud expressed his opinion as to what he thinks is wrong in the Lebanese situation, using the following words:

> "We are a collection of confessional entities sharing among ourselves benefits and privileges. When the State gains the upper hand, we unite against it to bring it down; when the State becomes weaker, we enter into a fight among ourselves bringing the nation down".[1]

The symmetry is made perfectly clear in the statement of the President: the State (and the Nation) on the one hand and confessional groups on the other. Conceptually speaking and in an abstract sense the statement has elements of beauty, but tested on the ground of reality it fails the test miserably. And this is for a simple reason that everybody knows, viz. that the State and religion in Lebanon have never been separated, and relationships between the two sides have never been counteractive, as the statement suggests, one opposed to the other, but rather interactive and complex. In a more practical sense it can be said that confessional groups inhabit the State or, more specifically, that the government frequently behaves like a conglomerate of religious or confessional interest groups. But even this is a simplification of the picture, for the fact is that, quite often, what is contested is the same old commodities of power and influence, which are variably distributed among the population, and in their drive to gain more of such commodities, contestants use religion as a convenient tool, sometimes bluntly and crudely, and other times in association with other tools such as money, or external pressure.

Rather than becoming embroiled into this discussion, what I want to do is to take note of the symmetry that the statement of the President suggests and move forward to talk about what has been happening in the country in the field of education in the last ten or twelve years. For illustration, I will take four case studies or stories – the first two

---

1 *An-Nahar* 2/8/2002

have to do with curriculum changes since Taif: one in the area of teaching of religion and the other in the area of teaching of history. The other two will deal with changes in the area of higher education, the first will focus on private institutions, and the second on the Lebanese State University. In all cases the theme I'll be developing is that of the breakdown or the disintegration of the mechanism of the State as a controlling or a guiding force vis-a-vis the influence of other groups mainly, but not exclusively, religious groups.

As a background, it is important to say that the Taif Agreement of 1989 covered educational matters in five points. Among these are "...revising school curricula... unifying textbooks in history and civics", "...safeguarding private education and strengthening State supervision over private schools", and "... reforming (and supporting) Lebanese State University".

In the area of curriculum revision a major project was started in 1993 dealing with changes in the educational structure as well as with the content of various subjects in all grades at the pre-university level. The results were included in a curriculum document approved by the cabinet on May 8, 1997 (Presidential Act No. 10227). This document has been taken since as the guideline for producing new textbooks and teaching material for all twelve grades, starting with 1997/98 and ending with 2000-2001. This year 2001-2002 is the first year when students sat for Baccalaureate exams based totally on the new curriculum.

Teaching of Religion

The old curriculum had one hour per week for religion, the teaching of which was left in the hands of religious authorities who would choose teachers for this hour and the government pays their salaries. More significant is that students were segregated during teaching, Christians would be exempted from attending classes when Islam is taught and conversely Muslims exempted when Christianity is the subject.

The new curriculum removed this one hour from the curriculum and left religion as a subject to be taught voluntarily in after hours, or on Fridays and Sundays depending on the wish of the parents.

It is to be mentioned that the new curriculum was to be mandatory only for government schools, which meant that private schools, many of which belong to religious associations, could remain free to include religion in their programs and teach it the way they wish. Total number of students in government schools has been in the range of 40% of the total, and the remainder in private schools.

As soon as word of the new curriculum came out, lobbying against it started in a concerted fashion. The opposition came not from one, but from all religious quarters, Christians and Moslems. No other issue except that of civil marriage, had unified all religious groups behind it to the extent that this one did. Even before the new curriculum was approved religious luminaries were quoted attacking the decision. Bishop of Beirut

Paul Matar said the following: *"Religion should be taught in the official curriculum so that students will grow believing in one God"* (March 17, 1997). Al-Sheikh Moh. Hussein Fadlallah: *"Government plan (to make religion an optional subject) aims to abolish religious education all together"* (March 17, 1997); Al-Mufti Moh. Rasheed Kabbani: *"Making religion an optional subject outside the official curriculum is in effect deleting it depriving new generations from religious and ethical guidance..."*(April 1, 1997); Al-Sheikh Moh. Mahdi Shamseddin: *"Requesting the State to reinstate religious instruction in government and private schools and including grades received in religion in determining success or failure of students in exams..."* (June 30, 1997); Bishop Roland Abou Jaoudi, spokesman for Maronite Patriarch : *"... we are against the plan to restrict teaching of religion in government schools to Fridays and Sundays as these are holidays for Moslems and Christians, and both are united in demanding that teaching of religion be on working days..."*[2]

The campaign became more heated as time went on, and instead of individual pronouncements or declarations, it began to take a more organized fashion where representatives of different religious groups would hold meetings, make official visits and appear together in press conferences. On September 9, 1998 an inter religious delegation appeared in a meeting with PM Hariri. The spokesman of the group Sheikh Taha Sabounji declared that, *"...discussion was on religious education after the cabinet made this an optional subject. We started our meeting with complaints and ended offering our thanks... the PM assured us that the question will be taken up in the up-coming cabinet meeting, and that he is in full support with our request as religious education is the foundation stone for the social, ethical and ideological existence of Lebanon..."*. The meeting included, in addition to Sabounji himself representing the Sunni Mufti, Mg. Aad Abi Karam representing the Maronite Patriarch, Father Hanna Dagher representing the Catholic Bishop, Al-Mufti Ghaleb Al-Usaili representing the Shiite Islamic Council, Father George Dimas representing the Greek Orthodox Bishop, Sheikh Marcel Nasr representing the Druze Council, among others.[3] A few weeks later, the Minister of Education, John Obeid, was visited by the same delegation with some replacements; their spokesman, Sheikh Sabounji declared that, *"we came to offer thanks to the Minister, and also to the Prime Minister for their support in the last cabinet meeting, for reinstating religion as a subject in the Curriculum... They were all loyal to their religion, and to the new generations..."*.[4]

It seems the support of the Minister and the Prime Minister did not produce immediate results, for we still find pronouncements, visitations and declarations in support of reinstating religious education. In early June 1999, Sheikh Shamsuddin received a delegation including university representatives, as well as Moslem delegates, and a declaration came out of the meeting emphasizing: *"the necessity of retracting the earlier deci-*

---

2   Quotations are from *Al-Marqab* Magazine (Fall 1998), published by the Center for Christian-Islamic Studies, University of Balamand.
3   *An-Nahar* 19/9/1998
4   *An-Nahar* 7/10/1998

sion to remove religion from the official curriculum and instead make it a basic component of it, with the understanding that selection, appointment and dismissal of teachers of religion should be in the hands of Christian and Moslem religious authorities, and that the State should carry the (financial) burden in the same manner that it does in supporting health, sport and civic associations in the country."[5] A few days later, a report appeared about a meeting of a Christian/Moslem delegation with the Minister of Education (a new one: Moh.Y. Beydoun), this time in the presence of officials in the Ministry of Education and the head of the Center for Educational Research and Development to discuss "*...reinstating religion in the curriculum, and exchanging views regarding some practical matters, ...and the Minister promised to bring these to the attention of the cabinet*".[6]

It seems more time was needed for further pressure. Then in November 12, 1999 we read that the cabinet in its meeting the day before had taken a decision to reinstate religious education in the official curriculum as it was before, for one hour per week, pointing out at the same time the need for a unified textbook in religion that the Center for Research and Development will be asked to prepare."[7] The decision was received with jubilant words from Mufti Kabbani and Sheikh Shamsuddin.

The decision, however, did not bring the story to an end; for it seems that the Center for Research and Development did not feel comfortable with this new assignment, and efforts to produce a unified book for religion did not go far. Soon afterwards we hear of talk about two books instead of one, and we learn of another decision taken by the Cabinet, on October 10, 2000, stating that the students will have: "one book for Moslems and another for Christians for each of the nine grades of the Basic education cycle, while for the secondary cycle there will be one book for both...". We also learn that on March 12, 2001, a committee of twelve persons was appointed to produce these books under the supervision and guidance of the Educational Research Center. But after a few meetings this committee asked for a time period of three years during which, "Christian sects and groups will endeavor to produce a unified Christian book, and Moslem sects will do the same..."[8]

The present picture is very confusing; so far no "unified books" are in hand on either side Christian or Moslem. The one clear achievement is that the hand of the government was forced down, and that under the combined pressure of Christian and Moslem clerics it had to rescind an earlier decision that it had made in 1997 regarding the subject matter of religion as part of a total curriculum package whose elements were carefully balanced and justified.

In a long interview with the Minister of Education (Murad: the third minister since the issue erupted) towards the end of 2001, the following dialogue was reported:[9]

---

5 *Al-Hayat* 6/6/1999
6 *An-Nahar* 30/6/1999
7 *An-Nahar* 12/11/1999
8 *An-Nahar* 12/3/2001
9 *An-Nahar* 1/11/2001

Q – *There are stories that the new curricula are not under proper evaluation, and that religious authorities are interfering...*

A – *No, religious authorities do not interfere; all what they are asking is that there should be one unified book for religion in Moslem schools and another one in Christian schools, and this is necessary and legitimate...*

Q – *What would you do with schools, which have mixed students?*

A – *Let the Christians learn in the Christian book and the Moslem in the Moslem book, each separately. There will be one book in one of the school grades which will concentrate on the common beliefs in both religions.*

Teaching of History

It is to be recalled that the Taif agreement had five points on education, and that the fifth one in the list had to do with revision of curricula and national unity with specific focus on civics, national education and history. That fifth point went as follows:

"Revision and development of curricula in such a manner as to strengthen national attachment and integration, encourage spiritual and cultural openness, together with unification of textbooks in the two subject matter areas of history and national education".

This same statement appeared as one of the goals in the "Plan for Educational Revival", which was approved by the Cabinet of Ministers on August 17, 1994.

One month later, the Center for Educational Research and Development (CERD) which is in charge of school curricula – had a new president appointed to it who went into the task of curriculum revision in full speed assembling a work team of some 350 persons divided into various groups and committees. First, the structure of the educational system was targetted and a new "ladder" was produced and approved by the Cabinet on October 25, 1995. Soon afterwards a plan with specific curriculum targets was produced and announced by the President of the Republic in a festive celebration attended by the Prime Minister, the Speaker of the Parliament and the three Ministers of Education. Subject matter committees began working on revisions and modifications; committees for all subjects were appointed and approved. The subject matter of history was singled out and delegated to a special committee including in its composition a carefully chosen team representing various religious/political groups. The work of this committee and its deliberations were handled almost like a state secret. Rumours leaked about arguments and conflicts among its members, and about resignations and reshuffling of membership, and when a copy of the new national curriculum was completed and submitted for government approval (which was obtained on May 8, 1997) all subjects were included, but not history.

It took exactly three years after that for the Cabinet to receive and approve a document entitled "General Principles and Specific Goals of the Teaching of History" – approved on May 10, 2000. When made public it soon became clear that it was a very tamed, desensitized, some would say emasculated document. And to be produced, clothed in the most carefully guarded and benign language, it took more than fifty meetings of a committee of six.[10] When finally presented to the press on May 10, 2000 only one member of the committee out of six had stayed with it from the beginning; all other five were either replaced or they resigned.[11]

We do not know why five of the six members were replaced or resigned. Two of the five had articles published in the press before the document became public, one in 1998 by A. Hoteit,[12] and the other by H. Moneimneh in 1999.[13]

Moneimneh's paper (1999), was described as one of individual papers that each of the committee members was requested to submit to guide its deliberations. Its author said that the committee did finally arrive at a joint paper which when it was sent for approval by a higher committee in CERD, it was returned for modifications. When the history committee refused to introduce modifications it, according to Moneimneh, was dissolved, and a new one appointed in its place.

Moneimneh's paper had all the characteristics of an academic treatise, debating matters that can hardly be controversial, such as the pedagogical advantages to be drawn from history as a school subject, historical authenticity, history and collective memory, and boundaries of inclusion, and similar matters. Hoteit's paper, on the other hand, was more informative as to events and proceedings. He reports that the joint paper agreed upon by the committee included one part on general objectives of history teaching, and another on objectives of teaching the history of Lebanon. Hoteit reports that it was on the second set of objectives dealing with Lebanon that the Higher Committee had objections hence returning the paper for modification. When this did not happen the history committee, or rather five of its six members were replaced.

We are fortunate to have in Hoteit's article part of the text of the joint paper that was submitted by the history committee (and returned for modification), as it gives us the chance to compare with the text that was finally approved by the Cabinet and issued on May 10, 2000. We will take from the original joint paper objectives that had to do with the teaching of the history of Lebanon (as these were the cause for the disagreement) – and they are four :

No. 1 – "Strengthening and deepening patriotic feelings based on the belief that Lebanon is a final homeland for all its people, and that it is Arabic in affiliation and identity, and that loyalty and identification with it as a country are essential. Likewise commitment to its causes and taking pride in it, so that a unified national outlook will emerge rooted in the political consciousness of the Lebanese with regard to

---

10 As reported by a member of the Committee (Hassan Muneimneh) in an article published in An-Nahar on 5/5/1999. Another member (Ahmad Hoteit) gives a total of 56 meetings (in *Al-Marqab* magazine Fall 1998). The President of CERD, M. Abou Asli reports a total of 1600 working hours (in an interview he gave in *An-Nahar* Annex, no. 280 – 8 –14/9/1998). Mr. Abou Asli's figure in hours appears to be an approximation of number of committee members multiplied by number of meetings and the average length of each meeting.

11 An-Nahar 20/5/2000

12 أحمد حطيط, "علمية كتاب تاريخ لبنان بين أزمة المنهج وهاجس التوحيد", مجلة المرقب, جامعة البلمند, العدد الثاني خريف 1998

13 حسن منيمنة, "مشروع (رفض) للمبادئ والأهداف العامة لتدريس التاريخ", النهار 1999/5/5

their Lebanese/Arab heritage and their Arab culture, reinforcing their unity as a nation rather than co-existing as religious groups".

No. 2 – "Deepening pride in Lebanese identity and in its Arab character, revealing solid connection between Lebanon and other Arab states, by cultivating Arab national feelings in the minds of its youth through textbook materials and teaching/learning activities. This is because Lebanese identity did not emerge from the void but is product of historical development and cultural heritage, making it essential that Arab history, ancient, middle as well as modern, is to be given attention and care."

No. 3 – "Commitment to Arab culture and highlighting the part played by the Lebanese in it, opening up to world cultures and human values, and recent discoveries, so as to contribute to the development of these cultures, enriching them and deriving sustenance from them."

No. 4 – "... that Christianity and Islam are basic sources for ideals and human values which run counter to political behaviour which aims at separating believers of one religion from believers in another, and that sectarianism is first and foremost an attack on principles and ideals of both Christianity and Islam and also on the ground roots of national unity."

The second document, which was approved by the Cabinet, also had a list of objectives for the teaching of Lebanese history. Comparing these with the four mentioned in Hoteit's original paper might give us a clue as to why the original paper was returned for revision, and, in addition, may shed some light on the whole business of historical writing.

In comparing, the first point that stands out is that the final version had eight main objectives for the "teaching of Lebanese history", three of which were broken down into sub-objectives, which makes the total number fourteen, as compared with four in the original. The final version turns out to be not only longer and more elaborate but, in terms of inclination, as cognizant as the original of Lebanon's (Arab) affiliation, and equally attentive to the need for Christian/Moslem accommodation. If anything, the final version does all the above using less "ideological" language than that in the original. Here are some specific points:

Objective No. 1, in the original is stated differently in the final version, which combines No. 1 and No. 2 and reads as follows:

"Deepening pride in the student's national identity and strengthening the feeling of loyalty towards Lebanon, and emphasizing the unity of the Lebanese rather than co-existence of religious groups, strengthening awareness of Lebanese identity and its Arab affiliation through highlighting common historical, geographic, human and cultural heritage in different ages, and cultivation of national and Arab feelings in the soul of our youth."

Objective No. 3, in the original, "committed to Arab culture..."was deleted from the section on "general objectives" and moved to that dealing with "objectives at the secondary level", with some modifications.

Objective No. 4, in the original (on Christianity and Islam) was entered as No. 1 in the final version, but after considerable revisions. It read in the final version as follows:

"Considering that Christianity and Islam are basic sources for ideals and human values which run counter to (so far, no changes, but then instead of the phrase: *"political behaviour which aims at separating believers of one religion from believers in another"* the new version continues to say...) *all forms and shapes of religious and sectarian fanaticism"*, (and then instead of the phrase: *"... sectarianism is first and foremost an attack on principles and ideals of both Christianity and Islam and also on the ground roots of national unity..."* (it goes on to say...) *"Exploitation of sectarianism is an attack on principles and ideals of both Christianity and Islam and on their values, and is also diminution of national unity and common life."*

Aside from these modifications, which are essentially attempts to tone down some expressions, the approved version adds new items, which were not included in the original. These include:

Objective No. 3: "Connecting the history of Lebanon to its unified geography ..."meaning that the history of "all" Lebanon not only "parts" of it should be taught; No. 5, referring to the "negative effects of conflicts among the Lebanese...", No. 6, which calls for "recognition of the role of foreign interventions and the influence of foreign countries on the course of events..." and benefiting from such knowledge to " strengthen feelings of common Arab destiny and appreciating the importance of Arab solidarity in the face of such interventions...", and finally objective No. 8, on the "Zionist danger" (which was not mentioned in the original paper).

The language and terminology in the final approved version was certainly milder than that in the original and it was, as we said before, equally attentive to all points and concerns that the four objectives in the original paper had. We have no way of knowing what viewpoints or arguments were exchanged during the long period of the work of the history committee (three years), and what caused change in membership, and more significantly, what reasons prevented the original committee from adopting modifications as requested by a higher one – particularly as the final version which was adopted by the higher committee seems to be a "better" one. All of such things can only be explained, perhaps, in the very peculiar way in which Lebanon's committees and individuals work!

Once announced on May 20, 2000, what remained to be done was perhaps more difficult, namely to translate these objectives into concrete teaching tools i.e. textbooks. In the meantime textbooks in all other subject matter areas were already issued and distributed to schools starting with the academic year 1997/98. Textbooks in history had to wait until 2001, when the first batch was produced.

The first batch included two textbooks under the title "A Window unto History", one for grade 2 and another for grade 3 elementary. Almost immediately after these books were distributed a campaign against them broke out. The attack focused on chapter 11 in the 3rd grade book, which dealt with independence. It had the title: "They all went and Lebanon stayed: independence of the nation.", and used a time line to show various peoples and states which occupied Lebanon at different points in time. When it came to the Arab period it referred to it with the words "Arab conquest" "احتفلي العرب" (p. 88). The words were immediately picked up and interpreted by some as equating the Arabs with other conquerors, and since the title used was that they "all went and Lebanon stayed ..."this meant that Lebanon was not an Arab country". The attack was spearheaded by a member of the parliament, a neurologist form Beirut. "... I have read the first chapters in the book and was surprised to see chapters which were different from history as we know it... it is true that Lebanon stayed, but it remained as an Arab country... a feature which is prevalent today and stressed in the Taif accord."[14] Almost immediately the Center for Educational Research and Development (CERD) issued a statement saying that page 88 in the book where mention was made of the Arab conquest will be removed, as "some interpreted this to mean that authors of the book classified the Arab conquest as similar to other occupations that the country has had... The questions found at the end of the chapter and the accompanying photos... prove the authors positive intentions."[15] In an interview with the Minister of Education, a few days later, he declared that the draft of the textbook was not submitted to him, or to any higher official, before it went to press. "...we are concerned with history textbooks and want them to be produced quickly, but we do not accept writings that declare that the Arabs were expelled from Lebanon... I had asked that the draft be submitted to me before printing but I have seen the book only after 70 thousand copies of it were printed..."[16] In another statement released by CERD a few days later, the readers were informed that "... in order to avoid further controversy the Center upon the request of the Minister had deleted the page under criticism in the book with assurances that it will be changed in future copies."[17]

So as a conclusion we can say that after more than twelve years since the Taif Accord, the teaching of history in the country remains as it has always been: subject to the interests and shifts of different groups, and that agreement to unify curricula and textbooks as a means to unify the people have produced nothing new, except more of the same debate and casuistry that goes as far back in the history of the country as the framing of the Lebanese constitution in 1926.[18]

---

14 *Daily Star* 24/10/2001
15 Ibid
16 *An-Nahar* 1/11/2001
17 *An-Nahar* 5/11/2001
18 In the 2nd session of the Parliament to debate the constitution (held on May 20, 1926), the following exchange took place on the interpretation of Article 10 of the constitution, dealing with "the rights of the religious communities to establish their own schools provided they follow rules and regulations issued by the State..."
Yusuf Al-Khazen: ... *"and what is meant by provided they follow rules and regulations issued by the State...?"*

Higher Education – Private

In a reply to a question after a Cabinet meeting on March 13, 1996, in which Michelle Eddé, Minister of Culture and Higher Education at that time submitted requests for licensing a large number of new private college and universities, Mr. Eddé responded by saying: "what can I do, if most applicants for new colleges and universities happen to come from the ranks of the non-secular...?"[19]

The number of institutions that Minister Eddé had carried to that meeting included: three new universities (one Shiite, another Sunni and a third Catholic), plus converting two colleges into full fledged universities, and expanding the number of colleges and institutes in existing universities and establishing new ones independently of universities – some thirtyfive in total, all in all. The request was met with angry opposition from a number of cabinet ministers, particularly from W. Jumblat who described the attempt as a "national catastrophe", and that it was simply an "apportionment among confessional groups."[20] That meeting ended with a decision to postpone the request for further study.

Shortly afterwards, the debate spilled over to the public. The head of the Shiite Supreme Council, late Sheikh Shamsuddin, declared in a speech a few days later, on March 29, 1996, that *"the Shiites do not have a project of their own; their project is that of a united Lebanon: one people and one state... The Islamic University is open for all, and is not a substitute for the Lebanese State University... If we are to strengthen higher education in the country we need not stop private colleges and universities, but rather raise standards... otherwise we should close all universities starting with the American and the Jesuit and develop the State University, then in that case the application of the Islamic University for a license will be withdrawn."*[21] At about the same time I. Hazeem, the Greek Orthodox Patriarch, was making a similar statement, and said on 28/3/1996: *"We are not opening a school for the Orthodox only... it is not true that we in the University of Balamand, add one drop of confessionalism or sectarianism to what is happening in other places... We are not a tribe, and we do not work as such... We do not discriminate."*[22] The head of the Hikmeh Institute Father P. Akl declared, a few weeks later, *"The University (Al-Hikmeh) is already licensed de facto... whether they say yes or they say no, we consider ourselves a University... I only notify them."*[23]

It took about half a year after that for the storm to subside, and on October 5, 1996

Shibl Dammous: ..."*it means unification of curricula of schools in the subject of sciences only...*"
Georges Zwayn: ..."*it means that the government issues certificates and lays down curricula for unification of education so that all schools will benefit...*" Yusuf Al-Khazen: ..."*The text is vague... all what it contains is against freedom which is in the text...*" انظر يوسف قزما خوري, البيانات الوزارية اللبنانية ومناقشاتها في مجلس النواب , المجلد الثالث 196.

19 *As-Safir* 15/3/1996
20 *As-Safir* 14/3/1996
21 *An-Nahar* 30/3/1996
22 *As-Safir* 29/3/1996
23 *As-Safir* 24/6/1996

five presidential Decrees were entered into the official Gazette, the last of which, No. 9278, approving all the requests for new colleges and universities that Minister Edde had requested earlier on March 13, 1996.

As for the remaining four Decrees, it is interesting that one of them, No. 9274, set criteria and conditions for establishing new universities and colleges or expanding old ones. Such criteria did not exist before. The other three Decrees (9275, 9276 and 9277) specified conditions for the study of law, medicine and engineering in the country and abroad.[24]

The claim about issuing all these Decrees at once, including the controversial one licensing new colleges and universities, was that the country was supposed to have turned a page in its legal history and that, henceforward, the hand of the government shall not be forced down. The new law detailing conditions and criteria was supposed to take care of that.

It is difficult to know whether cabinet ministers and other politicians and intellectuals, who had strongly opposed licensing new institutions a few months before accepted the government's line, but surprisingly not a word of protest came out this time. To the already existing eight private universities, two new ones were added (Antonine University and Beirut Islamic University), one was promoted from the status of a college to that of a university (Lebanese American University), and a number of new colleges and institutes were added to existing universities and others were licensed outside universities. Some of these were already operating without an official license and the new Decree, No. 2978 licensing new institutions "corrected" their status.

1996 was supposed to be a turning point as we said; henceforward all new developments will have to be strictly controlled by the new criteria and regulations.

But three years later, two new Decrees were issued, No. 1947 and No. 1948 (December 21, 1999) adding to the list of universities one more (Al-Jinan in Tripoli), converting Al-Hikmeh Institute into a University, and licensing nine new institutes outside universities, most of them for technical studies, and some in association with institutes or universities in other countries (mostly France and Canada). One year later, in 2000, a number of new Decrees were issued again, adding to the list four new universities: American University of Technology (Decree 2143 dated January 14, 2000), American University for Science and Technology, and Hawaii University (Decree 3585 dated August 7, 2000), and the forth one: the Arab Open University (Decree 3257 dated June 22, 2000). In addition, six new institutes were licensed the same year. In the following year, 2001, the Lebanese International University was licensed (Decree 5294 dated April 9, 2001) whose Board of Directors is headed by the present Minister of Education.[25]

No one seems to have remembered the criteria and conditions set in 1996 regulating

---

24 *Official Gazette* No. 51 for the year 1996
25 This last university located in Biqa', had an interesting name change; it was labeled Lebanese/Syrian when first foundation stone was laid in Biqa'. It later changed its name to Biqa' University (reportedly after Syrian objection to the original name), but when finally licensed it was given a new name: Lebanese International, with two branches, one in Biqa' and another in Beirut.

the opening of new institutions and universities. There were debates and complaints and objections, but none of it had to do with criteria and laws already issued a few years back, and whether these new institutions qualified. The complaints were directed at large: at the open door policy that the government seems to have adopted under pressure of forces on the ground, which had increasingly become an amalgam of confessional/and business interests. Beginning with 1998, what was almost a total monopoly of religious forces has now been joined by commercial interests and private individuals competing for profit. These complaints were particularly poignant as they were made at a time when the conditions of the State University were deteriorating further.

Early in 2001, an interview with the Minister of Education produced the following exchange:[26]

Q – Regarding university education, the number of private universities has become too big, do you agree?

A – The number is very encouraging.

Q – You think Lebanon can take this number?

A – Yes, and more. We have to support the Lebanese University first... but (other) universities have to be supported as well, because they constitute a treasure to Lebanon.

Q – But they are all sectarian.

A – Schools are also sectarian. This is our life. Do you think a Moslem Missionary can open a school in Kisirwan, for example? How do we get the schools to mix when such a mixture does not exist among the people? Sectarianism is not born in the schools; it exists in the media, clubs and associations. Briefly, it is in the laws.

It was a blunt statement coming from a Minister who thrives on a reputation of a secular Arab nationalist.

A few months later, a fellow's Cabinet member, the Minister of Culture Ghassan Salameh, made the following comments:[27]

"A government policy which supports a situation in higher education where one university, the State University includes 2/3 of the total number of students and, on the other hand, a government which grants in one Cabinet meeting Licences to nineteen private institutions – boutiques, which call themselves universities – where the remaining 1/3 of students pursue their studies – whose number had reached now fortyone private universities. ...is this globalization? This is nonsense... I hope Darwin's law will apply to these institutions soon so that they shrink in number..."

Until Minister Salameh's wish comes true, if it ever will, we'd do well to contemplate the story that the following Table (No. 1) summarizes, regarding the number of students enrolled in different institutions of higher learning in the country.

---

26 *An-Nahar* 21/1/2001
27 *An-Nahar* 1/10/2001

Table 1: Total Number of Students in Different Universities 1993/94 – 2000/01

	1993/94 N	(%)	1998/99 N	(%)	2000/01 N	(%)
Lebanese University:	36,503	(48.8)	59,728	(58.9)	71,050	(59.5)
Private Universities:						
1. Arab University	15,418		11,356		8,866	
2. A.U.B.	4,935		4,700		5,511	
3. U.S.J	5,563		6,667		7,696	
4. Kaslik	2,420		3,815		4,230	
5. L.A.U.	4,079		4,292		4,360	
6. N.D.U.	1,709		2,966		3,563	
7. Balamand	1,086		1,795		2,033	
Total	35,210	(47.1)	35,595	(35.1)	36,259	(30.3)
8. Other Private:	3,097	(4.1)	6,117	(6.0)	12,178	(10.2)
Total Private	38,307	(51.2)	41,712	(41.1)	48,437	(40.5)
TOTAL	74,810	(100.0)	101,440	(100.0)	119,487	(100.0)

Source: Statistical bulletins for relevant years, Center for Educational Research and Development.

The Lebanese State University

The previous Table (No. 1) shows that in a short period of seven years, the number of students in the Lebanese University almost doubled (from 36,503 to 71,050). Its share of the total also rose from a little less than half in 1993/94 to almost 60% of the total in 2000/01.

The growth pattern has mirrored the convulsions and tensions in the flow of events in the country very clearly. A turning point came in 1977, a couple of years after the war started, when a Decree was issued, known as the "Branching Decree" – No. 122, allowing for the establishment of university units, or branches in Beirut or other Mohafazats. A year later another Decree No. 810 was issued on January 5, 1978, defining duties and responsibilities of "Directors" of branches giving recognition, at the same time, to branches that had already been operating by force of events. A heated debate immediately broke out between two ideological camps: the "unionists", who opposed the branching policy as it would, in their views, cause partitioning of the country, and the "liberalists" who gave priority to independence and freedom of choice. The first camp was filled mostly by Moslems, and the second almost completely by Christians. With time it became clear that the process of branching was unstoppable – the number of branches quickly became 31 in 1982/83 only five years after the controversial law. Opponents soon realized that they were maybe missing the boat, and began pressuring for branches in their own areas. Though the slogan of "national unity" did not disappear completely, it was soon muffled or sidelined in favour of new ones, such as "regional development" or "equality"...

The number of branches stands now at 47 (71,050 students in total – in 2000/01), 13 in Beirut West (33% of total), and 13 in Beirut East (25% of total), eight in the North, seven in the South, and six in the Biqa', with a percentage of 16.6, 13.4 and 12.0 of the total number of students consecutively. Obviously, the number has become too big for any one campus, but the question of merging or not and which branches with which, where and how, remains one of the most contentious to this day.

On the surface "branching" is not all bad, as it does indeed open up opportunities for higher education to segments of the population who never had a chance, particularly in the outlying areas, and particularly for females.[28] Such an advantage disappears almost totally, when looked at in terms of standards or efficiency, as evidenced particularly in faculty hiring practices, or duplicating fields of study. In terms of social political associations, branching is frequently used as a high road for extracting benefits by local chieftains, and for reinforcing confessional/tribal loyalties. *"From the beginning..."* says one professor of sciences at the Lebanese University, *"confessional considerations and regional ones accompanied the establishment of the branches, leading to hiring of teachers as well as all branch administrators and workers exclusively from among followers of those chieftains who have political dominance in the region".*

The same professor goes on to say: *"Second branches (in the eastern parts of Beirut and the adjacent mountain areas), were and continue to be 'purely Christian' in terms of administrators, teachers and employees. From the beginning they could not contract one single professor on a full time basis who was not Christian, or maybe they did not want to... The same maybe said about First branches (in the Western parts of Beirut), which have been behaving in the same way, and the very few non-Moslems in them are left overs from pre-branching times, and they will soon disappear..."*

The professor concludes by saying: *"all these recent developments had nothing to do with the wish of one person or the other, or in accordance with a policy or a decision taken by one university body or another; all of it briefly is nothing other than a reflection of the political/religious balance of power in the various districts and localities..."*[29]

Polarization of the students clinches the story in a more dramatic way. An empirical research conducted in 1997 on a random sample of 3rd year students of the Lebanese University taken from all its branches and fields of study, reported the following distribution by religion, together with their responses to questions on some key issues. This is summarized in the following Table (No. 2)

Moslems predominate in all five branches except one, which is Beirut II (East) where Christians predominate; among the Moslems the Shiites are the majority in Beirut I

---

28 The share of the Biqa' and South branches of students has been consistently rising out of the total from 19.1% in 1993/94 to 23.4% in 1998/99 to 25.4% in 2000/01. In this last year 2000/01, female students constituted 61.2% of the total number of students in all branches.

29 علي دعيبس, "الفروع المطيّفة, كيف تتكامل ", النهار 1999/9/17

(West) and in the South, while the Sunnis are the majority in the North and in the Beqa'.

Among the Christians the Maronites are the majority and their heaviest concentration is in Beirut II (East). The one branch which has a more balanced representation than others is that of the North where Moslems do constitute the majority (about 2/3) but the remaining 1/3 of the Christians are more evenly divided between Maronites and Orthodox.

The religious polarization is clearly reflected in the responses students give to each of the three questions. There is almost a perfect alignment between these responses and the religious sects students belong to, on the one hand, and between these responses and the university branch in which they are enrolled, on the other.

While the majority on the "Eastern" side were happy to remain separate and "free" in their own branches, the government at the Center, and the remnants of "unionists" in the West, were not, and hence were always looking for ways to bring the Eastern elements into the fold. Various moves and demands were made at different times. A recent and one of the more significant decisions was made by the Cabinet in its meeting on May 10, 2001 to appoint a special ministerial committee to look into ways and means of unifying branches in Greater Beirut area i.e., branches in Beirut I (West), and in Beirut II (East). A couple of days later the press picked up discussions of what happened in that Cabinet meeting. It was said that the President of the Republic personally put forth the proposition remarking that, *"it is important that the University be united, so that it becomes a national university ... it should follow in the steps of the army which* (had fallen into divisions and...) *brought into unity in 1990, after it was segmented into different factions. The same should be done in the University, to bring about national integration..."*[30]

The decision was immediately met with protests and demonstrations on the East side. Even on the West side not all reactions were supportive, but reasons there were more often technical, citing the difficulty of attending to all students in one place before buildings of the new Campus are completed. The most serious objections however remained in the contest of religious dissonance. Boutros Labaki, Vice Chairman of the Board of Development and Reconstruction, put it succinctly when he said, *"... requests for unification could, very frankly, be simply a means of sectarian persecution..."*.[31] Maronite Patriarch Sfeir, expressed the same idea by saying, *"there are many voices opposed to unifying university branches under the pretext of integrating student groups... We hope these efforts do not produce the opposite... in our judgment integration does not mean unifying all views about all matters and suppressing democracy; it does not mean the dominance of one party, God unwilling ..."*[32]

---

30 *An-Nahar* 12/5/2001
31 *An-Nahar* 21/5/2001
32 *An-Nahar* 28/5/2001

Table 2: Distribution of Lebanese University Students by Religion in the Five Branches (%), and Their Responses to Some Key Questions (1997)*

Religion	Branch					
	Beirut I	Beirut II	North	Biqa'	South	TOTAL
Sunni	22.7	1.0	62.4	41.4	26.2	26.6
Shiite	56.9	0.6	2.7	28.8	63.9	29.3
Druze	11.1	0.3	-	9.0	5.8	5.8
Total Moslem	93.8	1.9	65.0	79.3	91.0	61.7
Maronite	1.4	68.4	15.0	5.4	2.5	22.8
Catholic	0.5	10.0	1.3	5.4	6.6	4.2
Orthodox	1.0	16.1	16.4	8.1	-	8.6
Total Christian	2.9	94.5	32.7	18.9	9.0	35.7
No answer	3.3	3.5	2.2	1.8	-	2.7
TOTAL	100.0	100.0	100.0	100.0	100.0	100.0
	(418)	(310)	(226)	(111)	(122)	(118)
Lebanon is Arab in identity and loyalty						
Agree:	83.9	33.7	70.5	80.2	87.9	
Disagree:	4.8	25.5	8.8	5.0	3.4	
Political sectarianism should be abolished						
Agree:	84.5	44.9	67.6	84.5	85.3	
Disagree:	4.7	26.9	24.6	5.8	3.4	
Change constitution, More power to President						
Agree:	14.1	56.1	31.6	27.3	13.6	
Disagree:	42.7	12.8	35.3	29.3	50.9	

* عدنان الأمين "الجامعة اللبنانية في ظلال العصبية الطائفية" مجلة المرقب، مركز الدراسات المسيحية الاسلامية, جامعة البلمند (1999) العدد (2)

Minister Ghassan Salameh entered the debate with a daring proposal: restructure and transform the present university into a collection of six universities: three in Greater Beirut (one for Sciences, another for Technology and a third for Law and Humanities); then each of the three other Mohafazats will have its own regional university – one in the North, a second in the South, and a third in the Biqa'. All six universities could have a central administration for coordination.[33]

So far, no unification or merging had taken place, and the debate comes and goes.[34]

---

33 *An-Nahar* 29/5/2001
34 It is noteworthy that branches in 4 professional Colleges, which started with 2 branches each, were quietly unified since 1998/99 without much noise, or debate in protestation. These are Colleges of Ag-

In the meantime, new private universities are licensed, and branches of existing ones are opened sometimes in the most unlikely places such as, for example, a new branch of a Catholic university (NDU), in the Shouf region this year.

The Bickering, the Dickering and the Horse-Trading

There is no doubt that the issue of branching and merging is deeply anchored in the fears and anxieties of the various religious/political groups. Such fears and anxieties (and competition for power and dominance) become more pronounced when appointments of senior university administrators are due. We have two occasions, one in the appointment of deans in 1997 and then in 2001, and another in the appointment of a new university president in 2001. The following is a narration of events related to these two occasions:

After the terms of office of the third president, George Tohme came to an end in 1998, that position was filled by a number of Acting Presidents until Asad Diab was appointed as the fourth President in July 1993. A couple of months after that a new group of deans and directors was appointed (September 27, 1993) who remained in office until the end of 1996, when the term of office of ten out of thirteen deans came to an end, and they had to be replaced.

The positions remained vacant for six months until the names of the new deans were declared (June 11, 1997). In a press conference held some seven weeks before that, president Diab went public to say that the delay in appointing the new deans was not caused by university authorities as these did their job, and the University Council had sent names of three candidates for each vacant position as regulations require, but that appointments were delayed because of "...Political interferences in the affairs of the university..."[35] The big surprise however, was that when names of the new deans were finally announced they included the name of a Shiite professor who was appointed to a faculty that, until that time, did not exist (Faculty of Tourism and Hotel Management). The head of the Union of Full-Time Professors, Isam Khalife had the following to say on this event: *"... in order to appoint this new dean the decision was made to establish a new faculty of Tourism without prior knowledge of the University Council and without a study of actual needs of the country... This decision was clearly taken to meet confessional quotas, and had nothing to do with academic matters."*[36]

Three years later the same story was repeated, but this time with double the complications: By mid 2000 the term of deans appointed in 1997 had come to an end, and the

---

riculture, Medicine, Dentistry and Pharmacy; the first 3 are all in East Beirut with one branch each enrolling 239, 680 and 141 students respectively, and the fourth in West Beirut with one branch that has 216 students (in 2000/01). The small size of these Colleges had certainly made it easier for their branches unity (or merge), but more importantly was quality control and attention given to standards as evidences in strict admission tests to these colleges.

35 *As-Safir* 2/4/1997
36 *An-Nahar* Annex 5/4/1997

wheels of fortune had to churn again. But then, a few months later, in November of the same year, President Diab, whose term had also come to an end, was appointed Minister of Social Affairs in a new Hariri cabinet, and a replacement had to be found for him as well. This took precedence over that of appointing new deans, and a situation of total limbo ensued, with deans waiting to be replaced, knowing that this will have to wait until a new president is appointed. In the meantime all university councils and boards were practically frozen, all headed by an Acting President. The only parts, which were still active in the whole structure, and in fact became more aggressive, were the "branches" with their Directors, who felt free to manage their branches as they wished.

This situation continued until the turn of the 2001-year when, on January 3, 2002, Ibrahim Kobeisy, the Dean of the Faculty of Law was appointed as the new President. A lot of haggling had gone before the decision was announced. To some it harboured on calamity. Samir Kaseer, one of the most trenchant columnists in An-Nahar, described Kobeisy's appointment as the "Mercy bullet": *"...the government could have waited another week, after all this waiting; it did not have to open the new millenium with a death sentence on its National University...* (Kobeisy's appointment) *reveals that the government of Lebanon and its ruling class has given up on any will to rescue the national university from its death.* (The appointment) *is the mercy bullet – that is it."*[37]

But there was still a lot of flesh in the dying body to be carved before it is put to rest. Almost as soon as the name of the new President was announced the focus shifted to that of appointment of deans. It should be mentioned first that when Kobeisy was declared as President, it was also declared that a special Ministerial Committee headed by Deputy Prime Minister was appointed to look into the affairs of the university and, *"submit a comprehensive review of university conditions and suggest, in coordination with the newly appointed president, a plan for its future development regarding all the different problems it faces"*[38]

In an interview given a few days later, on January 21, 2001, the Minister of Education commented on the appointment of the new president by saying: *"The religious identity of key persons in top administration has been set in the Taif agreement – positions such as that of governor of Central Bank, President of State University, President of Reconstruction and Development Board... such matters are not in my hands; they cover appointments in important positions all over – deans of faculties are to be half and half between Christians and Moslems... Let us hope we can select these from among those qualified in both groups."*[39] It was a long interview, but surprisingly the Minister did not mention any contribution or help that may come in the future from the Ministerial Committee appointed a few weeks before when a new university president was appointed.

A new school year started in October 2001 with no new deans appointed – more than

---

37 *An-Nahar* 5/1/2001
38 *As-Safir* 5/1/2001
39 *An-Nahar* 21/1/2001

a whole year since the position became vacant, and ten months since the appointment of Kobeisy as president. Professors began to clamour and threaten that without new deans they will not be willing to start the new academic year. A situation of almost total paralysis prevailed until finally, on October 31, 2001 the names of the new deans were announced – almost 16 months beyond the deadline. One day after that, the Minister of Education gave another long interview in which he explained reasons for delay in appointing new deans: *"...reasons are simple: we have a number of appointments in various government positions... those in the university were some of them. We could not agree on distributions. But it finally happened, yesterday, and names of new deans were announced."*

Q – Is the Ministerial Committee appointed to look into the affairs of the university still active?

A – No, it has been frozen."[40]

This was the Committee that was appointed some eleven months ago when the name of the new university president was announced. Its freezing brings back to memory decrees on criteria and conditions issued in 1996 related to the opening of new colleges and universities which was announced together with other decrees licensing some 20 new such institutions.

A final touch to be added to this irony is that in the middle of this morass of appointments and re-appointments, the director of one of the University branches (the 2nd branch in the Faculty of Information) resigned form his position, because his name was not among those submitted as a candidate for the position of deanship in the University. The position this director resigned from was not in the University, but in the Higher Council of Greek Catholics, on which he was a member. His reasons were explained in the following: *"The efforts of some persons on the Higher Council to impose or market names (for the position of deans...) is bound to create friction among council members... No authority should intervene in favour of one Catholic over another on grounds of political or regional favouritism."*[41]

Conclusion

Going over the chronology of events since Taif and declarations and developments associated with them, as illustrated in the four case studies reported in this review, one is justified in saying that the Taif agreement should have stayed away from education and not made any pronouncements on it. But since it did, and since the government accepted them, the rest of the story – its failures and successes, can be explained in terms of management or, more accurately, in terms of mismanagement of the affairs of the State. Here, two large questions emerge: one is related to philosophy of government, or rather to the science of politics which is, put simply, whether it is the job of the government to

---

40 *An-Nahar* 1/11/2001
41 *An-Nahar* 7/4/2001

lead the people or to respond to their demands. These two positions are certainly very crude polarities, and there are many shades or types of governing that lie in between which combine some portion of this and some portion of that. Clearly, how much of this and how much of that summarizes the whole field of political discourse since older times, and there are many in this room who can deal with this better than I. Suffice it to say here that President Lahhoud's statement, which I started my presentation with, clearly puts the controls in the hands of the government (to lead the people), and all other forces, particularly the religious, are seen as roadblocks or trouble makers to foil the efforts of the government in leading the people, or to use a more generic term, in nation – building. Now, anyone who is mildly familiar with the history of Lebanon or with the Lebanese society as it has evolved, would certainly find such a position too unrealistic, to say the least.

The second question is more specifically related to the functions of education and what it can do. Granting the desire and the need to use education as an instrument in nation – building (or social engineering), the question is whether education can do the job, or, the extent to which it can do the job and under what conditions. Again, this opens the door to a vast amount of ideas and debates that we need not go into at this point. The conclusions I wish to make are confined to what has in fact taken place since Taif as illustrated in the few stories or case studies I briefly summarized. What was to be done? What could have been done differently? I'll try to summarize my position in the following two major points:

First, I will have to assume that the government when it accepted the Taif agreement it accepted the responsibility of implementing its directives. From here on, the question becomes, as I said before, a question of management, more of social management than of social engineering. Management gives more room for negotiation, compromise, arbitration, and, equally important, it gives room for procrastination and delay. It is well known that many of the Taif points, some among the most important, failed until now to find their way to the agenda. This point of delay is particularly relevant to two of the four stories I told, both in the area of curriculum: teaching of religion and teaching of history. It should have been clear from the beginning that consensus on these two subjects is near impossible in Lebanon, and whatever time is spent on them will more likely be wasted. Hence as a strategy I would have dealt with the whole task of curriculum reform in a vertical way, that is subject-by-subject covering all grades, rather than horizontally taking all subjects in the various grades. I would have taken math and sciences first definitely, and perhaps foreign languages, technology, arts and crafts after, and then gradually Arabic in a third or fourth stage, and would have left religion and history until the very end, with the hope that, with some luck, I'll not reach there at all. Certainly there will be a lot of things to be done in the meantime, so that the whole curriculum revision process could garner more credibility and support: training of teachers, new school buildings, new technology, new teaching time tables and new salary scales, and so on, until one gets to a point where quality becomes the selling point to such an extent as to muffle, if not completely neutralize controversies embedded in decisions regarding the more sensitive subjects. Then and only then I would move into the subjects of religion and history.

In the second area which had to do with private higher education and the State University, the solution here is easier in principle, but more difficult in practice. Management in this area can be defined at the simplest level to mean putting laws already on the books in practice; seeing to it that these laws are not violated, not misused, not arbitrarily changed or discarded. At a more complex level, management here means inclusion, advice and consent, even handedness, fairness and, above all, a sense of legitimacy shared by the people, which is difficult to describe except to say that it is a feeling that people have, that their government is working for their interests, not the interests of its own individuals or the interests of others, and that it is doing this as best as it can. Failure then can be understood and forgiven, and maybe even become a source of more strength and fortitude for everybody.

The Postwar Economy:
A Miracle That Didn't Happen

BOUTROS LABAKI

Introduction

The present economic crisis is one of the main topics of debate in Lebanon as politicians exchange views and accusations against a background of various catastrophe scenarios.

This situation has lasted since the mid-90s, after the high hopes raised in the early years the last decade were disappointed.

Why did the economic hopes in the period 1991-1995 give way to desperation in the period from 1996 to the present? In this article I shall review and analyse the economic situation in Lebanon since the end of the "Wars for the Others" (1975-1990) in the hope of putting the current situation into perspective and indicating some way of overcoming the current recession.

Starting Point: The Prewar and War Economy of Lebanon

The prewar economy of Lebanon

Since the 1950s, the Lebanese economy had been characterized by relatively sustained growth based on the influx of capital and human resources from neighbouring Arab states (Palestine, Egypt, Syria and Iraq) and growing export markets for Lebanese services, goods and skilled labour in the Arab oil-exporting countries. This predominantly service economy, was not well balanced by sector, region or social stratum. Yet, thanks to government policies, the educational and social activities of the communities and the economic and social consequences of Lebanese emigration, disparities between regions and socio-economic strata had been diminishing since the early 1960s.[1]

---

1 Boutros Labaki: "L'Economie politique du Liban indépendant", in Nada Haffar Mills and Nadim Shehadi, *Consensus and Conflict in Lebanon* (Oxford and London: Centre for Lebanese Studies and Tauris, 1987).

The Lebanese economy during the wars (1975-1990)

The war period between 1975 and 1990 radically changed the Lebanese economy. The country suffered huge physical, human and economic losses: three percent of the population was killed, two percent displaced and 28 percent emigrated. The educational system was devastated. Losses in physical capital were estimated at between USD 10-12 billion and losses in income at more than USD 50 billion. Ranked fourth among middle-income countries in 1974, Lebanon ranked 20th in 1990.

In 1991, per capita income in real terms was 50 percent of the 1974 level. The public debt rose to the unprecedented level of USD 2 billion between 1988 and 1990.[2] At the sectoral level, half the telephone network was out of order, one third of the installed electric generating capacity was not functioning, 80 percent of the water table was polluted and half the hotels were not operating.[3] Such destruction and loss severely weakened Lebanon's regional and international economic position. This development was exacerbated by several changes in Lebanon's regional and international environment:

- The modernization of the Arab oil-producing countries – harbours, airports, commercial centres, banking and financial institutions, medical and educational institutions, technical services, and (often subsidized) industrial and agricultural sectors – negatively affected several Lebanese service, manufacturing and agricultural industries.
- The volatile revenues of Arab oil-producing countries affected Lebanese exports of goods, services and skilled labour to these countries.
- The diversification of Arab tourists' destinations (Greece, Spain, Morocco, Tunisia, Syria, Egypt, Turkey, France, the UK, etc.), deprived the Lebanese tourist industry of its traditional clients.
- The internationalization of banking marginalized Lebanon's banking industry.
- The cyclical decline in economic activity in Europe and North America from the mid-1970s onwards boosted the competitiveness of OECD countries in the export markets, particularly in Arab markets, which were traditional markets for Lebanese goods and services.
- The break-up of the Soviet bloc led to competition between its successor states in Arab markets to the detriment of Lebanese products.
- Industrial exports from Southeast Asia (above all China) to the Arab countries, and Lebanon in particular, deeply affected Lebanese industrial production.

---

[2] Boutros Labaki: "Liban: Economie politique des guerres pour les autres", in Fadia Kivan (ed.), *Le Liban d'aujourd'hui* (Paris, Beirut: Publications CNRS, CERMOC, 1995).

[3] Boutros Labaki: "Atouts et préparatifs libanais dans le cadre des économies et des rapports de forces régionaux", in Salgur Kançal and Jacques Thobie (eds.), *Enjeux et rapports de force en Turquie et en Méditerranée Orientale* (Paris: L'Harmattan, Varia Turcica, 1994): pp. 439-456.

Lebanon's comparative advantages at the start of the 1990s

Despite substantial losses and regional and international changes, Lebanon was not without some comparative advantages:
- the experience and competence acquired by Lebanese individuals and companies abroad;
- the considerable capital accumulated by Lebanese individuals and companies working abroad, mainly in Arab-oil producing countries, since the mid-70s. This capital is deposited and/or invested primarily in Western Europe and North America;
- no alternative centre to Lebanon has emerged in the Near and Middle East offering the variety, complexity and quality of service available in Lebanon.

The Beginnings of Recovery (1991-1994): The Hopes

Recovery efforts and their results

After the wars inside Lebanon ended in October 1990, the new Lebanese authorities undertook several measures to revitalize the economy.
- The Council for Reconstruction and Development (CDR) was reactivated in 1991: detailed plans for development and reconstruction were approved by the cabinet in spring 1992.
- As part of the political settlement of the Lebanese crisis agreed to in Taif in 1989, a campaign was undertaken, mainly in Western Europe and the Arab Gulf, to mobilize financial resources for Lebanese reconstruction.
- Implementation of infrastructure rehabilitation and reconstruction projects and programmes (electric power, telecommunications, public schools, airports and ports, highways, urban infrastructure, solid waste collection, water and waste water, public buildings, etc.) began in 1991.[4]
- In 1993, the Hariri cabinet asked the CDR to prepare a national development plan called "Horizon 2000" to prepare Lebanon for a peaceful future. The annual level of capital investment was raised from an average of USD 900 million in the 1992 Reconstruction Plan to USD 1,300 million in "Horizon 2000", which was supposed to be implemented in 13 years (1994-2007).
- The banking sector was gradually restructured: minimal capital requirements were increased, bank mergers were encouraged, liquidity ratios were raised and banks in financial difficulties were encouraged to liquidate.

---

[4] Sannan, Fernand (ed.), *Investir au Liban. Liban Guide* (Beirut: Pan-Arab Publishers, November 2001): pp. 115-124, 170-182, 199-209.

- Steps were taken to encourage investment: the maximum rate of corporate income tax was cut from 40 percent to ten percent. The Investment Development Authority of Lebanon (IDAL) was established in 1994 to help, encourage and promote investment. Restrictions on foreign ownership of real estate were relaxed. Financial markets were reorganized: the Beirut Stock exchange was reactivated, and the financial secondary market of Beirut was launched in 1994.[5]
- In 1992, the rent laws were liberalized for new rental contracts to encourage investment in rental accommodation.
- A real estate company, SOLIDERE, was created in 1992 with tax privileges and other advantages to rebuild the central district of Beirut. As shareholders it regrouped former owners and tenants, on the one hand, and financial investors on the other.
- To promote trade, investment and shipping, trade agreements were signed and ratified with Jordan (1993), Poland (1994), Syria (1994) and Turkey (1992).[6]

Thanks to peace inside Lebanon after autumn 1990, the above-mentioned efforts of the Lebanese authorities, the hopes raised by the first Hariri Cabinet in autumn 1992 and the sizable inflows of capital, the Lebanese economy grew rapidly:

Table 1: GDP Growth Rates (1991-1994)

Year	1991	1992	1993	1994
GDP growth in %	2,5	4,5	7	8

Sources: Lebanese Republic, Ministry of Finance; International Monetary Fund; Bank Audi, Quarterly Economic Report

We must emphasize that no official statistics for the national accounts have been published since 1974. GDP figures are estimates prepared and published by the Ministry of Finance, IMF and IBRD; usually the three sets of figures are similar.

Monetary and financial policies (1990-1994): The dangers

At the same time, the Lebanese authorities pursued monetary and financial policies that had negative long-term effects on the economy and society of Lebanon.

On the monetary side, the exchange rate of the Lebanese pound (LP) plunged from 500 LP/USD in early 1990 to around 3,000 LP/USD in summer 1992 owing to:

---

[5] Boutros Labaki: "Politiques de l'Etat et Reconstruction: Bilan des années 1991-2001", in *Travaux et Jours* (Autumn 2002).
[6] Ministry of Economics and Commerce, Information Trade Centre.

a) fiscal and monetary policies: public sector salaries were increased in early 1992, on the one hand, and the Banque du Liban (the central bank) stopped supporting the exchange rate of the Lebanese pound at the end of 1991 on the other;
b) a wave of speculation against the Lebanese pound in spring 1992;
c) the loss of public confidence in the Lebanese pound during and after the 1992 legislative elections, which were held on the basis of an unconstitutional electoral law, and involved other unlawful practices. These elections were widely boycotted.

The first Hariri government came to power in October 1992, and enforced a policy of high interest rates by issuing high-interest treasury bills denominated in Lebanese pounds. This policy had two main objectives:

a) to stop the massive flight into the US dollar and stabilize the exchange rate between the LP and the USD; and
b) to finance the growing public sector deficit by borrowing money in Lebanese pounds.

The public finances developed as follows:

Table 2: Basic public finance data (1993-1994) in billions of LP

Year	1993	1994
Total expenditures	3.069	5.379
Total revenue	1.855	2.241
Total deficit	1.214	3.138
Primary deficit	430	1.650
Debt service	784	1.488

Source: Lebanese Republic, Ministry of Finance, quoted by Iskandar Moukarbel (cf. note 7)

Between 1993 and 1994, debt service jumped from 40 percent to 60 percent of total government revenues. The primary deficit (excluding debt service) jumped from 23 percent to 73 percent of total government revenue.

Government expenditure rose by 75 percent between 1993 and 1994. In the same period, total government revenue increased only by less than 21 percent.

One-way regionalization and globalization: the unilateral openness of the Lebanese economy

Although the Lebanese government is supposed to have re-established its authority throughout the country, since the early 1990s the Lebanese market has been flooded by cheap smuggled goods, mainly from Syria, but also from Jordan, Egypt, China and other low-wage South and Southeastern Asian states.

As a result, Lebanon's agricultural and industrial sectors suffered from unfair competition as they tried to recover from the devastation of war. Farms and factories started losing markets. Many of them ceased operations completely.

Furthermore, cheap Syrian labour, used to wages on average only one quarter of those in Lebanon, flooded into the Lebanese market, displacing Lebanese workers.

Syrian service industries also competed successfully in Lebanon with their Lebanese peers, especially in the retail trade, transportation, personal and professional services.

In the meantime, Syrian markets and space were closed to Lebanese goods, services and transport. Lebanese goods, especially agricultural produce, also met with the same treatment in Jordan, Saudi Arabia and Egypt.

Markets in the Gulf gradually became less accessible to Lebanese goods as the respective governments implemented trade protection policies and paid subsidies to local producers.

Political events that influenced economic developments (1990-1994)

In the political sphere, this period was marked by several important events:
- In 1990: – Taif reforms were incorporate into the constitution.
  - The government of General Aoun was overthrown.
- In 1991: – Several militias were disarmed and some of integrated into the army.
  - Members were nominated to fill vacant parliamentary seats.
  - A Strategic Pact of coordination, cooperation and complementarity in political, economic, social, cultural, military and security matters was signed with Syria.
  - The Madrid Conference for Arab-Israeli peace negotiations opened.
- In 1992: – Parliament passed an unconstitutional electoral law.
  - The Omar Karameh cabinet resigned in May after widespread demonstrations against the hyperinflation that followed the depreciation of the Lebanese pound.
  - Legislative elections were held, despite a boycott by a very large majority of the population and widespread allegations of electoral fraud.
  - The first Hariri cabinet was sworn in, triggering an unprecedented wave of optimism in the economic future of the country.
- In 1993: – In July, Israel launched a large-scale attack on South Lebanon in retaliation for Lebanese military resistance to the Israeli occupation of South Lebanon; it caused widespread destruction and threatened the tourist industry.
  - In September, Israel and PLO signed the Oslo Accords.
- In 1994: – Samir Geagea, leader of the Lebanese Forces militias, was arrested in spring on several charges. The Lebanese Forces militia and party were

disarmed, disbanded and dissolved. Several members were also arrested.
- Jordan and Israel signed a peace agreement in Wadi Araba.

During this period, Syrian-Israeli and Lebanese-Israeli peace talks that had started in Washington stalled.

These political events had a positive effect on economic growth in the first two years (1990-1991) and a negative effect in the following three (1992-1994).

The incomplete and unbalanced implementation of the Taif agreement and the deterioration of the regional situation began to negatively affect economic developments in Lebanon.

From Slowdown to Recession (1995-2002)

Background

In 1995, the situation started to change: economic growth moderated, then fell sharply, and at the end of the decade Lebanon was on the point of recession.[7]

Table 3: GDP growth rates (1994-2000)

Year	1994	1995	1996	1997	1998	1999*	2000	2001
GDP Growth rate in %	8	6,5	4	4	3	±1	0	–

Sources: Lebanese Republic, Ministry of Finance, Beirut; International Monetary Fund, Washington DC; Bank Audi: "Quarterly Economic Report".
*In contrast to growth of one percent published by the Lebanese authorities,[8] some economists think that GDP contracted by one percent in 1999, a figure in agreement with IMF annual reports.

As a consequence of this slowdown, emigration, which had fallen to 40,000-55,000 persons per year in the early 1990s, jumped to levels unseen even in the war years between 1975 and 1990.[9]

---

7   Iskandar Moukarbel: "On the Reasons for Economic Stagnation in Lebanon" (in Arabic), in *Al-Nahar*, Beirut, 8 (January 2001): p. 15
8   Ibid.
9   Boutros Labaki: "From Regionalisation to Globalisation: Lebanese Emigration Since the End of the 'Wars for the Others' Inside Lebanon (1990-2000)", paper presented to the Lebanese American University Conference on Lebanese Emigration, Beirut, 28-29 June 2001, p. 6.

Table 4: Economic growth and emigration figures

Year	GDP growth (%)	Emigration
1991	2,5	50.000
1992	4,5	38.445
1993	7	48.050
1994	8	56.754
1995	6,5	106.812
1996	4	90.000
1997	4	152.704
1998	3	173.190
1999	1	276.676
2000	0	187.017

Sources: Tables 1 and 3, Lebanese Republic, Central Statistics Administration, Monthly Bulletin, Beirut.

At the same time, and notwithstanding the recrudescence of large-scale emigration, unemployment rate rose from seven percent in 1997 to ten percent in early 2001.[10] A survey of 1500 industrial and commercial companies conducted by the National Employment Office in 1999/2000 showed that the number of persons employed in these companies declined by five percent during 1999. The sectors with the largest increase in unemployment were construction, furniture, textile and clothing industries and hotels and restaurants. Sixty-six percent of the companies surveyed said they expected business to remain the same over the next three years, seven percent expressed their intention to liquidate their business, 12 percent said that they expected business to slow down and only 13 percent of the companies surveyed expected business to improve.[11]

The causes

The causes can be divided into two broad categories: economic causes and political causes.

1. The economic causes

The crisis in government finances

The direct economic cause of this long stagnation is high interest rates (which peaked at 35 percent in 1995) paid by the public sector to finance its deficit and to maintain an ar-

---

[10] Robert Kasparian: "Les problèmes de l'emploi au Liban", in *Travaux et Jours*, No. 67 (Spring 2001): p. 149.
[11] Lebanese Republic, Ministry of Labour, National Employment Office, Survey on Employment, Beirut 2000.

tificially high exchange rate between the Lebanese pound and the US dollar. The main indicators developed as follows:

Table 5: Basic public finance data (1995-2002) in billions of LP

Year	1995	1996	1997	1998	1999	2000	2001	2002 (Jan.-May)
Total expenditure	6342	7732	9662	8385	8911	10363	12600	3777
Total revenue	3033	3533	3752	4449	4868	4197	4500	2212
Total deficit	3309	4199	5909	3936	4042	6166	8100	1565
Primary deficit	1439	1546	2531	584	419	1969	3300	nd
Debt service	1870	2653	3378	3352	3623	4197	4800	1887

Sources: 1995-1999: same as for Table 2; for 2000, we included extra budgetary payments (CDR payments financed by loans, EDL payments, local government payments, CNSS, delayed payments to several creditors such as private hospitals and contractors. For 2001, the figures are estimates based on the same criteria used for 2000. For 2002: Lebanese Banks Association, Monthly Bulletin, May-June 2002 (No. 5-6), p. 55.

From Table 5 we can conclude the following developments between 1995 and 2001:
– total annual expenditure practically doubled (98,67 percent)
– annual revenue rose by 50 percent (48,37 percent)
– the total annual deficit rose by 144,78 percent
– the primary annual deficit rose by 129,32 percent
– the annual debt service rose by 256,68 percent

The rise in the primary deficit (excluding debt service) was caused mainly by the following:
1) the growth of current expenses (army, security forces, ministry of health payments to private hospitals, garbage collection payments to private companies);
2) uncontrolled spending of some autonomous bodies (Council for the South, Displaced Persons' Fund, etc.);
3) the inability of public utilities to cover the cost of services provided (electric power, water, etc.);
4) deficits of some autonomous bodies (Public Transport and Railways Authority, tobacco monopoly, etc.), and the bankruptcy of some state corporations (e.g. Middle East Airlines);
5) unequal and uneven tax collection in many sectors and regions and the reduction in the maximum rate of income tax from 40 to ten percent (subsequently raised to 15 percent); and
6) the overstaffing of several ministries and public bodies.

To finance the growing deficit, the government continued to borrowing at high interest rates, plunging the public finances into a vicious circle: total Lebanese public debt rose from USD 2 billion at end of 1990,[12] to USD 32.07 billion at the end of July 2002.[13]

This is equal to twice the GDP of Lebanon (according to official Lebanese figures). The breakdown of public debt as of 31 July 2002 was as follows:

Table 6: Lebanese public debt (31 July 2002) in LP billions

By currency	Debt in LP	Average interest rate (%)	Annual cost
In Lebanese pounds	29.012	13,84	4.015
In US dollars: 10.7 billion	16.063	9,684	1.555
In euro: 850 million	1.255	7,824	98
Other loans in USD: 1.326 billion	1.998	2,50	50
Total public debt service in LP billion			5.718

Source: Cf. note 13.

As Table 6 shows, in the early 1990s, most of this debt was held in Lebanese pounds; by July 2002, 40 percent of it was denominated in foreign currencies (mainly USD). The authorities justified this shift from borrowing in Lebanese pounds to borrowing in foreign currency by the need to curb the cost of servicing debt and extend repayment periods.

We suspect there is a third reason: the need to insure current and future creditors against the consequences of any change in the exchange rate of the Lebanese pound.

The very high rates paid on treasury bills (which reached 35 percent in summer 1995, 16 percent for three-month bills and 23,39 percent for two-year bills in December 1995[14] and finally 13,84 percent on average in July 2002) had the effect of "crowding out" the private sector, which found it increasingly difficult to borrow from commercial banks.

Given the competition from the public sector for banking sector funds, credit for private companies and individuals in Lebanon became very expensive. Lebanese companies found it increasingly difficult to obtain funds for current operations or capital investment. They started firing workers and many went bankrupt, as observed above in our discussion of the 2000 National Employment Office survey.

---

12 Cf. note 2.
13 Comments of Issam Fares (Deputy Premier of Lebanon) on the draft budget for 2003: "Questions on Ways to Curb Debt Service", in *Al-Nahar*, Beirut, 7 September 2002.
14 *Banque du Liban*, Quarterly Bulletin, No. 91 (Fourth Quarter 2001): p. 149.

The rise of the real effective exchange rate of the Lebanese pound
Thanks to Lebanese monetary and financial policies,[15] the nominal exchange rate between the LP and the USD rose from 1741 to 1 in 1993 to 1507 to 1 in 2000.

The real effective exchange rate of the Lebanese pound and is a trade weighted average that takes into account changes in nominal exchange rates with other countries and relative rates of inflation. In other words, this rate measures price competitiveness between Lebanon and its trading partners.

Taking 1993 as the year base, by September 2000 the real exchange rate of the Lebanese pound had risen 77 percent.[16] This development means that relative to its trading partners, the price of goods and services in Lebanon rose by 77 percent between 1 January 1993 and 30 September 2000. This explains the gradual decline in the competitiveness of Lebanese goods and services in the foreign markets, and the easy penetration of foreign production in the Lebanese market. At the risk of oversimplifying, the consequences of this development are much the same as if the exchange rate of the Lebanese pound and the consumer price index in Lebanon had not changed between 1993 and September 2000, but the Lebanese Government had imposed an export tax of 77 percent on Lebanese exports or paid a subsidy of 77 percent on Lebanese imports.

Inconsistent economic policies
Generally speaking, the economic policies of the different cabinets since 1995 have not been consistent. Some steps had positive effects on economic activity, others had negative effects. On the whole, though, these policies have not benefited the economy. The main developments during the period 1995-2002 were as follows:

a) Economic steps with a positive impact on economic activity:
- Two IDAL programmes: "Export plus" is a subsidy program for Lebanese agriculture, and the "One-stop shop" for investors seeks to reduce red tape by having investors deal only with IDAL for all their investment-related needs.
- The government provides interest-rate subsidies for bank credits to manufacturing, handicrafts, agricultural and livestock production, tourism and high-tech projects.
- Kafalat, a credit guaranty company founded by the government and the Bankers Association, guarantees 75 percent of loans in high-tech, tourism, agriculture, animal production, handicrafts and manufacturing industry; these subsidized loans must be repaid within seven years.
- The CDR has signed two agreements with the EIB (European Investment Bank). The first loan agreement provides EUR 30 million to repair or construct hotels outside greater Beirut at normal international conditions – which are excellent compared to Lebanese conditions – with long grace and repayment periods. Under the agreement, ten Lebanese banks have to provide a further EUR 30 million at

---

15 Ibid., p. 61.
16 Iskandar Moukarbel, op. cit.

the same conditions, so that the total amount of credit available is EUR 60 million.
- The second loan, to finance manufacturing industry, was signed with the EIB in 1999 and has similar conditions.
- The CDR is preparing a third loan, this one to finance agriculture, with the International Fund for Agricultural Development (IFAD) to finance agriculture.[17]
- Custom duties on imported inputs for the Lebanese manufacturing industry have gradually been reduced, so as to lower the cost of industrial production.
- A five-year development plan was prepared by the CDR in 1999 and approved by the government in May 2000. For the first time, a plan has focused on raising Lebanon's competitiveness and exploring investment possibilities for the private sector.[18] This plan has been practically ignored since the 2000 elections and change of government.
- In June 2000, the Lebanese government signed the Euro Mediterranean Association Agreement with the European Union, which opens up new opportunities for Lebanese products in the EU market.

b) Economic steps with a negative impact on economic activity:
  - Public spending on reconstruction

  Public spending on infrastructure, 80 percent of it under the aegis of the CDR, averaged USD 650 million per year from 1992 to 2001.

  Although initially small (USD 18 million in 1991 and 50 million in 1992), CDR investments rose to USD 1 billion in both 1997 and 1998, then declined to USD 500 million in 1999 and less in 2000 and 2002.[19]

  These expenses should have had a tremendous impact on economic growth. But this impact was lessened by various factors:

  - A substantial portion of the amounts disbursed were intended to finance imports that would encourage local value added. In the early 1990s, the government delayed the implementation of the law on national preference policy (15 percent) with respect to public sector purchases. Later, pressure from local manufacturers forced the government to change its attitude.
  - The bulk of the value added by foreign construction companies was transferred out of Lebanon (profits, wages, interest, etc.) These foreign companies subcontracted important parts of their contracts to local companies at low prices.
  - A few big companies accounted for most of the value added by local construction companies. This limited the social and geographic trickle-down effects of this infrastructural investment.

---

17 *CDR*, Annual Reports, Beirut.
18 *CDR*, "Five-Year Development Plan 2000-2004", Beirut, May 2000.
19 Boutros Labaki: "Politiques de l'Etat et Reconstruction", op. cit.

- Much of labour's share of value added in the reconstruction process went to foreign workers at the expense of more demanding local manpower.

For all these reasons, the multiplier effect of this huge spending on the Lebanese economy was limited.

- For political reasons, the government felt it was unable to cut the running costs of some public bodies, public utilities, autonomous bodies and state-owned enterprises.

For fear of displeasing banks, the government was not able to reduce its debt service payments, either. For both political reasons and administrative shortages the government was unable to collect all taxes from certain sectors and regions.

As a result, after 1998 the government decided to curb public expenditures by cutting the capital investment budget. Public investment peaked at USD 1 billion dollars in 1997 and 1998, although it was supposed to reach USD 1.5 billion a year under the then effective "Horizon 2000" development plan.

As a consequence, the growth rate, which had been declining since 1995, turned negative in 1999, according to IMF and some Lebanese economists. Construction and all the up-stream and down-stream sectors were heavily hit.

In 1999 and 2000, the government's policies in this field were similar in many respects to those of previous governments.

In autumn 2000, the new government lowered customs tariffs on the eve of negotiations with EU for the Euro Mediterranean Association Agreement. This move totally contradicts conventional negotiation techniques, which suggest raising tariffs before negotiating lower ones, in order to improve your bargaining power. Local production, already weak for the aforementioned reasons, took an immediate hit.

The second negative consequence was to deprive the government of a source of badly needed income.

In January 2002, the Lebanese government started to introduce a value-added tax, even before signing the Euro Mediterranean Association Agreement with the EU. The practical effect was to replace a tax on imports (customs) with a tax on exports and the local production of goods and services.

The effect of these two last steps was deeply detrimental to the Lebanese economy.

On balance, despite the positive steps mentioned above, the effects of inconsistent economic policies between 1995 and 2002 were negative.

The fall of crude oil prices (1996-1999)
Average crude oil prices dropped from USD 20.27/barrel in 1996 to USD 11.79/barrel in the first quarter of 1999, a fall of about 40 percent on average for oil-producing countries, before rising again to USD 29.38/barrel in August 2002.

In consequence, the income of Arab oil-producing countries declined sharply between early 1998 and mid-1999.

As the Lebanese economy is closely integrated with the economies of the Arab oil-producing countries, this loss of income also hit Lebanon, with a time lag. Remittances from Lebanese working in these countries declined sharply, as did income from Lebanese exports, and receipts from Arab Gulf tourists.[20]

2. The political causes
Several political events affected also negatively the level of economic activity between 1995 and 2002.

The extension of the presidential mandate in 1995
This move undermined trust among investors, in particular those with savings in Lebanese pounds, triggering a flight into US dollars and outflows of capital abroad.

To contain the situation, the Lebanese government issued treasury bills at 35 percent interest per year. Although this limited the outflow of capital, it has a very negative impact on growth by making it even more difficult for the private sector to obtain credit.

The Israeli attack of 1996
In spring 1996, Israeli launched a large-scale attack on South Lebanon, culminating in the Cana massacre. This attack took a heavy toll in loss of life and physical destruction, both of which affected economic activity. It also reminded the Lebanese that their country was still at war, itself a negative factor.

The legislative elections of 1996
The legislative elections in summer 1996 took place under an unconstitutional electoral law, and involved other unlawful practices. This, too, had a negative effect on economic activity.

The deterioration of the regional peace process (1996-1998)
The unravelling of the regional peace process accelerated after 1996, dashing expectations raised by the Madrid Peace Conference, the Oslo Accords and subsequent agreements.

The attempts at administrative and financial reforms in 1999
After the presidential election in autumn 1998 and the appointment of a new cabinet, a campaign buttressed by judicial and administrative sanctions was introduced to reform the civil service and eliminate corruption. Political pressures managed to derail it. In the

---

20 Boutros Labaki: "Politiques de l'Etat et Reconstruction", op. cit., and Iskandar Moukarbel, op. cit.

meantime, old and new high- and middle-ranking civil servants got cold feet and lost the initiative, paralysing the administration and the economy, too.

A plan of financial reform was drawn up in 1999.

This plan upset bankers, because it aimed inter alia to curb interest rates. But as it was not adopted, the hopes it raised in other sectors (manufacturing, industry, agriculture, tourism, etc.) quickly collapsed.

The consequence of Israeli withdrawals from South Lebanon in 1999 and 2000, and the Israeli attacks on infrastructure

These withdrawals raised hopes and enthusiasm. However, the government failed to take control of the liberated area, and the "no-war, no-peace" situation continued. Because the authorities failed to move quickly, enthusiasm soon gave way to disappointment, which in turn dimmed hopes and discouraged private investment. The regional and national economies failed to grasp an interesting opportunity. Israeli attacks in 1999 and 2000 badly damaged the electrical and transport infrastructure.

The legislative elections of summer 2000 and the manifesto of the Maronite bishops in September 2000

For the third time after the Taif agreement, legislative elections were organized on the basis of an unconstitutional law, this time a new one. The political balance in the country shifted again, and Prime Minister Hariri returned to power. Lebanon's relations with Syria were violently criticized during the no-confidence vote.

In September 2000, the monthly meeting of Maronite Bishops' Conference issued a formal analysis of the country's situation and criticizing in clear terms the legislative, executive and judiciary, questioning their legitimacy, criticizing the Syrian presence in Lebanon, and linking the economic crisis, emigration and unemployment to this Syrian presence and its political and economic consequences.

These developments unleashed controversies in political circles and the general public.

Political movements in Lebanon and attempts at political and economic reforms in Syria in 2000-2002

The death of the Syrian president in June 2000 raised expectations of economic and political reforms in Syria. A tentative push for reform started in autumn 2000, but all political reforms were put on ice a year later.

In Lebanon, the Israeli withdrawal, the new leadership in Syria and the legislative elections of summer 2000 inspired popular and youth movements for democracy, sovereignty and human rights. Political groups were founded and an important reconciliation took place in Mount Lebanon in summer 2001. These moves are being repressed by the local establishment in different ways. The way the public authorities are dealing with these political developments is unlikely to stimulate economic growth.

General Conclusion

In the first half of the 1990s there appeared to be a very real prospect of an economic miracle as peace returned to Lebanon, the government prepared an institutional framework, (numerous plans and programmes, dozens of steps, laws, decrees, promoting institutions, etc.), capital flowed in from abroad and reconstruction started. The initial spurt of growth slowed after 1995 and became negative at the end of the 1990s, largely owing to the government's monetary, financial and economic policies. Other influences included one-sided regionalisation and globalization, the change in the regional political environment, Lebanon's loss of competitiveness, the inconsistent economic policies of successive governments, and the fall in oil prices. Several local political factors also contributed to these negative developments.

Together, these factors were able to turn a promising economic miracle into a lengthy period of unprecedented stagnation and recession, with all the attendant economic, social, demographic and political consequences.

Abbreviations

BDL	Banque du Liban (Central Bank of Lebanon)
CDR	Council for Development and Reconstruction
CNSS	Caisse Nationale de Sécurité Sociale (National Social Security Fund)
EDL	Electricité du Liban (Lebanese Electric Power Authority)
EIB	European Investment Bank
IDAL	Investment Development Authority of Lebanon
IFAD	International Fund for Agricultural Development.
IMF	International Monetary Fund
LP	Lebanese Pound
WB or IBRD	World Bank or International Bank for Reconstruction and Development

The Sceptical Nation
Opinions and Attitudes Twelve Years after the End of the War

THEODOR HANF

By mid-1990, the Lebanese state had virtually ceased to exist. Fifteen years of parallel and coincident wars had made of the Lebanese a people hostage to internecine militias. Yet, surveys of Lebanese attitudes and opinions in 1982, 1984, 1986 and 1987 showed that the vast majority of Lebanese wanted to live in peaceful coexistence in one country. The conclusion could be drawn from these results that the Lebanese were in the process of becoming a nation.[1]

Twelve years later, the country has a state again, even if some of its powers are exercised at the discretion of outsiders. The former mercenary territories have disappeared. Reconstruction, though slower than many hoped, is impressive. But what has happened to the nation, whose emergence in the midst of war gave greatest cause for hope?

This was the subject of an empirical survey of the economically active population in Lebanon in 2002. The survey used the same methods and tools as in the wartime surveys, and a regionally weighted random sample (N = 983).[2] Owing to the state of official social and economic statistics, the quotas assigned to each region[3] – and hence the proportional representation of the different religious communities in each region[4] – are not beyond question. But this is not the place for a discussion of the different demo-

---

[1] Theodor Hanf, *Coexistence in Wartime Lebanon. Decline of a State and Rise of a Nation* (Oxford and London: Centre for Lebanese Studies and Tauris, 1993).
[2] One difference between this postwar survey and the wartime surveys is the considerably larger number of "No replies". During the war, respondents and interviewees were obviously interested in grasping every opportunity to express their opinions. The fact that the refusal rate is approaching that common in countries at peace indicates that life in Lebanon is returning to normal. It should be noted that just less than 4% of the respondents – particularly secondary-school students – refused to mention their religious affiliation.
[3] The most notable discrepancy between the earlier surveys and that of 2002 is in the region comprising Ashrafieh, East-Beirut suburbs, the Metn, Kisrawan and Jbeil: formerly, this region accounted for 28% on average of the economically active population, but only 17.1% in 2002 – a problematically low figure in the light of the economic density of this region.
[4] As a consequence of the low quota for the most heavily populated predominantly Christian region, the proportion of Christians in the total sample has fallen to 33% (compared with 48% in the early surveys); at just less than three percent, the Greek Catholics in particular are probably underrepresented.

graphic hypotheses,[5] about which the Lebanese – seldom without political nuances – argue with such authority. For our purposes, a sufficiently accurate comparison between the attitudes and opinions of respondents from different educational and income strata, regions and occupations on the one hand and different religious communities on the other is adequate.

Fear of the Future, Cautiousness, Powerlessness: Psychosocial Sensitivities

Lebanon – then as now – has always had the appearance of a country bursting with joie de vivre, full of hospitality and conviviality. Yet, in their attitudes towards life and their social environment, individual Lebanese leave one with the almost oppressive sense of palpable threat to this way of life.

"When I think of the future, I feel uncertain and afraid."
In the four wartime surveys, about 60% of the respondents answered in the affirmative. Now, no less than 81% do. Differences by education, income, place of residence, occupation and communal and religious affiliation are insignificant: four fifths of the Lebanese feel afraid when they think about the future.

Fear usually goes hand in hand with cautiousness and conservatism.
"Before you start something, you should know whether it will work or not."
"When you start changing things, they usually get worse."
During the war, between 71% and 74% of respondents were cautious in their dealings with people they did not know. Twelve years after the end of the war, this figure has risen to 81%. During the war 33% of respondents expressed strong scepticism about change and a fear that things would get worse; now 43% do.[6]

"You should always be careful. You cannot trust the people you live or work with."
A full 78% agree, women more than men. There is a direct and close correlation between mistrust of one's social environment and level of education, whereas level of income plays no role. Mistrust is particularly high in some regions: in the Beirut district of Chiyah 86% answered Yes, in Shuf 87%, in Zghorta 91% and in the Metn 92%.

So, whom do people trust?

---

5 Cf. e. g. the differences between the data of Kamal Feghali, *Les communautés du Liban. Approche démographique* (Zalka: Makhtariat, July 2002), and Boutros Labaki, *Données démographiques communautaires du Liban* (Beirut, 1996, idem, *From Regionalization to Globalization. The Lebanese Emigration since the End of the "Wars for the Others"* (1990–2000) (manuscript kindly made available by the author). Our sample uses Feghali's figures.
6 Responses to these two items do not differ significantly by social or cultural criteria, either. Only in the lowest income group is agreement with the second statement below average at 38% – and even this figure is higher than that for all respondents during the war.

	1987 survey	2002 survey
Close relatives	67	76
Friends	59	52
Colleagues	20	24
Superiors	10	24

Figures in %, rounded

The family is the repository of trust, even more so than during the war.[7] There are no significant differences by education, income or communal affiliation. Only half the respondents trust their friends, and not even a quarter their colleagues or superiors.

Only one fifth state that they trust members of their own religious community.[8] Seventeen percent trust fellow villagers, 16% their neighbours and just eight percent "all Lebanese". In short: the intact world is a very small circle. Intact is really only the family; many people do not even include "friends".

"People like me can't do anything to improve people's lives."
Reactions to this statement are a rough measure of how people assess their ability to bring about social change. Between 1982 and 1987 the feeling of powerlessness and helplessness rose from 66% to 80%. In 2002, it was still as high as 78%. Today, the Lebanese are no more likely than during the war to believe that they can contribute to change. Whereas during the 1980s the sense of powerlessness decreased with rising education and income, today it is spread more or less evenly across all strata and religious communities.[9]

"Even ordinary people can get ahead if they help one another and act together."
Almost nine in ten respondents believe that help for self-help can be successful. However, this conviction falls linearly with rising income. This view is shared by 85% of Muslims and 94% of Christians. Those who earn less – and those who feel their position is weak – are slightly more likely to think that solidarity can help them to overcome their powerlessness.

In summary: the psychological sensitivities of the Lebanese in 2002 do not give much ground for optimism. Four in five respondents are afraid of the future, extremely cautious and mistrustful. Four in ten respondents go as far as to fear that any change will be for the worse. People trust only their families and a few friends, otherwise virtually nobody. Finally, four fifths are convinced that they can do nothing to change their lot.

---

7 This is more pronounced in rural areas than in Beirut. Trust in the family is above-average in the Bekaa, Baalbek-Hermel, Zahle and Nabatieh.
8 Income, education and communal and religious affiliation played no role.
9 In the lowest age group the sense of powerlessness was below average. The sense of powerlessness is above average in Ashrafieh, the Metn, Kisrawan and Zahle.

These attitudes correlate only marginally with educational and income status, and even less rarely with communal affiliation. In other words, they are characteristic of the entire Lebanese society, and just as strongly now as in the war years, if not more so.

Entrepreneurial Spirit in Unfavourable Circumstances: Attitudes to the Economy and Society

The following question measured preferences for investment or consumption:
"Imagine you won some money in the national lottery. What is the first thing you would do with it?

	1981	1984	1986	1987	2002
Buy a house or property	37	33	26	19	18
Spend on myself and my family	5	3	3	4	11
Start my own business	42	46	57	51	45
Put the money in a good bank investment	16	17	14	26	25

Figures in %, rounded

Both during the war and in the postwar period consumption was way at the bottom of the list and commercial independence at the top. Whereas men would like their own business, women prefer bank investments. There are no significant differences by education or income.

But In 2002, the differences between the individual religious communities are significant,[10] in particular between Muslims and Christians as a whole.

	Muslims	Christians
Buy a house or property	21	13
Spend on myself and my family	13	6
Start my own business	39	51
Put the money in a good bank investment	25	26

Figures in %, rounded; totals below 100 because of multiple replies

Muslims opted for consumption twice as often as Christians, and Christians considerably more often than Muslims for their own business. Despite this, even among Muslims the propensity to invest is far greater than that to consume.

This finding is substantiated by the reactions to the following statement:
"I don't want to work for someone else all my life; some day I want to be my own boss."

---

10 Sunnis exhibit a comparatively stronger preference for property, Shi'is and Druzes for consumption, and Maronites, Greek Orthodox and Catholics for their own business.

More than four fifths of the respondents[11] – including 79% of Muslims and 87% of Christians – agreed, though less frequently than average among the lowest and highest income groups.

"In your opinion, which of the following factors counts most for success in life?"

	1987	2002
Religious beliefs	*	22
Education/Training	16	19
Achievement	21	18
Luck	14	7
Experience	21	7
Team work	*	7
Astuteness	7	6
Connections	16	4
Inheritance	5	4
Other	*	6

Figures in %, rounded; * not asked

In 2002, "Religious beliefs" was rated highest. This factor was not asked in the wartime surveys between 1981 and 1987, so we cannot say whether this reflects a change in mentality and attitudes or not. The answers given during the war show the great majority of people to be performance-oriented. In 2002, non-achievement factors such as luck, connections and inheritance are still rated very low, but so is experience. And more than one fifth of all respondents rate religious beliefs as the most important factor for success. Among Muslims this figure rises to 25%, and even among Christians it is 17%.

A possible interpretation is that this is a reaction to a fairly desperate economic situation, in which neither luck nor connections offers much hope of success, and people can only put their trust in God's helping hand. This view is supported by the replies to other questions.

"One man says:
'I'd rather work hard, build up my own business and take risks to get ahead and make a lot of money.'
Another says:
'I'd rather have a safe job with a regular income so that I don't have to think about the future.'
Do you agree with the first of the second man?"

Between 1981 and 1987, agreement with the first option rose from two thirds to almost three quarters. In 2002, it draws the support of just under half the respondents. The

---

11 During the war the figure was about three quarters.

Lebanese have become much less risk tolerant, and in the lowest income group tolerance is lowest. In economically backward regions it is far lower than elsewhere.[12] Christians (56%) exhibit a greater willingness to take risks than Muslims (41%). More than two thirds of respondents who refused to mention their religious affiliation chose the first option.

What about job satisfaction?

	1987	2002
"Of course, everyone would like to earn more, but I'm satisfied with my salary."	24	37
"On the whole, I'm satisfied with my boss."	47	61
"It's a pity, but I don't have any prospects in my job."	47	62
"If I could, I'd like to have a different occupation."	70	76
"If I could, I'd like to work in the Gulf."	52	54

Agreement in %, rounded

Today, more respondents are satisfied with their salary[13] and their boss[14] than during the war. This is only because there is no other alternative, as the responses to the other statements show: people's sense of no career prospects in their present jobs has risen considerably[15] and more people would like to change their occupation.[16] Although earnings prospects in the Gulf are no longer what they were in the 80s, more than half would still grab the opportunity if offered it. Remarkably, communal or religious affiliation does not significantly affect job satisfaction – with the exception of the desire to work in the Gulf, which is considerably weaker among Christians than Muslims. Compared to the war years,[17] today Lebanese of all confessions are dissatisfied with their career prospects.

The depth of the economic crisis is reflected in opinions about living standards and future prospects from a transgenerational point of view.

---

12 Risk tolerance is below average in Chiyah-Gobeiri (31%), Akkar (31%), Jezzine (32%) and Tripoli (33%) and above average in the suburbs of East Beirut (70%), Jbeil (67%), Ras Beirut (61%) and Ashrafieh (60%), in Zghorta (58%) and in Sidon (54%).
13 Agreement rises with income, but even in the highest income group reaches only 46%.
14 Satisfaction with employers rises with education and income.
15 Agreement falls with rising education. Nonetheless, almost half of all university graduates agreed.
16 The desire for a career change falls with rising education and income, but even in the highest status groups two thirds of respondents still share this view.
17 Cf. Hanf, op. cit., pp. 466ff.

	1987	2002
"Compared to how my parents lived, I think I'm much better off."	71	57
"I fear my children won't have it as good as me."	66	85

Agreement in %, rounded

More than half the Lebanese still think their generation is better off than their parents'. In the mid-80s, however, this view was even more widespread. Although education and income are not determinants, age is: in the 2002 survey respondents who share this view are a minority in the lowest age group – the generation that experienced their parents' economic decline.[18]

During the war fears that the next generation would be worse off were already widespread; since then they have grown. They are shared by the vast majority of respondents across all levels of education and income, and all regions and communities.

How do respondents feel about social distinctions in Lebanese society and the distribution of prosperity and economic power?

	1981	1984	1986	1987	2002
"The differences between the social groups have widened since 1975 (2002: in the last five years)."	90	91	94	96	87
"In Lebanon a rich minority is buying up everything, and the large majority is losing out."	87	92	94	95	89
"In Lebanon the majority of people are middle-class, with only a few rich people and not very many poor people."	68	54	46	17	43
"It doesn't matter what the workers do, they can never win against the bosses."	25	37	40	52	54
"When I see people from the wealthy parts of town, I think to myself that's how I want to live, and I have a right to live like that."	66	67	63	72	72

Agreement in %, rounded

In the view of the Lebanese, neither the war nor the past five-year period was the great leveller.[19] Then as now the overwhelming majority of people agree with the topos of the "rich minority". The competing view of a middle-class society, which was shattered in

---

[18] Communal affiliation has low significance. The proportion of Shi'is who think that their parents were not better off than they are is above average, an indication of this community's relative economic advance.
[19] In this assessment there were no differences by education or by religious affiliation.

1987, had regained support by 2002, but remains the dream of a minority.[20] More than half of all respondents believe that the power of employers is unassailable. In view of the social crisis, it is not surprising that social envy of people living in well-to-do areas has grown – across all education and income groups and all religious communities. Indeed, it has fallen only among the very people that live in so-called better parts of town.

To summarise: Attitudes and opinions about the economy and society in 2002 were either little changed from those in the war years – or were more pessimistic. The majority of Lebanese would still like to be independent businessmen, but the proportion of people willing to accept the risks associated with entrepreneurial activity has declined. Although most people are convinced that achievement, education and experience are the main factors determining success in life, a substantial minority thinks religious beliefs are more important. Job and career satisfaction have dropped. People are even more pessimistic about their children's prospects than they were in the war years. Social differences have widened and social envy increased.

And hopes of a better future have fallen.

"The services that Lebanon provides for the region are unique. Despite the crisis, Lebanon has consolidated its position."

Between 1981 and 1987 more than four fifths of the respondents agreed with this statement. In 2002, just two thirds did. Looking on the bright side, despite all that the country has been through, two thirds still think Lebanon has consolidated its position.

A Nation of Believers

"Even cautious interpretation and allowance for 'socially desired' responses cannot disguise the fact that the economically active Lebanese population interviewed is strongly influenced by religion. West European clergy can only dream of such figures."[21] This comment about our results in the 1980s is even truer today.

Although religion and religious practices may mean less and less to West Europeans, this is not true of the Lebanese.

	1987	2002
"I believe in a life after death, in which the righteous will be rewarded and the wicked will be punished."	71	85
"I try to live by the teachings of my religion."	75	80
"I often visit a place of worship."	38	60
"I can be happy and enjoy life even if I don't believe in God."	11	11

Agreement in %, rounded

---

20 This minority does not differ from the majority by economic markers. The number of Christians with this view is disproportionately high: 52% of the Christians vs. 38% of the Muslims continue to believe in a middle-class society.
21 Hanf, op. cit., p. 480.

The number of Lebanese who state that they are believers has risen in the postwar period: more try to live according to the teachings and observe the rites of their religion. Although a good tenth of the respondents declared that they were not religious, this figure is no higher than 15 years ago. One could hardly speak of growing secularisation then, and today even less so.

Belief in a life after death and divine justice for all runs through all income groups and all religious affiliations without any significant distinctions. The figure of 80% for university graduates is only marginally lower than that for people with less formal education. Astonishing in this connection, though, is the indirect correlation with age; or to put it another way, the younger the respondents, the more likely they were to agree with the statement.[22] This phenomenon has been recorded only once before – in Georgia, a country that, like Lebanon, has been through a war and is in a severe economic crisis.[23] In Georgia, however, this behaviour was observed only among the (Orthodox) ethnic Georgian majority; in Lebanon it is characteristic of all communities. There are no significant differences by age, education, income or religious affiliation among the four fifths of all respondents who stated that they tried to live according to the teachings of their religion. Religious attendance declines slightly with rising income, but otherwise varies in accordance with the directives and practices of each community. Among the one tenth who are cheerful non-believers the highest levels of education and income are slightly overrepresented, but there is no significant difference by religious affiliation. Once again, it is notable that respondents under the age of 25 are underrepresented.

To summarise: The Lebanese, already pious during the war, have become more pious. But there is little difference by socio-economic markers. There is no significant difference in the degree of religiosity of the different communities and the two major religious groups: the Lebanese are a nation of believers, the young even more so than their elders.

Kinship: Attitudes to Family and Society

Although deep family loyalties may compete with loyalty to one's religious community, it also constitutes the social foundation of the latter. According to Fuad Khoury, familialism is a more traditional form of kinship loyalty, and loyalty to the community a more modern form.[24]

The responses to the following statements measure the strength of familialism:

---

22 Results from the highest to the lowest age group: 82% – 82% – 82% – 88% – 89% – 92%.
23 Cf. Theodor Hanf and Ghia Nodia, *Georgia Lurching to Democracy. From Tolerant Agnosticism to Pious Jacobinism* (Baden-Baden: Nomos, 2001).
24 Fuad I. Khouri, *From Village to Suburb. Order and Change in Greater Beirut* (Chicago: University of Chicago Press, 1975): pp. 201ff.

	1987	2002
"Stand by your brother, be he oppressor or oppressed."[25]	45	47
"If my family disagrees with the dominant political tendency in my community, I'll side with my family."	50	48

Agreement in %, rounded

In the war years, agreement with the saying: "My brother, right or wrong" rose from one quarter in 1981 to almost one half in 1984, where it still stands 15 years later.[26] Respondents are more or less equally divided over conflicts between family and community interests.

The replies to the following statements indicate the strength of community identity:

	1987	2002
"It doesn't matter whether they are rich or poor, I feel close to all members of my community."	58	66
"It is good if there are no conflicts between the sons of the same community."	91	78
"One man says: 'It is not so important if my daughter marries a man with a different religion, as long as she loves him." A second man says: 'Marriages between people of different religions are not good and are often unhappy. I don't want my daughter to marry someone with a different religion.' Do you agree with the first or second statement?" Agree with the first statement:	40	39
"I prefer neighbours who have the same background as me."	55	48
"If my colleagues are honest and cooperative, I don't mind what group they belong to."	90	92
"The identity and uniqueness of my community are more important to me than loyalty to my country."	12	34

Agreement in %, rounded

Solidarity with a religious community has continued to strengthen in postwar Lebanon: two thirds expressed it. This feeling is somewhat stronger among women than men. There are no differences by education or by community.

There is less concern now about conflict within the community, since conflicts are no longer settled at gunpoint.

---

25 Lebanese proverb, the equivalent of "My brother, right or wrong".
26 It falls slightly with rising education, but does not exhibit any correlation with income. It is particularly strong in Baalbek-Hermel, in the Shuf and in Baalbek. It is above-average among Armenians and Druze, but below average among the Shi'is.

Attitudes towards mixed marriages have not changed. Acceptance is greater among university graduates. The influence of income is insignificant.[27] The differences between Muslims and Christians are not statistically significant, but those between the different communities are. Druze and Greek Orthodox have the fewest problems with mixed marriages, whereas disapproval is above-average among Sunnis, Armenians, Greek Catholics and members of smaller Christian communities.

The proportion of those that would prefer neighbours with the same background has fallen slightly, but still makes up almost half of all respondents. Whereas neither education nor income plays a role, religious or communal affiliation does: only 42% of Muslims, but 60% of Christians, want people like themselves as neighbours.

As in wartime, religion and communal affiliation are largely irrelevant in the working environment.[28]

The hard core of community loyalists feel that their community is more important than the nation-state. Their proportion has almost doubled since 1987.[29] Today, they account for just under one third of all respondents.[30] Such extreme community loyalty is higher than average among Armenians (67%) and Druze (46%) and lower than average among Greek Orthodox (21%) and Maronites (29%).

To summarise: Both familialism and community loyalties remain very strong; the latter has even strengthened a little since the war years. Every second Lebanese ranks the family above everything else, two in three feel that they have very close ties with their community, one in two prefers people like themselves as neighbours, and one in three feels greater loyalty to the community than the state.

But nine in ten have no problem working with members of other communities, which bears out J. S Furnival's classic observation: "two or more elements of social order which live side by side ... in one political unit. ... there is one place in which the various sections of a plural society meet on common ground – the market place."[31]

Strata, Communities and Identity

As in all plural societies, three question complexes dominate academic and political discussion. The first concerns the connection between economic stratification and group affiliation, the second citizens' perception of this connection (which is not always the same thing) and the third group and transcendent identities.

The first of these questions, the "incorporation" of strata and communities, has been coloured for decades by the topos of the "rich Christians" and the "poor Muslims", ex-

---

27 In the surveys conducted in the 80s, women were generally more supportive of mixed marriages than men. In 2002, by contrast, gender plays no role.
28 Least of all among university graduates, 95% of whom agreed.
29 Question asked for the first time in 1987.
30 There are no differences by education. Members of the middle income groups are more likely to belong to the hard core than members of the lowest and highest income groups.
31 J. S. Furnival, *Netherlands India. A Study of Plural Economy* (Cambridge: Cambridge University Press, 1939): p. 449.

acerbated by the thesis of "communal class". It is not our intention to add to this body of literature,[32] mainly interpretations of aggregate data. Sample surveys provide only approximations; they cannot replace exact socio-economic census data. Our surveys in the 80s established that, with minor variations, all communities were stratified by income, i.e., each had its wealthy, average and poor groups. Whereas Shi'is alone were underrepresented in the highest income group, the lowest group – quite correctly termed poor – had more or less equal percentages of Shi'is, Greek Catholics, Armenians and Maronites.

In the 2002 study, the connection between communal and religious affiliation on the one hand and income stratification on the other is statistically insignificant. In other words, although the distribution of income as a whole may have grown more unequal, there are no longer rich communities and poor communities.

There are still connections between stratification by education and religious affiliation: Muslims are overrepresented in the lowest educational group and underrepresented among university graduates. However, the Christians' one-time educational advantage[33] has narrowed substantially. But there is a difference between Muslims and Christians by occupation: Christians are frequently overrepresented in industry, trade and the hospitality sector, Muslims on the other hand in agriculture and the public sector. However, the Lebanese labour market has little in common with the "ethnically" divided markets found in many plural societies.

How do the Lebanese perceive their social positioning?

"Every society has social classes. Which class do you think you belong to?"

highest
upper middle
middle
lower middle
lowest.

The answers to this question correlate with income data as follows:

Income	Highest	Upper middle	Middle	Lower middle	Lowest	Income groups total
up to $166	2	7	55	27	10	40
up to $362	9	3	49	32	7	20
up to $500	5	10	48	31	7	19
up to $8,000	6	10	55	25	5	21
Overall estimate	5	7	52	28	8	100

Figures in %, rounded

---

32 An excellent critical survey will be found in Farid el Khazen, *The Breakdown of the State in Lebanon 1967–1975* (Cambridge: Harvard University Press, 2000): pp. 29ff.
33 Cf. Theodor Hanf, *Erziehungswesen in Gesellschaft und Politik des Libanon* (Düsseldorf: Bertelsmann Universitätsverlag, 1969).

The urge to be middle-class is very apparent. Respondents may no longer believe that Lebanon is a middle-class society, but they do see themselves as middle-class. About half of all respondents across all income groups thought they belonged to the middle class, and another quarter to the lower middle class. Even in the lowest income group only one tenth felt they belonged to the lower class.

As shown above, the relationship between income stratification and community is not significant. The connection between social self-categorisation and community affiliation, however, is.

	Upper class	Upper middle class	Middle class	Lower middle class	Lower class	Community as a whole
Sunnis	5	7	47	30	11	23
Shi'is	4	5	51	31	10	35
Druze	12	19	46	19	5	6
Maronites	3	7	60	36	4	19
Greek Orth.	2	6	61	28	2	9
Greek Cath.	8	15	42	19	15	3
Armenians	17	-	67	17	–	1
No reply	–	8	56	31	6	4
Average categorisation	5	7	52	28	8	100

Figures in %, rounded

Druze, Armenians and Greek Catholics have the fewest reservations about classifying themselves as upper or upper middle class. Maronites and Greek Orthodox are more likely than others to view themselves as middle class and less likely to categorise themselves as lower class. The most surprising detail is that only one tenth of Shi'a respondents regard themselves as members of the class that they previously described as "deprived". They are a little less likely than Maronites to classify themselves as lower middle class, but their representation in the middle class is almost exactly average. In short: despite a few discrepancies, communal awareness appears by and large to have caught up with economic reality.

Going beyond social positioning, how do the Lebanese perceive themselves? How do they define their identity?

"*Each of us belongs to several groups simultaneously: each person is either male or female, belongs to a religion or a community, is rural or urban and has a political viewpoint. And different people attach different importance to each factor.*
If you were asked who you are, how would you describe yourself?"
    first
    second, and
    third?"

The answers ranked by frequency of the first identity choice are:

	1st place	2nd place	3rd place
Lebanese	41	21	12
Normal person	8	2	1
Personal characteristics	7	10	16
Arab	6	10	4
Muslim	5	9	9
Christian	4	4	2
Occupation	3	4	4
Other*	8	15	15
No reply	18	25	37

Figures in %, rounded
* includes religious or political choices and place of origin

How do the groups of respondents as classified by first choice differ? There are no significant differences by area of residence, professional activity, education, and income. On the other hand, differences by individual community as well as between Muslims and Christians as a whole are significant. People who identify themselves as "Lebanese" first are overrepresented among Maronites, Greek Orthodox and Druze; Sunnis are more likely to call themselves Arabs. Sunnis are also more likely than Shi'is to identify themselves as Muslim first, and Greek Catholics, Armenians and members of smaller Christian communities as Christians. Overall, 48% of Christians opted for Lebanese first, compared with 38% of Muslims. Nine percent of Muslims and one percent of the Christians regarded themselves as Arab first.

Correlation of the first, second and third choices reveals the full complexity of the identity patterns.

1st place	2nd place	3rd place
Lebanese	16% Lebanese 15% Arabs 14% Muslims 10% Personal 7% Christians	17% Personal 12% Lebanese 12% Muslims 4% Arabs 1% Christians
Arabs	61% Lebanese 24% Muslims 2% Arabs 2% Personal	42% Muslims 22% Lebanese 10% Personal 2% Christians
Muslims	54% Lebanese 27% Arabs 8% Muslim 2% Personal	24% Arabs 22% Lebanese 14% Personal 8% Muslims

Continued:

1st place	2nd place	3rd place
Christians	27% Lebanese 27% Christians 8% Personal 5% Arabs	30% Lebanese 22% Personal 3% Christians
normal person	30% Lebanese 30% Personal 6% Arabs 4% Muslims 1% Christians	27% Personal 17% Lebanese 10% Arabs 9% Christians
Personal characteristics	34% Lebanese 20% Personal 3% Arabs 1% Christians	37% Personal 16% Lebanese 7% Muslim 1% Arabs 1% Christians

Figures in %, rounded

Taking the respective first choices, it is possible to trace different types of complex identity. Each type, regardless of political leanings, has a strong Lebanese component, and also includes an Arab element in varying degrees.

Almost three quarters of the respondents see themselves as Lebanese – whether first, second or third. For one third religious affiliation is important, more often among Muslims than Christians. One fifth emphasise their Arab identity. For four in five, non-political and non-religious characteristics are also part of their identity. This is a pattern of identity typical for an open society – complex, but obviously at peace with itself.

The questions asked above can be answered unequivocally. First, our data does not demonstrate any linkage between economic stratification and group affiliation. Second, allowing for nuances, there is an overwhelming tendency across all communities for people to categorise themselves as middle-class. As for the question of an identity that transcends community, in so far as any political identity was articulated, it was, again allowing for nuances, also clear that the respondents regard themselves as Lebanese.

How do respondents view the relationship between economic stratification and religious cleavages on the one hand and its political consequences on the other? This question was examined using the following statements:

	1987	2002
"Of course there are political and religious differences in this country. But the differences between rich and poor are more important."	59	66
"People who try to exploit differences between the communities in politics do this to hide the real differences between rich and poor."	52	72

Agreement in %, rounded

In short: two thirds think that the most important cleavages are economic, and even more are convinced that the purpose of the traditional politics of politicising communities is economic. In 2002, more the ever, the main problem facing Lebanon is not its identity, but its economy and, as we shall see below, its politicians.

Snapshots of Political Systems and Political Orientations

"In your opinion, which of the following groups has the greatest influence in Lebanon?"

	before 1975[34]	1981	1984	1986	1987	2002[35]
Large landowners	7	4	7	2	2	2
Religious leaders	11	7	10	12	3	7
Bankers	2	5	5	-	8	3
zu'ama	57	6	17	18	38	27
Merchants	3	13	16	17	14	3
Party leaders	4	54	38	41	30	10
Industrialists	2	4	1	-	1	1
Ministers	9	1	-	3	1	20
Military officers	4	5	6	6	3	12

Figures in %, rounded

The state has made a comeback, but it is not the state the Lebanese once knew. Respondents think that the executive branch and the armed forced exercise much greater power. The prewar state was dominated by the *zu'ama*, the traditional notables who formed a sort of executive committee in parliament and government that continually negotiated new compromises between family, regional, communal and personal interests in frequently changing coalitions. After the outbreak of war, these notables were displaced by "party leaders", in effect the militia leaders. When it became obvious to all that the latter had plunged the country into chaos, the *zu'ama* regained some of their influence. In the picture of Lebanon reflected in the 2002 survey the *zu'ama* still play a significant role, while the influence of the party leaders has been in decline since peaking in 1981. But the influence of the latter is still greater than it was in prewar Lebanon.[36]

Today, the parliamentary state run by the notables has to share power with the civil and military executive.

All other leadership elites have been marginalised: large landowners,[37] bankers, industrialists[38] and merchants, people the Lebanese feel have failed them in economic crisis.

---

34 Estimated in the survey of 1981
35 In the 2002 survey, 14% of respondents gave more than one answer.
36 Above average among Shi'is, Muslims in general and the inhabitants of the southern suburbs of Beirut.
37 Druze still regard them as relatively important.

It is noteworthy that evaluations of the powerful reveal no significant differences by education and income, only by religious affiliation and region.[39]

What do respondents think of politicians?

	1987	2002
"The time of the old politicians is finished. The new leaders represent the basic feeling of the country and function better."	62	32
"The old politicians are better than the new generation. At least they are tolerant, moderate and realistic."	37	62

Agreement in %, rounded

The standing of the *zu'ama* compared to the party leaders has changed spectacularly in the past 15 years. Support for the old politicians is overrepresented in the lowest age group in particular.[40]

How do the Lebanese feel about becoming politically involved?

"If you keep out of politics you have peace and quiet and a clear conscience."

In 1987, 62% of respondents agreed with this statement. Today 69% do. The depoliticisation of Lebanese society is far advanced. While 15% of the respondents said they belonged to a political organisation,[41] only two thirds of them name the organisation. A full two percent of respondents are members of Amal or Hezbollah and one percent admit to being members of the Communist Party; all other organisations receive less than one percent of the responses.

The replies to the question of the most and least popular politicians also reflect a profound rejection of politics.

	Favourite politician	Least liked politician
None	23	9
All	-	11
No reply	16	21
Executive office holders	12	28
Pro-government politicians	4	10
Opposition politicians	38	14
Foreign politicians	3	4
Others[42]	4	3

Figures in %, rounded

---

38 Above-average support among the Greek Orthodox.
39 Cf. the previous footnotes.
40 There is no significant variance by other characteristics.
41 Shi'is and Druze are above average in this group. Education and income play no role.
42 All less than one percent.

Almost one quarter of the respondents do not have a favourite politician, and one tenth reject all out of hand. When negative ratings are subtracted from the positive, few come off well.

The harshest judgments are reserved for the incumbents of the highest executive offices: their negative ratings are more than twice as high as their positive ratings. Government's supporters do not fare any better. By contrast, the approval ratings of opposition politicians are, on the whole, much higher than their disapproval ratings.

Who likes whom? Most politicians are the favourite sons of their own communities; patterns of admiration point to the strong persistence of confessional monocultures. The same it also true for patterns of dislike. As reflected in respondents' opinions, animosity towards individual politicians is stronger within than between communities.

How strong is respondents' support for their favourite politicians, how do supporters assess politicians' overall support, and what do they think about their effectiveness?

	2002
"Even if the politician that I prefer does something I don't agree with, I will continue to support him."	21
"Most people in my community support this leader."	36
"In the present situation these politicians cannot do much for us."	60

Agreement in %, rounded

The appeal of unconditional loyalty is limited;[43] only a good third believe that their favourite politician enjoys wide support, and no less than 60% think their politicians are more or less powerless in the current situation.[44] In short: respondents have few illusions on this score.

Does political orientation play a role in the popularity of individual politicians? This is less obvious in 2002 than in wartime. The following table shows trends over time.

Trend	1984	1986	1987	2002
No reply	20	16	46	16
None	12	22	20	23
"Decoupled voters":				
total	32	38	66	39
Christian *zu'ama*	11	5	7	7
Muslim *zu'ama*	9	7	3	9
"Government"	-	-	-	4

---

43 Most common in the lowest and highest income groups, in Chiyah and Bourj al-Barajneh as well as in Ashrafieh, the Metn and Zghorta.
44 This view is contradicted above all in the Shuf. Maronites in particular think that the politicians they support are powerless.

Continued:

Trend	1984	1986	1987	2002
"Opposition"	-	-	-	7
Others	5	3	2	2
Notables, ind. parliamentarians:				
total	25	15	12	29
Militant Christians	16	24	7	6
Amal	16	11	7	5
Islamists	1	1	2	9
PSP	7	9	4	4
Left	3	2	2	8
Party politicians:				
Total	43	47	22	32

Figures in %, rounded

"Decoupled voters" is not meant to imply that the respondents in this category will not vote at the next elections; it serves as a general term that embraces both the trend towards political abstinence and the refusal to take part in politics. In the difficult circumstances of 1987, a very high percentage simply refused to reply; in 2002, this category is a relatively low 16%. More meaningful is the increase in the number of people who expressly state that they do not like any politician, more or less doubling between 1984 and 2002. Almost four in ten Lebanese now stay away from political home games.

The notables have seen their support recover after bottoming out in 1987. Yet, it is still less than half that of the "old politicians", as shown above. Obviously, many Lebanese who want "tolerant, moderate and realistic" politicians are not very happy with the current choice of notables. That said, although the *zu'ama* have often been declared dead, they are not a threatened species.

Although party politicians and representatives of particular ideologies are no longer as popular as at the height of militia power, in 2002 they were still somewhat more popular than traditional politicians. This figure is crucially affected by Jumblatt's classification: is he thought to owe his support to his position as party leader or his position as traditional Druze leader?[45] If the latter, the proportion of notables will obviously rise.

Be that as it may: the support of those who actually subscribe to the views of one or other politician is divided more or less equally between representatives of traditional politics and those that represent a party or political movement. The most notable developments among the latter are the rise of Islamic leaders on the one hand and the resurgence of the Left on the other.[46] As the interests and policies of these parties and movements are diametrically opposed, the notables – who, although competing with

---

45 It is not far-fetched to assume that in the Shuf Jumblatt would retain a considerable body of support if he resigned from the Socialist Progressive Party and assumed the leadership of a liberal party.
46 Najah Wakim's personality plays a considerable role, as does the persistence of the Lebanese Communists.

each other for a larger slice of the cake, largely agree on power-sharing mechanisms – will probably have the greater say for the foreseeable future.

On balance, the most important finding for an understanding of the political landscape in present-day Lebanon is that more people have turned their backs on politics than support the notables and party leaders. They see the power of the government, the army and the parliamentarians – and do not like what they see.

If the respondents are deeply sceptical about the status quo in Lebanon, what are their desires and ideals?

"Which country do you think is the most perfect country?"

The list, ranked in accordance with the answers of the 2002 survey, is as follows:

	1984[47]	1986	1987	2002[48]
Switzerland, Scandinavia	30	33	47	20
France	7	8	9	16
Other EU countries	10	8	10	11
Western immigration countries	1	2	12	10
No country	10	19	3	10
Lebanon	15	8	4	6
Syria	-	-	(0.2)	4
Iran	7	3	2	3
Other Arab countries	5	4	-	2
USA	4	6	6	3
Israel	1	1	1	(0.3)

Figures in %, rounded

About one tenth did not think any country was ideal; Shi'is were overrepresented in this group. In all the surveys more than half the replies name western democracies.[49] Switzerland and Scandinavia – small and prosperous – take first place. France's standing has risen considerably. A good five percent resolutely favour their own country.[50] The attraction of Iran and most Arab countries excluding Syria – the ideal of four percent[51] – has declined over the years, and people are more sceptical about the USA. By 2002, Israel had lost virtually all its admirers, who were never numerous at the best of times.

How do respondents assess the influence of the international environment on Lebanon?

---

[47] Not asked in 1981.
[48] In 2002, ten percent did not reply to the question and five percent of replies mentioned other countries.
[49] The replies reflected the composition of the Lebanese diaspora. With above-average frequency Shi'is mention Germany and Switzerland, Shi'is and Maronites France, and Shi'is and Sunnis Scandinavian countries.
[50] Above average among Shi'is and Maronites.
[51] Overrepresented among Shi'is. Even so, only 6% of all Shi'a respondents regard Syria as their ideal country. Only 2% of all Christians share this opinion.

"*Here is a list of organisations and countries that may exercise some influence on Lebanon. Please tell us whether you think the influence of each is positive, negative or ineffective?*"

The replies in 2002 were as follows:

	Positive	Negative	Ineffective
France	64	11	25
Syria	50	35	15
Iran	43	32	25
Saudi Arabia	42	19	39
UN	40	23	37
Vatican	37	13	50
EU	36	18	47
Arab League	31	16	53
USA	22	65	14
Egypt	16	23	61
Iraq	16	22	62
PLO	16	52	32
Jordan	11	24	65
Russia	14	16	70
Israel	5	82	13

Figures in %, rounded

The influence of France is seen by most as positive and least often as negative.[52] The view of the United States is almost the reverse.[53] The assessment of Syria reflects a parting of the ways by community. Syrian influence is held to be positive by up to 70% of Shi'is, 57% of the Druze and 56% of Sunnis, while Christians in general and the Maronites in particular[54] judge it as negative. A positive view of Syria is particularly common among the inhabitants of Nabatieh, the Akkar, Zahle, the Bekaa and Tripoli. The influence of Iran is thought by 72% of Shi'is and 60% of all Muslims to be positive, and by 60% of all Christians to be negative. The positive view of Iran correlates inversely with education, and is far less common among women than men. In the light of Lebanon's experience of the PLO, it is hardly surprising that so few view its influence as positive and a clear majority as negative.[55] It is even less surprising that the most negative results are those for Israel – without distinction between communities and religions.

---

52 There are no significant differences between Christians and Muslims.
53 Christians take a slightly more positive view than Muslims of the USA. The positive assessment correlates inversely with income.
54 67% opted for "negative".
55 Positive assessments of the PLO reached 28% among the Sunnis, a view shared by only 18% of the Shi'is and just 7% of the Christians.

There is a fundamental difference of opinion among the Lebanese by community and religion over the influence of Syria and Iran. The differences in the assessment of Syria are even sharper in the replies to the following statement:

"Lebanon and Syria are one people in two states."[56]

A total of 35% of the respondents agreed. There were no differences in agreement or disagreement by job, education or income.[57] Agreement is lowest among the Christians, just 20%.[58] Among Shi'is and Sunnis, on the other hand, 42% and 44%, respectively, agree. An interesting finding is that agreement falls linearly from the highest to the lowest age groups; among the young just 29% are agree.

To summarise: the respondents regard the executive (and the military) as powerful, but do not like them much. The most important pillars of the state attract more disapproval than admiration. Political abstinence and rejection have risen. Differences in opinion are most pronounced over whether Syria is just a neighbouring country or a brother country. Half the respondents think Syria's influence is positive, a good third regard the Syrians and Lebanese as one people, but only 4% see in Syria a model. These trends differ by community and between Christians and Muslims as a whole – similar to the nuances about identity. While a plurality of respondents see themselves primarily as Lebanese, a strong absolute majority regard themselves as an independent people.

Democrats by conviction and necessity

"Think of a country in which you would like to live. Which of the following do you think is best for that country?"

	Democratic option
One party that unites the country or *Several parties citizens are free to choose between.*	57
Judges that follow directives from the government or *Judges that only follow the laws without listening to the government.*	80
Press censorship to prevent propaganda that causes strife or *A free press that can criticise politicians as it likes.*	70

Figures in %, rounded

---

56 A statement of the former Syrian president Hafez al-Assad.
57 By region, agreement was strongest in Burj al-Barajneh and in the Bekaa.
58 Maronites 15%, Greek Orthodox 31%, Greek Catholic 27% and Armenians 17%.

Most respondents have democratic views, but a substantial minority do not. Support is strongest for an independent judiciary – which is, of course, not incompatible with a proto-democratic state. The idea of a free press is already less popular, and a multiparty system finds only a small majority.

Who likes a one-party system? Support is overrepresented among people with middle incomes and average education, and includes 29% of Muslims[59] and 19% of Christians.

Nine percent of both the Shi'is and the Druze believe judges should obey the government, compared with just 5% of the Sunnis and Maronites – and not one Greek Orthodox in our sample.

Support for press censorship declines with rising education and income. It meets with the approval of 18% of Muslims and 10% of Christians.

Assuming that the Lebanese are more or less democratic, what economic and social policies do they prefer in 2002? The findings are surprising for a country that was a by-word for laissez-faire economics. Only 51% of the working population favour private ownership of the means of production, while no less than 38% would like the state to take charge of the economy. The latter view is held by an above-average 44% of the Shi'is. The lower respondents' incomes are, the stronger their support for a state-controlled economy: in the two lowest income groups support for the free market fell (just) short of a majority.

Hence, it is not surprising that a broad majority favours economic and social policies that promote equality.

"What is best for the country in which you would like to live:
A policy that aims to create as much equality as possible in between salaries, living conditions and study opportunities,
or
A policy that allows people who work hard to earn more and live better than others?
No less than 75% chose the first option. Support is above average among women (81%), Greek Orthodox (89%) and Maronites, and substantially below among Druze (68%) and Greek Catholics. Education and income did not affect this choice. By region, support for equality was strongest among the inhabitants of Zghorta, Kisrawan, the Metn and the region around Jbeil: these are clearly the regions where people feel most neglected.

The economic crisis has obviously undermined the belief in the superiority of a free-market system and in the wisdom of laissez-faire policies. Naturally, this also influences people's choice of government.

"Which would you prefer:
An honest and clean government that rules with a firm hand,
or
A government that is perhaps a bit corrupt but respects civil freedoms?"

---

59 The Druze in particular are overrepresented: one in three prefers a one-party state.

Two thirds of the respondents favour clean, firm government and only one fifth more freedom even if a bit of corruption is inevitable. It is impossible to avoid the conclusion that indignation about perceived injustice and corruption is challenging the liberal convictions of Lebanese society. This indignation is found without any significant differences across all educational and income levels in all communities.

Against this background what are the opinions and attitudes about the current Lebanese system of government and possible alternatives?

"There are many countries that, like ours, have a variety of different groups – language groups, religious groups, ethnic groups and others. Together these countries have different systems of government and there are differing opinions about the best system. We would like to present some of these opinions. Please tell us for each opinion whether you think it is acceptable or unacceptable for Lebanon.

	1987	2002
"The country should be partitioned and each group have its own state."	4	11
"The strongest group should govern. The other groups must accept what this group decides."	20	8
"The numerically strongest group should govern. The other groups must accept what this group decides."	6	12
"One group should govern, and groups that don't like it must leave the country."	10	9
"One single party that everybody can join should govern without an opposition."	35	28

Continued:

	1987	2002
"Everybody votes for the party of their choice. The party or parties that win form the government; the other parties remain in the opposition."	71	54
"Everybody votes for the party they want, but the government should be formed on the principle that all groups have a share of power."[60]	80	65

Agreement in %, rounded

The first point to note is the increase in support for partition, in particular among the young: an above-average 29% find it acceptable. Although there are no significant differences between Muslims and Christians, there are between the individual communi-

---

[60] In 1987 the item read: "Given the nature of Lebanese society, all important political decisions must have the agreement of all large communities." The new formulation was chosen to facilitate international comparisons.

ties: 15% and 16% of the Druze and Maronites, respectively, have no objection to separate states for different groups.

Support for domination by the strongest group has fallen by more than half. Acceptance declines with rising education.[61] There were no significant differences by either religion or community.

By contrast, it appears that twice as many respondents as in 1987 are ready to accept domination by the largest group. This opinion is not significantly influenced by education or income or communal or religious affiliation. Agreement with this concept is above average in a few regions: the southern suburbs of Beirut and in Nabatieh.

The extreme form of domination – if you don't like it, get out – is primarily a product of poor education: acceptance declines linearly from 20% among the least educated to 6% among university graduates.[62]

The one-party system continues to find support among a good quarter of the respondents: Christians at 21% are underrepresented. This system is most popular among people in the lowest education groups.[63] Remarkably, almost half – 46% – of the youngest age group among the respondents are ready to accept a one-party state.

More than half of the respondents approve of a first-past-the-post system of majority democracy, and almost two thirds support the traditional Lebanese system of proportional democracy.[64] Compared with the results during the war, support for both of the democratic alternatives has declined considerably.

In 2002, the survey did not only ask about the acceptability of various types of government, but went on to ask which one of the alternatives respondents thought was best. This produced the following results:

Partition	4
Domination by the strongest group	1
Domination by the largest group	2
Extreme domination of one group	2
One-party system	9
Majority democracy	21
Consociational democracy (proportional representation)	35
Majority democracy or proportional representation	4
Other double responses	4
No reply	18

Almost two thirds of the respondents think one of the democratic solutions is the best option. Just under one fifth chose other options and an equal number did not reply. In Lebanon there is a solid, but by no means overwhelming, majority in favour of democracy.

---

61 Nearly linearly: 19% (lowest) – 13% – 8% – 5% – 7% (highest).
62 Overrepresented in Chiyah, Bourj al-Barajneh, in the Bekaa, Baalbek-Hermel – and in Zahle.
63 Agreement falls linearly from the lowest level of education to university graduates.
64 No significant difference by stratification or communal or religious affiliation.

Neither education nor income played a role in these preferences,[65] in contrast to community affiliation:[66]

	One-party system	Majority democracy	Proportional representation
Sunnis		25	35
Shi'is	11	18	38
Druze	12	17	37
Maronites	9	23	35
Greek Orthodox		20	34

Figures in %, rounded

In other words, about one third of the respondents from each of the five largest communities think that the best solution is to share power. One quarter of the Sunnis and the Maronites prefer simple majority democracy; among other groups this option draws the support of only one fifth or less. About one tenth of the Druze, the Shi'is and the Maronites – i.e., the communities that have or had parties with claims to leadership – think a one-party system is the best solution.

The responses to the following statements indicate that the plurality in favour of sharing power does so for reasons of necessity rather than conviction:

	1981	1984	1986	1987	2002
"Because of the nature of Lebanese society, important decisions need the agreement of all large communities."	*	*	*	80	77
"Lebanon won't have a strong and united government until authentic representatives of the communities have a share in power."	67	79	73	66	72

Agreement in %, rounded
* Between 70% and 80%

Social characteristics played no role in agreement to the first of these statements. Three quarters of the Muslims and four fifths of the Christians agree with it, though members of the smaller communities – Druze, Greek Catholics and Armenians – less frequently, possibly on account of the formulation: "all large communities".

Over the years, and again in 2002, at least two thirds of the respondents have agreed with the second statement.[67] This is higher than the level of support for proportional representation – let alone the percentage that regard it as the best solution – and higher

---

65 Almost half the civil servants among the respondents prefer proportional representation.
66 The table lists only figures that were above average.
67 There are no significant differences by socio-economic characteristics or religion.

than the percentage of respondents who, through their support for multiparty democracy and freedom of the press, showed themselves to be true democrats.

In short: The Lebanese are in favour of a system of democratic power-sharing because they do not see any viable alternative. A majority are democrats by conviction, and a larger majority by necessity.

Perspectives of coexistence

	1987	2002
"Perhaps it doesn't look like it, but it is possible that the political system can be changed in the near future."	35	50
"The strength of the different communities makes fundamental long-term change in the political system impossible."	52	62

Agreement in %, rounded

The statements contradict each other to some extent: the first expresses a wish, the second an insight. In 2002, neither of them correlated with any social or cultural characteristic. Whereas half hope for change, almost two thirds think it is impossible.

Against this background, how do people view possibilities and forms of coexistence?

	1981	1984	1986	1987	2002
"During the crisis the regions had to get by on their own. Perhaps decentralisation is a good thing.	52	61	46	31	62
"Coexistence between the communities would be easier if each community had its own region."	*	23	25	18	28
"Most regions in Lebanon are mixed. All Lebanon is for all Lebanese.	*	86	85	70	76
"Whatever the political solution, Lebanon must remain a single economic entity.	*	86	85	70	90

Agreement in %, rounded
* not asked

In 2002, "decentralisation" may no longer have the connotations it did in the war years, when it was associated with the idea of partition or "cantonalisation". Today the concept again finds acceptance among nearly two thirds of the respondents.

By contrast, only a good quarter of respondents approve of the idea of a separate region for each community. Support for this view is above-average in the suburbs of East Beirut, in the Metn and the Kisrawan as well as in Baalbek-Hermel, Tripoli and the Akkar – for the most part regions that are fairly homogeneous.

The principle of freedom of movement throughout the territory of Lebanon and the necessity of preserving the economic integrity of the country in all circumstances are far less contentious. Three quarters agree with the first statement and nine in ten with the second.

How do Lebanese view the relationship between religion and politics?

	1981	1984	1986	1987	2002
"One should not mix religion and politics."	84	84	87	93	78
"The best solution to Lebanon's present dilemma is a completely secular state and society."	*	75	52	63	57
"Every Lebanese should have the right to join a secularised community that has the same rights as the other communities – personal status law, political representation, etc."	*	*	*	50	54
"It doesn't matter what anyone wants, secularisation doesn't seem to have a chance in Lebanon. Community membership is a reality you have to accept."	*	*	*	54	64

Agreement in %, rounded
* not asked

A general formulation on the desirability of separating religion and politics draws strong support, but not as strong as in the war years. This view is shared by more than four fifths of the Christians and three quarters of the Muslims.

Support for more precise proposals for separation is considerably weaker. Christians are still slightly more favourably inclined than Muslims. The attitudes towards the creation of a secular community, which people can opt to join voluntarily, are particularly interesting. This proposal does not go as far as the call for a fully secular state, but it is more concrete – and it finds less agreement. Agreement correlates directly with income.[68] Although religious affiliation plays no role, there are differences between the communities: whereas only 45% of the Maronites and 49% of the Sunnis favour a secular community, 55% of the Greek Orthodox are in favour, 56% of the Shi'is, 61% of the Greek Catholics and 67% of the Armenians. Not only have the religious authorities in Lebanon always unanimously rejected this first step towards secularisation, but even among the general public it finds only a bare majority, rather than widespread support.

Hence, it is not surprising that almost two thirds accept community affiliation with all its consequences as a fact of life.

If the Lebanese have to come to terms with the diversity of communities in their country, how do they view coexistence between them?

---

68 From 47% in the lowest income group, through 56% and 58% in the middle groups, to 60% in the highest.

	1984	1986	1987	2002
"In the last 10 years,[69] horrible things have happened. I fear that this has made coexistence between the communities very difficult."	48	44	21	43
"In spite of the recent terrible events, I believe that coexistence between the communities is still possible."	82	79	86	80

Agreement in %, rounded

Remarkably, 12 years after the end of the war twice as many respondents regard coexistence now as more difficult than in 1987, and about as difficult as in the worst war years of 1984 and 1986. In 2002, this view is shared by 52% of the Christians; it is far less prevalent among Muslims at 39%. We suspect that this perception of "difficult" has less to do with the experiences of the war years than with the dissatisfaction with postwar politics. Notwithstanding this, four in five respondents believe that coexistence is possible in the future. What about the one fifth that does not share this opinion? Maronites (26%) and Greek Catholics (35%) are overrepresented. Above all, among these that believe that coexistence is no longer possible, there is a very high proportion of university graduates (25%) and members of the youngest age group (34%). Scepticism about coexistence is also stronger than average among the most educated and among the youth – who have little experience of the war.

What do people feel about the balance of power, militancy and peaceful resignation?

	1987	2002
"With the strength and determination of our group we will eventually achieve our goals."	72	59
"Victory isn't worth the sacrifices and losses my community would suffer."	62	68
"In the struggle between the different communities in our country we're all losers."	77	83
"In the present situation, given the strength of the different communities, it is necessary to search for a compromise and come to some agreement."	92	80

Agreement in %, rounded

In general it is clear that people have learned some lessons from the war: they are less certain about victory[70] and less willing to accept losses, while the realisation is more

---

69 In surveys during the war years: "In recent months, ...".
70 Social and religious characteristics play no role. Two thirds of both the Greek Orthodox and the Maronites say they are confident of victory – more to talk up their courage than out of genuine conviction.

widespread that everybody loses when the communities fight against one another.[71] The understanding of the need to compromise is not as strong as during the war years, but still accepted by four in five respondents.[72]

Opinions differ more widely on the external and internal causes of the conflict.

	1984	1986	1987	2002
"Despite all that has happened, we Lebanese could reach agreement among ourselves if foreign forces would stop interfering in our affairs."	79	69	75	79
"Even if foreigners stayed out of Lebanese affairs, it would be hard to reach an understanding; it is possible that the conflicts between hostile Lebanese groups would break out again."	*	*	50	66
"If foreigners stayed out, conflicts in Lebanon would never end in victory or defeat for anybody."	*	*	56	70

Agreement in %, rounded
* not asked

In 2002, almost four fifths of the respondents believed that outside forces were responsible for the conflicts, but at the same time two thirds think war could erupt again even without foreign intervention.[73] Such a fear may have a healthy influence on politics, particularly if it goes hand in hand with the conviction that there can never be a clear winner in internal Lebanese conflicts.[74]

Finally, we look at a few opinions and attitudes that are fundamental for coexistence between different communities and groups.

	1981	1984	1986	1987	2002
"Whether we like it or not: when different language, religious, ethnic or racial groups live in the same country, they must either dominate or be dominated."	*	*	*	53	60
"Very different religious, ethnic, language or racial groups can live together in the same country, accept one another and respect each other's rights."	*	*	*	70	86

---

71 Among those that do not share this conviction, the Druze are overrepresented at 20%. Agreement rises in direct correlation with education and income.
72 Christians somewhat more often than Muslims, otherwise there are no significant differences by strata or community.
73 This fear is disproportionately strong among women, 74% of whom share this view.
74 "Neither winner nor loser be" is more popular among Christians, 82% of whom agree, than among Muslims, but even 64% of them concur. Agreement correlates directly with education.

Continued:

	1981	1984	1986	1987	2002
"A country with groups with different traditions is wealthier for it and its society benefits."	*	*	*	64	80
"The monotheistic religions like Christianity and Islam believe in the same God and teach similar ethical and social principles."	92	82	88	91	81
"A good friend is a good friend, whether he is called Georges or Muhammed."	96	96	96	98	92

Agreement in %, rounded
* not asked

The conviction that people must either dominate or be dominated has grown in postwar Lebanon. It is particularly strong among Christians (71%), but also shared by a majority of Muslims (55%). At the same time, the view that different groups can also accept and respect one another has also gained support.[75] And the proportion of those who are convinced that cultural diversity enriches a country has risen substantially in postwar Lebanon.[76]

Four fifths of the respondents in 2002 agreed that Islam and Christianity had a lot in common. One cause for concern is the underrepresentation of the youngest age group in this respect: just 68% share this view.[77] This finding is substantiated by attitudes to friendship across religious barriers: the younger the respondents, the fewer that agreed. However, this concern should not be exaggerated: even among the youngest respondents Muhammed can have a friend called Georges, and vice versa.

To summarise: About half of the Lebanese would prefer another political system, but an even greater number believe this is impossible. Similarly, half favour political decentralisation, but only one quarter would like separate regions for each community. Large majorities are in favour of freedom of movement and a single economic entity.

Similarly large majorities favour the separation of politics and religion, but there are only very narrow majorities in favour of a secular state and society, or of creating an optional secular community. For the most part, people accept affiliation with one or other community.

A growing minority believe that coexistence between these communities has become more difficult – but 80% still think such coexistence is possible. One lesson people have

---

[75] Significant differences in agreement or rejection do not correlate with any social or cultural characteristic.

[76] At 74%, Druze agreement is below average, while Greek Orthodox agreement of 89% is above average. The influence of social characteristics is insignificant.

[77] Agreement is also below average among respondents in Nabatieh and the Metn. The question here, as in other respects, is whether relatively decoupled confessional subcultures have developed in these areas.

learned from the war is that no conflict is worth the losses involved, and that in the end everybody is a loser. Thus, one has to compromise.

Regardless of whether the respondents think the wars were caused by internal or external factors, 70% of them are convinced that in internal conflicts no group will prevail.

Cultural tolerance is high and diversity is regarded as a treasure. A large majority recognise the common ground between Islam and Christianity, and an even larger majority agree that friendship across religious barriers is possible.

The question asked at the beginning can now be answered. All the results of the 2002 survey – like those conducted in the war years – indicate that the Lebanese accept themselves as they are: different from one another, but forced to live together. They view their coexistence with scepticism, albeit as a possibility that may even be an enrichment. The Lebanese may be a sceptical nation, but all the findings show that a nation is what they now are.

Zur Reihe

Ethnischer Konflikt ist gegen Ende des 20. Jahrhunderts zur Hauptform gewaltsamer Konflikte geworden. Untersuchungen zu Konfliktursachen, -genese, -verlauf und -regelung sind nötig, um Möglichkeiten der Vorbeugung zu ermitteln. Wenn ethnische Gruppen gleichzeitig Religionsgruppen sind, werden Konflikte zwischen ihnen mit besonderer Schärfe und Bitterkeit ausgetragen. Gleichwohl ist zu beobachten, daß religiös begründete Toleranz Bereitschaft zur Gewalt mindern kann. Daher erscheint es angezeigt zu prüfen, ob und wie religiöse Lehren gelebte Religiosität prägen und damit Konfliktverhalten beeinflussen. Eine dauerhafte Regelung ethnischer Konflikte bedarf der Zustimmung von Mehrheiten aller betroffenen Bevölkerungsgruppen – und damit letztlich der Demokratie.

Die Studien dieser Reihe analysieren die Bedingtheiten ethnischer und ethno-religiöser Konflikte in unterschiedlichen Ländern. Ihr Schwerpunkt liegt auf empirischen Untersuchungen von Einstellungen zu Ethnizität, Religion und Demokratie, die Vergleiche ermöglichen.

Sur cette série

Le conflit ethnique est devenu, vers la fin du 20ème siècle, la forme prédominante des conflits violents. Afin d'explorer les possibilités d'une prévention de ces conflits, l'étude de leur causes, de leur genèse, de leur déroulement ainsi que de leur issue s'imnpose. Ces conflits sont particulièrement aigus et acerbes quand ils opposent des groupes définis à la fois par leur ethnicité et leur religion. Cependant, l'on peut également observer qu'une tolérance fondée sur des convictions religieuses puisse mettre un frein au recours à la violence. Il paraît donc indiqué d'analyser l'impact des doctrines religieuses sur la religiosité vécue qui peut restreindre un comportement conflictuel. Toutefois, uni règlement durable d'uni conflit ethnique nécessite l'accord de majorités de tous les groupes impliqués – et donc, en fin de compte, la démocratie.

Cette série de publications se propose l'étude des conflits ethniques et ethno-religieux de pays différents dans leur contexte particulier. Elle privilégie les enquêtes empiriques, permettant la comparaison des attitudes envers l'ethnicité, la religion et la démocratie.

On this series

Towards the end of the 20th century, ethnic conflict has emerged as the pre-eminent expression of violent conflict. Before we can explore ways, means and prospects of preventing ethnic conflict, we need to analyse the causes, genesis, course and outcome of conflict. When groups in conflict are defined simultaneously by ethnicity and religion, the conflicts between them appear to be exceptionally bitter and destructive. At the same time, it has been observed that religiously based tolerance can reduce the readiness to resort to violence. Hence, it appears appropriate to examine the impact of religious teachings on religion in practice and how this influences conflict behaviour. As a rule, sustainable regulation of ethnic conflict requires the agreement of a majority of each of the population groups involved – in other words: democracy.

This series of publications is intended as a collection of analyses of ethnic and ethnoreligious conflicts in different countries within their particular context. Accordingly, the series will focus above all on empirical surveys of attitudes towards ethnicity, religion and democracy conducted with instruments that facilitate comparison.

Theodor Hanf/Ghia Nodia

Georgia Lurching to Democracy

**From agnostic tolerance to pious Jacobinism:
Societal change and peoples' reactions**

Georgien ist schnell, aber nicht gradlinig in die Demokratie »hineingeglitten«. Freien Wahlen folgten Sezessions- und Bürgerkriege, bevor die graduelle Stabilisierung einsetzte. Eine Erblast des Sowjetsystems ist die Politisierung von Ethnizität.
Einer Darstellung des Wegs zur Unabhängigkeit folgt eine Analyse der jüngsten Prozesse sozialen und politischen Wandels. Wie reagiert die Bevölkerung hierauf? Anhand der ersten Repräsentativbefragung, die im Lande durchgeführt wurde, werden sozial-psychische Einstellungen, Bilder von Wirtschaft und Gesellschaft, Religion und Identität, politische Präferenzen, Einstellungen zur Demokratie und interethnischen Koexistenz geprüft. Wichtigster Befund ist hierbei der Gegensatz zwischen »agnostischer Toleranz« und »frommem Jakobinismus«. Der Umgang mit ethno-religiöser Vielfalt erweist sich als ein zentrales politisches Problem.
Allen an Georgien und an Ethnopolitik Interessierten bietet der Band neue, empirisch gesicherte Einsichten.
Die Verfasser, Direktoren des Arnold-Bergstraesser-Instituts bzw. des Caucasus Institute for Democracy, lehren Politikwissenschaft an den Universitäten Freiburg bzw. Tiflis.

1. Auflage 2000, 156 S., brosch., 30,– €, ISBN 3-7890-7010-6
(Studien zu Ethnizität, Religion und Demokratie, Bd. 3)

◆ **NOMOS Verlagsgesellschaft
76520 Baden-Baden**

Theodor Hanf (ed.)

Dealing with Difference

Religion, Ethnicity, and Politics: Comparing Cases and Concepts

Nach dem Ende der bipolaren Welt verschärfen sich in vielen Staaten alte Gegensätze zwischen Religions-, Volks- und Kulturgruppen. Neue Konflikte entstehen.
In diesem Band werden gängige Deutungsmuster alter wie neuer Differenzierungen einer Kritik unterzogen. Fallstudien zu Schwarzafrika, Lateinamerika, dem Vorderen Orient und Europa zeigen die Komplexität unterschiedlicher Konfliktlagen. Weitere Studien untersuchen Südafrikas bemerkenswerten Versuch, Gegensätze friedlich und demokratisch zu überbrücken – die Faktoren, die ihn ermöglicht haben, aber auch die Gefährdungen, denen er ausgesetzt ist. Im Gegensatz sowohl zu liberalen als auch zu marxistisch inspirierten Deutungen des Modernisierungsprozesses belegen mehrere Beiträge die zunehmende Bedeutung von Religion als Faktor sozialer Differenzierung.

Abschließend werden drei kontrastierende Konzepte für eine Regelung ethnischer und religiöser Konflikte vorgestellt: Entnationalisierung des Staates, Übergang zu einer post-nationalen Republik und Domestizierung von Ethnizität durch den Nationalstaat.

Die Autoren sind renommierte Sozialwissenschaftler aus dem In- und Ausland.

Mit Beiträgen in englischer und französischer Sprache.

1. Auflage 1999, 456 S., brosch., 62,– €, ISBN 3-7890-6243-X
(Studien zu Ethnizität, Religion und Demokratie, Bd. 2)

**◆ NOMOS Verlagsgesellschaft
76520 Baden-Baden**